The
Scotch
WHISKY BOOK

Dedication:

'To K with love'

First published in Great Britain in 2002 by
Lomond Books
36 West Shore Road
Granton
Edinburgh EH5 IQD

Produced by Colin Baxter Photography Ltd

Copyright © Colin Baxter Photography Ltd 2002

A CIP catalogue record for this book is available from the British Library

ISBN 1-84204-021-9

Printed in China

Text copyright © Tom Bruce Gardyne 2002

All photography copyright © Glyn Satterley 2002, except for the following:

Photography copyright © Anthony Blake Photo Library / Carol Sharp – Front Cover

Photography copyright © Mary Evans Picture Agency 19, 32, 38, 40, 43 top & bottom

Photography copyright © Public Record Office Image Library 8, 13, 16, 20, 26, 30, 35, 36, 39, 45

Photography copyright © Scottish Life Archive, National Museums of Scotland 10, 11, 12, 14, 17, 21, 33 top & bottom, 34, 37

Photography copyright © John Dewar & Sons 22, 23 (top & bottom), 42, Glenfarclas 24 (top & bottom), 25 (top & bottom),
Glenmorangie 28, Guiness UDV 15, 18, 27, 29 (top & bottom)

Maps copyright © Wendy Price Cartographic Services 70, 72, 122, 168, 202

Whisky Label Credits

Allied Domecq: 217 (centre), 225 (left), 229 (bottom centre), 232 (centre), 233 (right), 234 (right) **Bacardi:** 215 (left), 222 (top right), 230 (centre),
235 (bottom right) **Bruichladdich Distillery Co. Ltd:** 219 (bottom right) **Burn Stewart:** 222 (bottom centre), 232 (top right), 235 (top left)
Cutty Sark International: 221 (centre) **Diageo:** 217 (top left), 219 (top left), 219 (top right), 221 (top left), 221 (bottom left), 221 (right),
222 (bottom left), 224 (bottom centre), 227 (right), 228 (top right), 228 (bottom right), 229 (top left), 229 (bottom left), 229 (right), 231 (top left),
231 (bottom left), 232 (top left), 232 (bottom left), 234 (left), 235 (centre) **Edrington Group:** 218 (top right), 223 (bottom left), 226 (top left),
226 (bottom right), 227 (bottom centre), 229 (top centre), 230 (top right) **Glen Katrine:** 224 (right), 227 (top centre) **Glenmorangie Plc:**
216 (top left), 216 (right), 224 (top centre), 226 (bottom centre) **Gordon & Macphail:** 218 (centre) **Inver House:** 215 (right), 217 (left),
217 (bottom left), 227 (left), 231 (top right), 232 (bottom right) **Inverarity Vaults:** 228 (top left) **Isle of Arran Distilling Co.:** 228 (bottom left)
J & G Grant: 225 (top centre) **J & A Mitchell:** 233 (bottom left) **Kyndal:** 220 (top left), 222 (top left), 228 (top centre), 231 (centre),
235 (top right) **Nikka:** 218 (top left) **Pernod Ricard:** 215 (centre), 218 (bottom left), 220 (bottom right), 220 (bottom left), 223 (top left),
224 (top left), 224 (bottom left), 226 (top centre), 230 (top left), 233 (centre) **Peter J Russell:** 228 (bottom centre) **Pràban na Línne:**
231 (bottom right), 234 (centre) **Raymond Armstrong:** 218 (bottom right) **Speyside Disillery Co.:** 233 (top left) **Suntory:** 216 (bottom left),
219 (bottom left), 223 (bottom right) **William Grant & Sons:** 225 (bottom right)

Back cover photographs: top: Highland Park; second: Highland Park; third: Dalmore; bottom: Bunnahabhain;
Page 1 photograph: Shop, Tomintoul; Page 4 photograph: Talisker, Skye

The *Scotch* WHISKY BOOK

TOM BRUCE-GARDYNE
with photographs by GLYN SATTERLEY

LOMOND BOOKS
EDINBURGH · SCOTLAND

CONTENTS

INTRODUCTION

————◆—◆————

Scotch whisky is a weird paradox of a drink. It is made from a few, very humble ingredients and yet is infinitely varied and often incredibly complex. It soothes away stress one moment and fires up passion the next. It is a beguiling temptress that allows one dram to slip smoothly into another by night, only to turn into the most vicious, vengeful demon in the morning. It is, as many have claimed, a distillation of its homeland that manages somehow to capture a little of the bitter-sweet, melancholic beauty of the place. For millions around the world, it is Scotland in a bottle, and yet its very 'Scottishness' is now almost taboo in the way it is sold. It is currently the hip drink in downtown Barcelona and Madrid, but is considered hopelessly uncool in the style bars of Glasgow where vodka reigns supreme. It has been praised by politicians for its success abroad and contribution to the balance of trade, while being simultaneously milked for every last penny of tax at home.

What is also weird is the way it has developed a split personality, as though blended Scotch and malt whisky were two totally separate drinks. In fact considering how they are written about, marketed and therefore perceived one starts to wonder if they are from the same planet. At first blends did all the running, and it was left to a few die-hards like the novelist Neil Gunn to keep the flame alight for the other side. As he wrote in 1935, in 'Whisky and Scotland' 'the future of Highland malt whisky, other than as a flavouring ingredient of patent spirit, is very obscure'. He had good cause for concern for there were just nine distilleries in Scotland actually making malt whisky at the time. Today there are around 80, and in almost every case a little of what they produce is on sale somewhere as a single malt. These are then endlessly picked over by the 'experts', while blended Scotch barely gets a look in. The trouble with delving ever deeper into the subject is that it tends to leave the rest of us out in the cold. Yes, there are those who are truly fascinated with every strain of barley and type of

barrel used, and who go off bagging distilleries like others bag Munros, but it is not the world where most of us whisky drinkers live.

The truth is, both types of whisky can be superb and both can be sorely disappointing. It was ridiculous to suppose in the 1960s, when Glenfiddich began to appear south of the border, that single malts would be too strong a flavour to ever catch on among the whisky-drinking masses. But it is equally absurd to assume that malts are somehow naturally superior to blends.

Fashions are fickle by their very nature, but what is obvious the moment you scratch beneath the surface of Scotch whisky is that malts and blends are joined at the hip. Out of every 100 bottles of Scotch drunk, 94 are blends which on average contain somewhere between a quarter and a third malt whisky and the rest grain whisky. That means that very few malt distilleries could begin to survive on what they bottle themselves as a single malt. There are one or two exceptions like the odd boutique distillery, but for the vast majority, the business of swapping casks, selling fillings and making blends is what keeps them in business. As a result there is no sense of 'them and us' within the trade nowadays because the few key players who dominate tend to be involved in every aspect. They might be shipping grain spirit in bulk one day and bottling rare expressions of their most precious malts the day after.

Scotch needs to celebrate its diversity as a drink with deep roots and one which has no need to get precious about itself. Whether poured into a tall glass over ice, mixed with soda or coke, sipped neat or knocked back as a chaser after a pint, there are countless ways to enjoy it. Besides, what will always matter more is where and with whom one is doing the drinking. Like the beard and sandals brigade with Real Ale, the anorak tendency among whisky drinkers can get a bit righteous at times. So let's leave them to their own devices and go and explore the origins of what is without doubt one of the greatest drinks in the world.

**Sunset off Ullapool,
West Highlands**

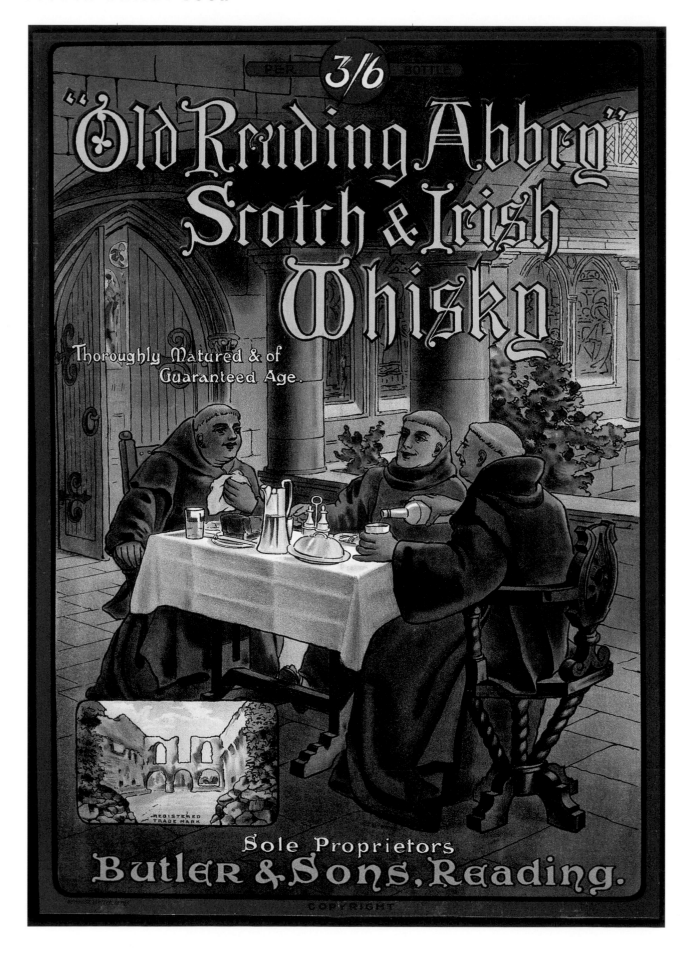

ORIGINS OF WHISKY

Alcohol is the product of nature. With wild yeast blowing freely in the wind, the fermentation of grain and grape happens spontaneously of its own accord. To turn this into beer or wine requires very little on the part of man – just a big tub and a rough idea of when to cover it up. Covering it up restricts the amount of oxygen causing the yeasts to react with the natural sugars present and convert them to alcohol. Not that any of the early brewers or vintners knew that at the time, or indeed needed to.

To take this a step further and turn fermented liquor into spirits does require a touch more sophistication – not much, but a little. Again the precise science of distillation was only understood relatively recently, while Arrack was being distilled in India as far back as 800 BC and some form of rice spirit was probably being made in China even before then. What is clear is that you hardly need a degree in nuclear physics to make a drink like whisky, but you do need some knowledge, and this knowledge seems to have spread slowly westwards from the eastern fringes of the Mediterranean.

In the fourth century BC, the Greek philosopher Aristotle was studying the weather and trying to work out how rain forms. From this he devised a method of distilling sea water by boiling it in a pan and suspending balls of wool in the steam to capture the vapours. The balls presumably were to imitate clouds. Distilled water is some way off from making whisky of course, but making sea water drinkable did demonstrate how distillation can separate a liquid into its various parts. It showed how the vapour could rise up leaving, in this case salt, behind. The reason why it works with whisky and other spirits is, as every distiller knows, because alcohol has a lower boiling point than water.

The Ancient Egyptians had long since stumbled on the art of distillation though their interest was principally in perfume and making aromatics. The word 'alcohol' may be derived from *al kohl*, with *kohl* being an Egyptian pigment used for eye-shadow, though the connection between make-up and hard liquor is not at first obvious. Another possible derivation comes from the eighth-century Arab scholar, Geber, who wrote of something he called *al ghul* or the evil spirit. He was pretty obtuse on the subject, however, as with most things – in fact the word 'gibberish' is said to be derived from his name.

The search for an elixir of life was a common fascination among the early physicians and alchemists. Indeed the use of the word 'spirit' is no accident, for distillation, like death, allows the spirit to rise up and leave the body behind. The first book on the subject by Hieronymous Braunschweig, published in 1500, defines distilling as the 'puryfyeng of the grosse from the subtyll and the subtyll from the grosse'. If this essential essence could be captured, then perhaps it really could enable us to live for ever.

No wonder the ancient monasteries and universities of Europe became obsessed with this quest for what the thirteenth-century Catalan, Ramon Lully, had dubbed 'aqua vitae' – the water of life. Lully believed its taste and smell exceeded all others and that aqua vitae was an unrivalled stimulant to soldiers before battle. His contemporary, Arnold of Villanova, was also studying the rejuvenating effects of alcohol and its ability to warm and relax the body. 'Our medicine has power to heal all infirmity and diseases, both inflammation and debility; it turns an old man into youth.' Sadly much of this, especially the last point, is all in the mind.

So how did this knowledge reach Scotland? Well the short answer is, no one really knows. The romantic response, if not the most likely, is that whisky was invented by accident. It was known that to re-heat a stew made the day before was to reduce it and make it rich and strong, so might not the same effect be achieved with ale? Only of course in this case it was what left the pot in the form of steam that was the stronger. If, thanks to the cold autumn air and a bit of luck, this vapour could somehow be caught and returned to liquid then something wonderful would

Early Whisky Advert from 1905

Note the words 'thoroughly matured and of guaranteed age'.

9

An Eighteenth-century Image of Contentment
The dram at the end of the day.

have been discovered. It was a very impure science to be sure — a momentary accident that would sometimes work but most often not. Yet this in itself would have increased its allure and sense of magic. In a similar vein, learning about distillation once and for all proved as elusive as the fickle vapours themselves. The early knowledge appears to have been snuffed out by the Dark Ages, which is where the Irish claim comes in.

Just as it is easy to tease Italians by telling them pasta was invented by the Chinese in the form of noodles and was brought home to Italy by Marco

Polo, so the Irish can have fun with whisky at the expense of the Scots. The theory goes as follows. Christianity came to Ireland in the fourth century AD and was kept alive for the next four or five centuries while the rest of Europe was plunged into darkness following the demise of the Holy Roman Empire and the arrival of the Barbarians. By the ninth century, Ireland, the 'land of saints and scholars', was attracting students from all over the known world to study at its monasteries. Some time before then, missionary monks had brought the secret of distillation back from the Middle East.

In 1170 King Henry II of England and his troops landed in Ireland where they are said to have developed a taste for *Uisce Beatha* even if they never managed to pronounce it properly. A century later, near the site of the present-day Bushmills distillery, Sir Thomas Savage was wont to fortify his troops with a mighty draught of the hard stuff, or so it was claimed. It is true that an ancient 'worm' — the copper coil used to condense spirit — was found preserved in an Irish bog, but its date was 1400 at the earliest. It was also supposedly around then that the Irish chieftain, Richard MacRanall, made history by becoming the first known case of someone drinking themselves to death — a cruel blow for one who had merely indulged in the elixir of life. But by then, according to the nineteenth-century scholar Samuel Moorewood, the Genoese had been selling small bottles of grain spirit for a high price for well over a century — so perhaps the Italians had the last laugh.

The writer Michael Brander in his book *The Original Scotch*, puts in a claim for the sixth-century

What is this...Whisky?

It would be a long time before anyone thought to describe 'whisky' — a word which did not appear in print until 1736 when Bailie John Steuart of Inverness wrote to his brother-in-law urging him to 'keep a sober regular dyet' and 'forbear drinking that poisonous drink, I mean drams of brandie and whisky.' Its name evolved from the Scots Gaelic translation of *aqua vitae*, the water of life, as in — *uisge beatha* (pronounced 'oosh-key-ba') or *uiskie* as it became in the seventeenth century.

Today whisky is very tightly defined — no additives are allowed along with the malted barley and unmalted grain. Originally it would have been made from whatever cereals were available and was frequently 'compounded' or mixed with sugar, herbs and spices. It was often the only way to achieve

something remotely drinkable. Fynes Morrison, the Elizabethan writer, wrote that the 'usquebaugh' he knew was produced with raisins and fennel seeds. Though whether the Scots were growing fennel in their *kail* yards is another question. In Dr Johnson's famous Dictionary of 1755, 'Usquebaugh' was defined as: 'a compound distilled spirit, being drawn on aromaticks; and the Irish sort is particularly distinguished for its pleasant and mild flavour. The Highland sort is somewhat hotter and by corruption in Scottish they call it whisky'.

Johnson only drank whisky once in his life on his Hebridean Tour with James Boswell 20 years later. He declared it drinkable — a better endorsement than the 'malt brandy' he had tried in England which he called 'repulsive'.

Celts in Wales and speculates that they may have passed the knowledge to the Irish when they drove the Picts out of Scotland. However, he then concludes 'It is only certain that when the English first invaded Ireland in the twelfth century, the Irish were making a spirit from distilled grain, and clearly the Scots also possessed the art by this time.' If true, no one in Scotland was exactly racing to take the credit for making the first dram. It was not until 1494 that we finally get our first Scottish mention of what would eventually become known as whisky. As the Exchequer Roll for that year states: 'To Friar John Cor, by order of the King, to make aquavitae, VIII bolls of malt.' With eight bolls equivalent to 1120 pounds of grain – enough to make just over 400 bottles of today's standard strength Scotch – it was presumably not just for personal consumption. The fact that the first record refers to a monk, a member of the Benedictine Order at Lindores Abbey in Fife, is no surprise. After all monasteries were then at the cutting edge of scientific knowledge. What is faintly depressing, however, is that the Exchequer Roll implies an interest in the financial side by the State, from where it is but a short hop to taxation.

If 1494 was the first written mention of aqua vitae, one can only speculate how many years before that the first recognisable drop of whisky was produced. With necessity being the mother of invention it is tempting to suggest the Scots did not have to wait until then, did not have to endure so many cruel winters before discovering the soothing balm of *Uisce Beatha*. Perhaps some heather ale that had turned sour was boiled up and some small trickle condensed. Apart from the physiological need for strong drink to numb the pain of feeling permanently cold and damp, whisky was a medicinal spirit to cleanse cuts and rub on aching bones. There was also the fact that without modern day fridge freezers and sell-by dates, much of the food eaten would have been 'off'. Being a natural antibiotic, whisky would help kill the bacteria before the bacteria killed the patient.

In other words whisky was a wonder drug – a universal panacea which made the claims for the potions pedalled by the medicine men of the Wild West centuries later pale by comparison. For Peter Morwyng who wrote one of the first books on the subject in 1559, there was little a distilled spirit could not do. It was a cure for tired eyes, palsy, poor memory, ringworm and spots: 'It is mervelous profitable for frantic man and such as be melancholy … it taketh away sadness, pensiveness; it maketh men merri, witti and encreaseth audacitie'. Two decades later, Raphael Holinshead, whose 'Chronicles' of England, Wales and Scotland were a famous inspiration for William Shakespeare, went one further. 'Being moderately taken… it kepyth and preserveth

The Kilted Warrior

In a secret bothy beside his illicit still - the very picture of Highland defiance, albeit highly romanticised (c18th century).

the eyes from dazelying, the tongue from lispying, the teeth from chatterying, the throte from rattlying, the weasan from stieflying, the stomach from womblying, the harte from swellying, the belie from wirtching, the guts from rumblying, the hands from shivering, the sinews from shrinkying' … and on and on *ad infinitum*. Just imagine seeing that on the back label of a bottle of Bells. In fact if Holinshead was half right, the idea of not drinking whisky sounds too horrible to contemplate.

One final reason for believing that whisky-making might have been around longer in Scotland than the Exchequer Roll would have us believe, is that distillation tended to be a jealously guarded secret by alchemists and physicians. Beyond the four elements of earth, air, fire and water of which all terrestrial things were made, philosophers believed there was a 'quintessence' or fifth essence of which the heavens were composed. Some felt that, as well as being able to free one from earthly concerns, which it still can, the water of life held the key to transforming base metals into gold. It would thus be able to cure the national debt forever. This was something of a holy grail for a cash-strapped monarch like James IV of Scotland. It was also a pretty wild claim to make and any sensible alchemist would be inclined to keep quiet until he could prove his magic potion actually worked.

SCOTCH WHISKY 1494 – 1788

Whatever the truth about the early, unwritten history of whisky in Scotland, after 1494 references come thick and fast. Within just nine years, Edinburgh's Guild of Surgeon Barbers (the fore-

runner of the Royal College of Surgeons) were granted exclusive rights for making aqua vitae in the city – a deal that lasted over two-and-a-half centuries. A similar monopoly in England was revoked by Queen Elizabeth I in 1601 who declared that her citizens should 'have all the cheap aqua vitae they wanted to warm their chilled stomachs'. It was during the previous century that whisky evolved from a surgical spirit and tonic into an increasingly popular drink.

First a little technology was needed. At some point it was learnt that if you ran the pipe protruding from the top of the still, known as the worm, through a tub of cold water far more spirit would trickle out the end than if you relied on cold air. By the mid fifteenth century it was discovered that if you coiled the worm like a cork-screw, even more of the hot,

alcoholic vapours would condense. At the same time the still itself was beginning to stretch into its familiar pear-shape. As to what the first faltering attempts by the early distillers tasted like it would have been nothing like the whisky you and I might drink today. The first dram drunk in Scotland was no smooth-tasting single malt. It did not slip down the throat like treacle, spreading a gentle warmth as it went. No this would have blistered the tonsils like sandpaper and smacked you between the eyes for good measure.

Yet suddenly there was a whole new demand for barley whose principal use had been in making bread and ale for as long as anyone could remember. This had serious implications whenever the harvest came in short, prompting the parliament of Mary, Queen of Scots to make the first attempt at restricting the use of barley in 1555. Anticipating another bad harvest, an Act of Parliament in 1579 spoke of a great quantity of malt being used to make aqua-vitae and actually banned whisky-making for a year. The only exceptions were Earls, Lords, Barons and Gentlemen for their own consumption.

The government's other interest in all this soon became apparent. In 1644 came the first-ever tax on spirits in Scotland. It was levied at 2s 8d on every Scottish pint ($^1/_3$ of a gallon) sold, in order to raise money to pay for the Duke of Montrose's Highland army to fight for Charles I. It was a one-off tax that was soon allowed to lapse. Yet that was hardly the

'I have seen a troop of thirty of them riding Indian file, and in broad day, through the streets of Brechin, after they had succumbed in disposing of their whisky, and as they rode leisurely along, beating time with their formidable cudgels on the empty barrels to the great amusement of the public and the mortification of the excisemen, who had nothing for it but to bite their nails and stand as best they could, the raillery of the smugglers and the laughter of the people …. Everybody with few exceptions, drank what was in reality illicit whisky – far superior to that made under the eye of the Excise – lords, lairds, members of parliament and ministers of the Gospel, and everybody else'

From the Autobiography of Thomas Guthrie (b. 1803)

Early advertising of Scotch whisky tended to eschew subtlety when it came to hammering home the national stereotype. Only the proverbial shortbread tin appears to be missing.

point, for having supped on this sweet source of revenue, the powers that be were not about to lose the taste. By the end of the century the taxation of hard liquor was here to stay. With the Act of Union in 1707, excise duty on drink would be one of the principal sources of income for the new administration. In the Act was the provision to charge the same rates of duty in Scotland as in England, but the English trod carefully. It took five years for them to extend the malt tax to Scotland, and only then at half the rate down south. Ten years after the first Jacobite Rising of 1715 had been safely defused, the duty was raised to 3d per bushel of malt. This provoked a violent reaction on the streets of Glasgow. Eleven people were killed and the local MP, Daniel Campbell, found his fine townhouse burnt to the

ground. The Shawfield riots were really about beer, but the £9000 compensation paid to Campbell (some £1.2 million in today's money) allowed him to buy Islay. This was to have a huge impact on farming and distilling on the island, as we will learn later.

If the malt tax switched people from ale to spirits, the Gin Act of 1736 was a boon to whisky. The writer Geraldine Coates has compared England's early eighteenth-century gin craze to the epidemic of crack cocaine that recently hit the American inner cities. It hardly seems an exaggeration when you consider that at one stage three quarters of the children christened in London were being buried before the age of five. Parliament's belated reaction to 'Mother's Ruin' was just one example of how government policy has undoubtedly done more than

anything to affect the evolution of drink. Nothing has swung people's taste like taxation, especially when it comes to whisky.

Though widespread, whisky-making was a part-time activity that began shortly after the harvest and was well over by spring. It was made privately and on farms in small stills, which would rarely hold more than 50 gallons. At most it was a cottage industry and was firmly wedded to the farmyard. The one exception was Ferintosh. Despite unsubstantiated claims by the Haig whisky dynasty, this was the oldest recorded distillery in Scotland, built on the Black Isle near Dingwall in the 1670s. Its owner, Duncan Forbes of Culloden, was a prominent supporter of the newly crowned William of Orange, which was the reason why a band of Jacobites burnt the distillery to the ground in 1689. It was recorded that he had 'suffered the loss of his brewery of aqua vitae by fire in his absence … and all the whiskie pits destroyed...' The Scottish Parliament felt obliged to offer some form of compensation. The package they presented was, depending on your point of view, either the dumbest or most brilliant deal ever struck by a parliament. According to Charles Craig in *The Scotch Whisky Industry Record* Forbes was excused the £40,000 payable every year in duty so long as he paid the Exchequer an annual sum of 400 Scots merks — about £22. Not surprisingly the Forbes family became exceedingly rich. Their duty-free status lasted almost a century, until the Crown bought them out for £21,580 in 1784. By then the family had built three distilleries on the site, and had created the first ever brand of Scotch whisky well over 100 years before 'Johnnie Walker' had even been thought of. Compared to the mean mouthwash coming from most other legal distilleries, Ferintosh was clearly quality stuff. Its demise prompted the national bard, Robert Burns, to pen the following lines:

Thee Ferintosh! O sadly lost!
Scotland lament frae coast to coast!
Now colic grips, an' barkin hoast
May kill us a';
For loyal Forbes' charter'd boast
Is ta'en awa.

By the mid eighteenth century the licensed production of whisky had soared to around half a million gallons a year. This boom persuaded a few larger distilleries to join Ferintosh and start producing on a commercial scale. There was Dolls, (later Glenochil) at Menstrie and Gilcomston in Aberdeen, which went bust 12 years later. Clearly much of the whisky then being drunk, was being made privately for home consumption and a bit on the side for selling locally. A certain amount of smuggling was doubtless going on, but not on any great scale. What tipped the balance was the government's decision, after the disastrous harvest of 1756, to ban all distilling in Britain for the next three years. By the 1760s it was estimated that ten times the quantity of whisky was being produced 'privately' than by licensed distillers. Gradually these 'private' stills began to supply a wider demand, provoking an

Whisky Barons – Peter Mackie

While Tommy Dewar was still a teenager in Perth, Peter Mackie, the father of White Horse, had just begun working in his uncle's whisky business in Glasgow. He was just 23 and keen to get on in life, when he was sent on an apprenticeship to Lagavulin on Islay which was leased by his uncle at the time. His time at the distillery instilled a deep fondness for the island which he never lost.

Back in Glasgow 'Restless Peter', as he was later dubbed, set about expanding sales of Laphroaig and Lagavulin, and working on the firm's prototype blends. Having set up an office in London six years earlier, the name 'White Horse' was registered as a brand in 1890. The name came from the famous inn in Canongate on Edinburgh's Royal Mile where the Mackies had owned the next door house since the seventeenth century. It was called something else then, but was re-named after its owner had won a hefty bet on a white horse at Leith Sands. Having hosted George III who apparently stayed there incognito, on his way to Rothesay to meet the Earl of Bute, the White Horse became popular with travellers, actors and eloping couples.

By the end of the nineteenth century White Horse was being plastered over newspaper adverts and billboards and slapped across thousands of bottles that rattled down the bottling line in Glasgow. In 1901 with overseas sales running at 24,000 bottles a year, it was decided to launch the brand in Britain. Yet unlike the nag at Leith Sands 'White Horse' hardly took off at a gallop, and four years later Peter Mackie was having to concede to an embarrassing flop that had cost the business £30,000.

Restless Peter seemed frustrated by the endemic ignorance among the whisky drinking classes. 'There is a section of the public who know quality,' he fumed, 'but there is a larger section quite indifferent who are only influenced by extravagant and persistent advertising'. If the great unwashed were unable to recognise the superiority of White Horse on taste alone then so be it – advertising it would have to be. Between 1902 and the outbreak of the First World War, Mackie spent £90,000 on marketing in the UK and saw domestic sales rise from 700 to 70,000 cases per annum. For a man who purported to despise advertising he became quite a convert. And curiously when a German firm decided to hedge its bets and bring out a copy-cat brand called 'Black & White Horse' it was Mackie and not Jimmie Buchanan who sued.

Having learned his trade on Islay and made Lagavulin the heart and soul of his top-selling blend, Peter Mackie was more wedded to malt whisky than his rivals. But he also knew that without blends, malt whisky would be decimated.

Despite failing to get a minimum age for whisky enshrined in law, something that did not happen until 1915, Mackie campaigned vigorously against the chancellor, Lloyd George, whose draconian taxes threatened to destroy the industry. By the outbreak of the First World War, sales of White Horse, plus a couple of stable-mates, Logan's Perfection and Logan's Superb, were running at 190,000 cases a year with South Africa the biggest market. Mackie was spending increasing amounts of time playing the laird in full Highland dress at his two estates in Argyll and Ayrshire.

But his entrepreneurial drive never left him. He was forever dreaming up new ideas from manufacturing carrageen moss and concrete slabs to weaving Highland tweed. His most bizarre brainwave was an apparent attempt to create a new breed of brawny Scotsmen. It was a brand of flour called BBM or Brain, Bone and Marrow milled directly beneath the company's Glasgow boardroom which all staff had to eat. Perhaps Restless Peter had been taken in by the kilted shot-putter that stared out at him from the packet of porridge oats on the breakfast table?

White Horse distilleries owned a half share in Cragganmore, the Hazelburn distillery in Campbeltown and Craigellachie on Speyside, which Mackie had built as a modern, large-scale distillery in 1890. In 1921 he finally bought his beloved Lagavulin outright. Having turned down an earlier invitation to team up with Buchanan-Dewar, Sir Peter Mackie remained an independent force to the end. The merger did go ahead, three years after he died in 1923.

inevitable crack down from the government as they saw their revenue from the legal trade melt away. In 1774 a law was passed outlawing wash stills of a capacity less than 400 gallons and spirit stills of 100 gallons. The aim was obviously to make unlicensed stills easier to spot, but the effect was merely to discourage any new distiller to take out a licence. Meanwhile illicit stills were starting to operate in caves and bothys, but also in town, where it was doubtless easier to hide the smells of distillation amidst the smoke and squalor of the tenements. In Edinburgh it was said that only eight of the city's 400 stills were licensed. The rest bubbled away in secret, their fumes lost in the stench of 'Auld Reekie'.

Despite the rise of smuggling and competition from Ferintosh which was then making two thirds of the legal whisky in Scotland, the 1770s saw the emergence of the great Lowland distilleries under the Steins and their cousins, the Haigs. James Stein's Kilbagie Distillery in Clackmannanshire was apparently the biggest in the country and had a staff of 300. It had cost £40,000, or something over £4 million in today's money. Everything was geared to producing volume from specially designed flat-bottomed stills in an attempt to flood the market with cheap booze. Whether Kilbagie ever produced good

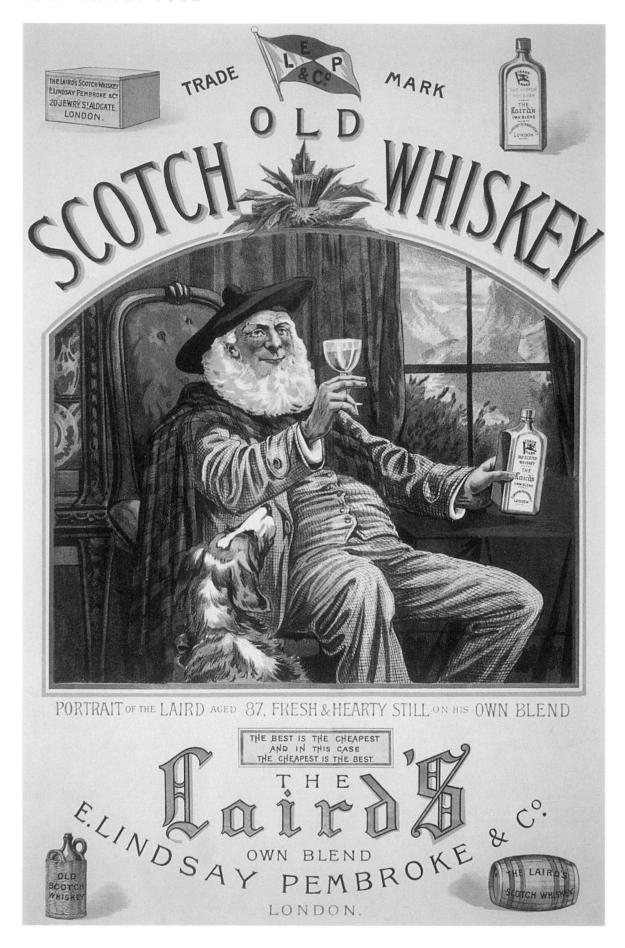

whisky is not known, but when it stopped distilling in the midnineteenth century it was converted to a manure factory. This might not have surprised one contemporary who claimed that the spirit produced here was 'only fitted for the most vulgar and fire-loving palates'. There was also big business to be had exporting bulk spirit to England for rectifying into gin – a trade which by 1782 had jumped from 2000 to 184,000 gallons in just five years.

Whisky-making in the Highlands was a very different beast, and this difference was enshrined in law with the Wash Act of 1784. Following a failed harvest, which had provoked virtual famine in parts of the country, the government sought to acknowledge the problems in the north. Anyone north of the Highland Line was exempt from malt tax, but stills had to be small and the barley could only come from the local parish. This caused resentment among Lowland distillers, so it was further decreed that Highland whisky could not be exported out of the region. The trouble was the whole country had by then developed quite a taste for the pure malt made in the north, after a gentle distillation in a small pot still, and the fact it was illegal only added to its allure.

SCOTCH WHISKY 1788 – 1823

'The whisky of this country is a most rascally liquor, and by consequence drunk by the most rascally part of the inhabitants.' – Robbie Burns writing from his Dumfriesshire home in 1788.

By 1788 distilling was very much part of the fabric of Scottish society, split between a small number of operators in the Lowlands and a vast number in the Highlands. The former were very much part of the nascent Industrial Revolution that had seen the first cotton mills established at New Lanark, and Deanston in Perthshire, a few years before. The latter

Morning Break

Distillery workers on Islay take a break after a hard morning cutting peat (c. 1880).

Poster, 1888

Wearing an unlikely-looking beard, and for once no kilt, a Scottish laird toasts himself with a dram of his own blend. Note the spelling of 'whiskey'.

Alexander Walker

The real hero of the
Johnnie Walker brand.

Whisky Barons – Johnnie Walker

To judge by the familiar strapline on the world's best-selling Scotch whisky – 'Born 1820. Still going strong' – it would appear that Johnnie Walker was the oldest whisky baron of them all. The family was certainly quick on the scene as blended whisky began to take-off, but its claim to fame is not quite that old. Indeed the first recognisable forerunner of the Johnnie Walker brand probably appeared after John Walker's death in 1857.

Back in 1820, when our hero was supposedly strutting round his native Kilmarnock in top hat and tails, he was actually just 15. He had recently inherited £417 from his father which was to be held in trust until he was old enough to open a grocery shop in the town. John no doubt taught his young, teenage son, Alexander all about blending tea, but whether he progressed to whisky we don't know. If he did, it would have been more a case of vatting malts, since it was not until the Spirits Act in 1860 that what we would know as blended Scotch, would take off. The Act allowed malt and grain whiskies to be blended before duty was payable, for the first time.

The world-famous logo of the Regency dandy in mid-stride was sketched on the back of a menu in a London restaurant in 1908 by Tom Brown, a well-known cartoonist and commercial artist. It was at the end of what was presumably a good lunch with George Pattison Walker, the company chairman, whose grandfather was probably chuckling in his grave. Kilmarnock was a boom town of the newly industrialised Scotland whose population tripled in the first half of the nineteenth century. But grocers, even successful ones, did not go around looking quite like that.

Just before his father died, Alexander Walker was brought into the family firm having served an apprenticeship in the whisky trade in Glasgow. With blends given the green light, this side of the Kilmarnock business began to grow and by the mid-1860s the firm was selling 100,000 gallons of whisky a year in Glasgow and beyond. In 1867 he registered the name 'Walker's Old Highland Whisky' and began putting the blend in bottles with a slanting black and gold label. A few years later the familiar rectangular bottle started to appear.

Alexander was quick to spot the opportunity in Australia where 'Walker's Kilmarnock Whiskies' won a string of medals at trade shows across the country in the 1880s. The brand's success down under was one reason why Australia became whisky's largest export market until the Second World War. Four years after Alexander's death, John Walker & Sons bought its first distillery – Cardhu in 1893, and leased another, a now defunct distillery in Dumfriesshire. In time the empire spread to include Coleburn, Mortlach, Talisker and Clynelish to ensure sufficient fillings for Walker's blends.

The name 'Johnnie Walker' was not actually registered until 1908, but there was already a well-defined range of whiskies. They stood out from the crowd thanks to their distinctive packaging and from each other because of their different coloured labels and variety of ages. The 12-year-old 'Extra Special Old Highland Whisky' was already simply called 'Johnnie Walker Black Label'.

At first, advertising had been limited to the occasional etched glass in a pub or grocer's shop and the odd placard in a railway station. This was soon given a mighty boost to compete with the Buchanan's Black & White and Dewar's 'White Label' which together with Walker's formed 'the Big Three' who by now dominated the trade. The 'Striding Man' began to appear in newspapers, magazines, posters and billboards in the far-flung corners of the Empire inspecting the natives and talking to tea planters. It is all a far cry from Harvey Keitel and the New York tightrope walkers of Johnnie Walker's recent multi-million pound campaign. What has hardly changed at all is the logo itself. While Scottish Widows has transformed its image into a set of very young, glamorous-looking 'widows', old Johnnie Walker is still strutting away in his top hat and tails. Talk about a contemporary icon – he hasn't even got a mobile phone!

After his death, Alexander's son, Alec, became the driving force behind the business. He was equally obsessive in maintaining the quality of the blends up in Kilmarnock. Apart from building himself Piersland House, a fairly modest home at Troon in Ayrshire that is now a hotel, profits were ploughed back into the business. Compared to the flamboyant Tommy Dewar, Sir Alec Walker, as he became in 1920, was distinctly shy. In James Stevenson, he had a brilliant co-director who became Minister of Munitions during the First World War and sponsored the Act of Parliament that set the minimum age of whisky at three years.

In 1920 Johnnie Walker joined its erstwhile rivals and became part of the burgeoning Distillers empire. Sir Alec was still very active and when brought before a Royal Commission in 1930 to investigate the Scotch whisky industry's involvement in flaunting US prohibition, he was wonderfully blunt. Asked if the industry could cut off most of the supply, he replied 'Certainly not', and when pressed, added, 'we would not if we could'. Later he became a close friend of Winston Churchill during the Second World War, and used to have him to stay in Troon. By the time he died in 1950 at the ripe old age of 81, Johnnie Walker was the brand to beat.

were anything but. Distilling in the Lowlands continued to be dominated by the two great whisky dynasties – the Steins and the Haigs – who between them controlled almost half of all the licensed production in Scotland. But despite their industrial muscle, the next 40 years proved to be a time of strife – between London distillers in the south desperate to cling on to their market and bitterly resented competition from the Highlands. On their side they had Scotland's farmers who were by now locked into a cycle of growing barley for the whisky industry which produced the draff they needed for cattle feed.

First though, was the problem of debts. After two years, trading at a loss to compete in the English market, the Haigs and Steins ceased trading, owing £700,000 in excise – equivalent to a staggering £20 million in today's money. The creditors had no choice but to write off the debts and the firms survived. In a few years, however, they were squealing again at the end of the eighteenth century with a five-fold jump in tax to help fund the war with France. Because the tax was calculated per gallon of still capacity, the Lowland distillers were forced to run their stills at full throttle, up to 25 times a day compared to once or twice in the past. James Stein at Canonmills was even managing 47 distillations in 12 hours at one point, to stave off bankruptcy, which was beginning to claim a fair number of his fellow Lowland distillers. And to add to his woes, there were the first mutterings of concern against the demon drink and its place in a newly industrialised society. It was reported in Govan, then a small weaving community on the outskirts of Glasgow, that consumption among the 279 families living there was running at 6000 gallons a year. A few drinks back then would have you weaving in more ways than one – a dram was not today's meagre dribble of a few millilitres from a sealed optic, but a third of a pint at 50 per cent proof.

Meanwhile up in the Highlands, the frantic pace of distillation and desperate search for new methods to make whisky-making viable was unknown. From much smaller stills, using weaker washes, a far superior spirit was distilled on average about six times a day. But for Ferintosh, whose spirit was being sold as far afield as Glasgow under its name as the first ever brand, whisky-making in the Highlands offered little more than temporary employment after the harvest. The customers were largely local, though word was seeping southwards that there was more to whisky than the 'rascally liquor' described by Robbie Burns. As long as the big producers saw their main opportunity as making raw spirit for rectification into gin, there was no contest on grounds of quality. As the Irish said of poteen, illicit Scotch was 'superior in sweetness, salubriety and gusto to all that machinery, science and capital can produce in the leagalized way'.

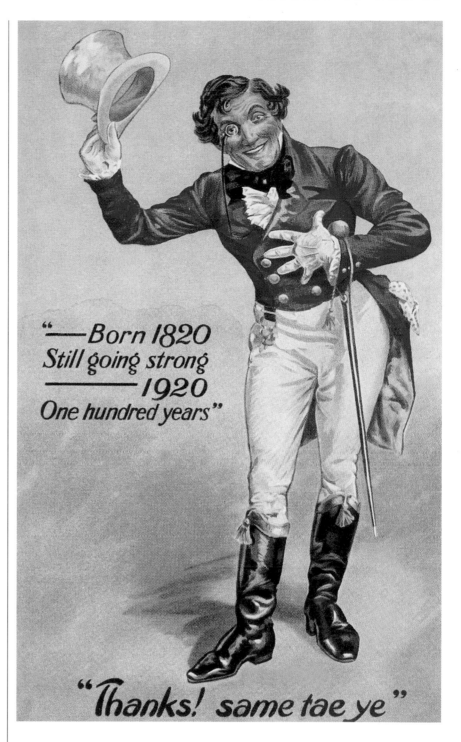

"—Born 1820
Still going strong
—1920
One hundred years"

"Thanks! same tae ye"

Johnnie Walker
Before he got into his stride (c.1920).

The government had taken a pragmatic approach to tax, keeping it low in order to encourage Highland distillers into the fold of the law, and partly out of recognition that barley yields were considerably lower further north. By the end of the eighteenth century, there were still only 58 licensed distillers there, while on an island like Tiree it was said that every farm operated at least one still. But an attempt to reduce the 'Highland advantage' and extract more tax, to the undoubted delight of the Lowland distillers, completely backfired.

**Delivery at
Glen Garioch**

Barley arriving by ox and
cart at the Aberdeenshire
distillery (c.1890).

Higher taxes did nothing to quench demand, it merely caused the price of whisky to soar. Smuggling suddenly took off as a highly profitable business. Glen Livet, where it was claimed there had been almost no illicit distilling before 1794, became a one-industry glen overnight devoted to making 'moonshine' with at least 200 illicit stills. As routes south became cut off by the first fall of snow, Glen Livet would begin to retreat in on itself behind the bulk of the Cairngorm mountains. From hidden caves and isolated bothys, wisps of smoke would start to curl upwards into the cold air to be followed by the sweet vapours of distilled spirit. Beside the still itself, an elder of the clan would tend to business, his senses straining to hear news from a lookout perched on some nearby crag that the dreaded gaugers were closing in. The image was simply too romantic to resist – at least for the later Victorian artists. How true to life it was, one wonders.

When Walter Adams was caught making whisky near Castle Huntly in November 1798, he simply told the exciseman to get lost. When the exciseman

Andrew Usher

In the mid-nineteenth century, a wine and spirit merchant at 34 West Nicholson Street, Edinburgh, had just launched 'Usher's Old Vatted Glenlivet' – taking advantage of a change in the law allowing inconsistencies between casks and vintages to be smoothed out by vatting. Not that he knew it at the time, but Andrew Usher had just pioneered the first step of a process that would revolutionise whisky. In a few years time, with another change in the law, he would move from vatting malts to creating one of the first examples of blended Scotch whisky as we know it today. He was a man ahead of his time, for it was to take the advent of bottling lines, grocery chains, mass advertising and greatly improved transport to build blended whisky into a world force. The family became wealthy benefactors to the city of Edinburgh and bequeathed £100,000 in 1898 to build the Usher Hall. As a brand of Scotch the name lives on as 'Usher's Green Stripe' but it has long been eclipsed by brands like White Horse, Bells and Famous Grouse.

A 1904 Advertisement

'Old Vatted Glenlivet' – the flag-ship brand of Andrew Usher, the great pioneer of blended whisky.

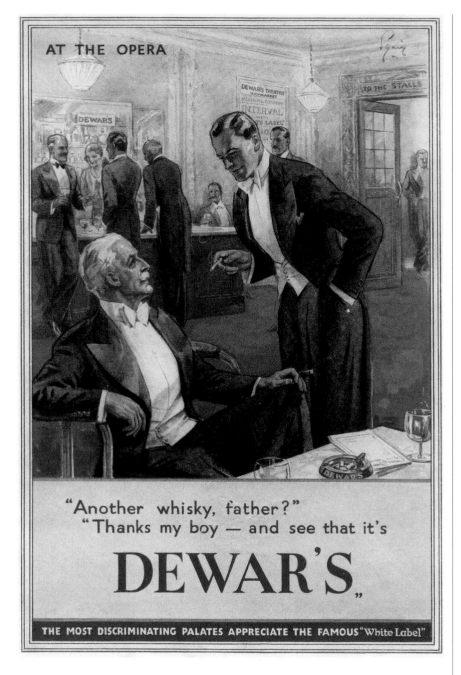

AT THE OPERA

DEWARS

DEWAR'S THEATRE
HAYMARKET

INTERVAL

TO THE STALLS

"Another whisky, father?"
"Thanks my boy — and see that it's

DEWAR'S

THE MOST DISCRIMINATING PALATES APPRECIATE THE FAMOUS "White Label"

1934 Advertisement
Like the characters in this ad in the 'Illustrated Sporting & Dramatic News', Dewar's White Label saw itself as a pillar of the establishment.

returned with reinforcements the next day, Adams was still at it. It was a lot more risky getting the whisky to market via the old droving routes to the outskirts of Perth or Dundee. Here, there would be a pre-arranged rendezvous with the agents or 'blethermen' of existing customers. But even if caught, the fines were seldom harsh especially if the magistrate happened to be the notoriously lenient William Grant — the peg-legged Justice of the Peace from Aucharachan. Even by 1819, a quarter of the 4200 cases were being thrown out. Alternatively by pleading guilty one moment and volunteering for military service the next, all charges would be dropped. Getting whisky over the Highland Line past Stirling could be tricky because of the number of

troops garrisoned there. But it was not impossible, as one smuggler gleefully explained in 1804. A couple of men, some knackered old nags and a few casks would be sent out as a lure to tempt the excisemen out of their quarters. On being seized the men would 'make a great feigned resistance, but at last after a great deal ado, they are taken and carried off by the officers in triumph, who congratulate themselves on being very successful'. Meanwhile a veritable flood of illicit hooch with nothing to fear was flowing via another route.

Even the government's offer of £5 to anyone reporting an illicit still was turned against them. Once the copper worm, the most expensive single piece of distilling apparatus, wore out, the bootleggers would simply leave it behind as evidence, move their dismantled still elsewhere, and claim the reward. No wonder the licensed distillers were upset. That said, it was in their interest to paint the blackest picture possible in the spirit of what the Germans call *zweckpessimismus* or self-serving pessimism. John Stein of Kilbagie, the biggest distiller in Scotland, told a House of Commons Select Committee in 1798 that over half the whisky consumed in Scotland was illegal. The Highland response sounds a touch disingenuous:

'All that is contended on behalf of the Highlander,' wrote John Grant of Balnagown near Grantown in 1798, 'is that he shall have the liberty in moderate terms suited to the poverty of his circumstances to convert the growth of his own soil through his personal industry to the necessary beverage of wholesome spirit, whether diluted with water as grog … or taken as a cordial dram to brace, sometimes the humid, sometimes the piercing winds of the north...'.

For all the talk, however, the biggest threat to distillers in the Highlands, whether licensed or not, came from poor harvests as in 1813 when many parts of Scotland were faced with famine and distilling was banned throughout the country. Yet while the government cannot have relished having its newly minted laws treated with such derision, what mattered most was how to squeeze as much tax from whisky as possible. It was always going to be easier to tax the large Lowland distillers than their unlicensed cousins in the north for the simple fact that their stills stayed put unlike those in the Highlands. Only when revenue fell because of a slump in production due to harvest failure, a flood of French brandy or increased smuggling, did the government resolve to do something.

By 1810, the Scottish Excise Board realised that the gaugers were not going to win the war on their own without the support of the Highland lairds. That is unless the ongoing clearances that began in

Whisky Barons – Tommy Dewar

For sheer bravado there was no greater whisky baron than Tommy Dewar, the son of a small-time blender from Perth, who was sent to London in 1885 aged 21 to 'wake up the south'.

Unfortunately, of his two business contacts it transpired that one had died and the other had gone bankrupt. It was not the most promising start, and yet within 50 years Dewars became one of the most powerful dynasties the trade has ever known.

Unlike their arch-rival Jimmy Buchanan, the Dewars were a double-act from the word go. While Tom played the witty, irrepressible front man, his brother John was the shrewd but dour Scot who ran the production-end of the business in Perth. Tommy Dewar was a consummate salesman who set off on the first of two global sales trips in 1892 aboard the City of Paris bound for New York. He returned two years later having visited 26 countries and appointed 32 agents, some of whom were to last over 50 years. The cost had been a staggering £14,000 – more than half a million pounds in today's money – yet any doubts there may have been up in Perth had long faded – orders were pouring in.

Tommy Dewar understood the power of advertising better than almost any of his contemporaries on either side of the Atlantic. For him it was to business 'what imagination is to poetry'. Long before Coca-Cola discovered how to use neon to its best advantage, Tommy Dewar had attached a 200 foot Scotsman to the side of a disused tower on the south bank of the Thames. Londoners were transfixed by this giant Highlander, made of hundreds of light bulbs, whose kilt appeared to sway in the breeze as his right hand repeatedly raised a glass of Dewars White Label to his lips. Other tricks included showing a film version of the long-running 'whisky of his forefathers' campaign from the roof of a New York skyscraper. In it an Anglo-Scottish gent sits in his baronial home nursing a glass of Dewars while his ancestors reach out from their portraits behind him to try and grab the bottle.

The unsung hero behind the scenes was Alexander Cameron who joined the firm in 1890, and whose lifetime achievement was White Label – a blend with up to 40 different malts that was launched at the turn of the century. He understood the importance of maturation like few others and pioneered a method of pre-vatting malt and grain whisky according to provenance, and only blending them together when each was just right. Dewar's had first leased the Tullymet distillery from the Duke of Atholl, before building their own in 1898 at Aberfeldy in Perthshire, a couple of miles from John Dewar's birthplace. From then on the malt of Aberfeldy was to be the sweet, heathery heart of White Label. By 1900, production had passed the one million gallon mark while yearly profits had jumped to £59,000 from £1231 in 1880.

With Edward VII on the throne, the two brothers were clambering up the social ladder as fast as their legs would carry them. Both were now in politics, John a Liberal MP for Inverness and Tom a rather unlikely Tory for Tower Hamlets in London's East End – a constituency he lost in the Liberal landslide of 1906. Back in 1895, he had acquired what was said to be the third motorcar in Britain – a three hp chain-driven Benz. The first belonged to the Prince of Wales and the second to his friend and fellow tycoon, Sir Thomas Lipton.

Believing that 'competition is the life of trade, but the death of profit,' Dewar bowed to the inevitable as he saw it, and merged with Buchanan in 1915. A decade later they became the first of 'the big five' to join up with William Ross in his burgeoning empire at DCL. By then Dewar's had acquired three further distilleries – Lochnagar, Aultmore and Ord, while annual profits had passed £1 million.

When Tommy Dewar was knighted two years after his brother became Baron Forteviot, he choose as his family crest a scarlet cock crowing from a bed of thistles. It seemed to sum up this larger than life character who lived out his days at Dewar House in London's Haymarket and at his Sussex estate where he bred racehorses and tried in vain to win the Derby. The two brothers died within six months of one another in the winter of 1929-30 and left estates worth around £5 million each.

Top:
Tommy Dewar
Whisky baron and sheriff of London in 1897, two years after becoming the proud owner of Britain's third motorcar.

Bottom:
John Dewar
Founder of a dynasty.

John Grant

He bought Glenfarclas distillery on Speyside in 1865.

the 1750s were carried to their ultimate conclusion, so that the entire population were replaced with sheep. 'While any is left here, they will continue [as] whisky smugglers and of course sheep stealers' argued James Loch – the Duke of Sutherland's infamous factor. Incidentally it was the Highlander's taste for robust whisky which they took with them on their mass-migration to Glasgow and across the seas that inspired the whisky-making boom in Campbeltown at the foot of the Kintyre peninsular.

Loch grumbled that 'the skill displayed cheating the Revenue is regarded rather as proof of

Distillery Workers

Outside Glenfarclas in the late nineteenth century.

praiseworthy dexterity than as a crime to be punished'. What must he have thought when George IV arrived on the royal yacht for the start of his famous state visit to Edinburgh in 1822? With his 20 stone bulk swathed in tartan and flesh-coloured tights, the King had barely waddled ashore before he was demanding 'Highland whisky' and, as he soon made clear, that meant illicit Glen Livet. A contemporary analogy would be Prince Charles asking where he might 'procure a bit of wacky baccy' for his next trip to Balmoral. That same year, however, his Government launched its most serious attempt yet to stamp out illicit distillation. Fines for keeping an 'ungauged still' or smuggling leapt to £200, and JPs could no longer impose discretionary sentence in case of hardship on the part of the defendant. If that had been the stick, 12 months later came the carrot with a halving of duty rates and a significant rebate on malt to encourage licensed distillers to use more of it and thus improve quality.

This was the Excise Act of 1823, which meant that for the first time ever small distillers could compete fairly on price and quality with those on the other side of the law. A distiller could now choose the strength of his wash, the size of the stills and the quality and flavour of his whisky. As for those left out in the cold, the choice was simple – whether to fight on against gaugers now equipped with newly sharpened teeth, or pay the £10 and get a licence. In just two years the number of licensed distilleries in Scotland shot from 111 to 263.

SCOTCH WHISKY 1824 – 1900

With the Excise Act, the whisky industry may have come of age, but its problems had only just begun. As the number of players in the market swelled to take advantage of the newly liberalised conditions, the industry grew increasingly complicated. Add in the wild swings in taxation which depressed or inflamed demand depending on which spirit, whether brandy, rum, whisky or gin was being targeted. Then sprinkle with the whims of fashion and you have a monster of instability, lurching after its market like a drunk in pursuit of a clockwork mouse.

First however, was the question of what was to happen to all the illicit distillers. Some were a quick case of poacher turned gamekeeper like James Robertston of Crathie who set up the first Lochnagar distillery on Deeside. Some took up other professions like weaving instead. But others, notably around Speyside, were determined to go down fighting. With no tax, and an established clientèle willing to pay an extra £1 an anker (a ten gallon cask) if it came from Glen Livet, there was no lack of incentive. When

George Smith went legal and applied for a licence for his distillery at Upper Drumin he won few friends in the neighbourhood. A couple of none too distant distilleries had already been torched by smugglers, so to protect himself and his business from a similar fate, he kept a brace of hair-trigger revolvers tucked in his belt. And he was not afraid to use them. Once, when holed up for the night at an inn by the Spittal of Glenshee, he found his bedroom invaded by a smuggling gang led by a thug named Shaw who threatened to disembowel him on the end of his butcher's knife. Smith whipped out his guns from under the bed clothes, held one to Shaw's head and fired the other up the chimney. With a deafening blast and a cloud of soot, they fled.

The whisky gold rush inspired a building boom in the industry. This was the time that new distilleries like Glendronach and Ben Nevis were born, others like Bowmore and Highland Park were brought back to life, and dozens more licenced for the first time. Around Campbeltown alone, no less than 27 distilleries were opened between 1823 and 1837. How many had paused to consider such trifles as having a ready supply of grain and peat or whether there really was a demand, is not known and many new ventures soon ended in tears. That said, production trebled to ten million gallons within five years of the Act.

In the rush to the market, there was no time for the niceties of maturation, and next to the lazy rhythms of pot-still distillation in the Highlands, the pace was frantic and soon non-stop. Robert Stein produced his patented continuous still in 1827, and three years later Aeneas Coffey launched his version in Dublin – a bizarre invention to come from the city's Chief Excise Officer. The Coffey Still involved two columns separated by a set of perforated plates and was a definite improvement on Stein's. The wash was heated up to near boiling point, passed down the first column and pumped to the top of the second where it met low-pressure steam. This caused it to vaporise, allowing the more volatile spirit vapours to rise to the top where they were condensed by the cold wash coming into the still. Unfortunately, it tasted foul and was only suitable for rectifying into gin. Once copper was used instead of cast iron, however, the result was certainly palatable if not brimming with personality.

These innovations took production of patent still grain whisky to new heights, which added a certain urgency to the quest for new markets. Glasgow's Dundashill distillery was the first to send whisky to India, but it turned in the tropics and was pronounced undrinkable on arrival. It took a couple of decades before regular consignments of grain whisky were being shipped down the Clyde to New

George Grant of Glenfarclas
He went into partnership with his father, John, as J&G Grant in 1870.

York and Newfoundland, Canada in one direction and Ceylon, now Sri Lanka and Madras, India in the other.

Back home criticism of the 'devil's drink' was growing more vociferous. From a first outpost in Greenock in 1829, 'temperance' societies spread like a rash across Scotland and into England preaching moderation and more tax. The counter-argument, as expressed by the anonymous author of *An Apology for Whisky*, went as follows: as 'the fruit of our own farmers, the manufacture of our friends and brethren' whisky was the patriotic thing to drink. 'In

Glenfarclas
With George Grant astride a barrel surrounded by his children and staff.

Whisky Barons – James Buchanan

James Buchanan, the man behind 'Black & White', was very tall and slim, was always immaculately turned out and seemed to exude style and panache wherever he went. He slipped into London completely unobserved to begin his career in whisky aged 30 and emerged some 20 years later as one of the undisputed titans of the trade.

Buchanan was born in Brockville, Ontario, Canada in 1849, the youngest son of Scottish emigrants who soon decided to return home. After leaving school at 14 he began work in Glasgow as a Customs House clearing clerk on £20 a week, before joining his brother who was a grain merchant in the city. Somehow this must have brought him into contact with the whisky trade and convinced him that the place to be was down south as London agent for a firm of blenders. After five years in the 'big smoke', he reckoned the time was right to set up on his own. He had no capital, and no family firm behind him – not even a little grocer's shop in Perth, but he had contacts and he had supreme self-confidence. The first step was to find a backer to put up the money and someone to supply the malt and grain to create 'The Buchanan Blend of Fine Old Scotch Whiskies'. The solution to both was the firm of WP Lowrie of Glasgow who had their own malt distilleries and were early converts to blended Scotch. This was quite rare – most malt distillers behaved like farmers – supplying a commodity to be processed and packaged for the end consumer whom the distillers had no particular interest in.

With whisky about to enjoy an unprecedented boom in England, the timing was spot-on, but there was no guarantee that it would be Scotch and not Irish, and no certainty that blends would outshine malts. Some have since argued that if the same drive and determination had been applied to malt whisky from the very start, they could have captured the market that blends quickly dominated. But it seems Buchanan's instincts were right – that English taste would favour something lighter, less assertive and above all consistent. Malt whisky could vary dramatically and one duff cask could lose Scotch whisky hundreds of potentially life-long drinkers, possibly for good.

Though he had a definite brand he was selling his whisky in bulk to bars, pubs and music halls. In the 1880s the first bottles of 'Buchanan's Blend' appeared with the less than hard-hitting strapline 'suitable for Grog or Toddy'. But the bottles were black and the labels were white, a fact eventually registered as a brand name in 1905.

His pursuit of the big London customers was masterful for its patience and cunning. He went after them as he later fished for salmon, gently coaxing them onto the end of the hook followed by the perfect strike before carefully reeling them in. Perhaps his greatest coup was becoming sole supplier to the House of Commons, not so much for the amount MPs drank in those days, but for the prestige which could be milked a hundred fold. This and winning lots of gold medals which again were heavily publicised, was the way Buchanan built the reputation of Black & White. For 30 years there was also the daily parade of Buchanan's beautiful horse-drawn carts in London that came to rival the trooping of the colour. Yet when it came to exploiting the black art of advertising he was a novice compared to his arch rival, Tommy Dewar.

He sailed through the stormy waters of the Pattison crash unscathed and held the confidence of investors when he converted James Buchanan into a limited liability company in 1903 with an authorised capital of £1 million. By now he owned the first of a number of malt distilleries and had bought out his former backer WP Lowrie. Having supplied the original loan, Lowrie had soon come to rely on Buchanan as his major customer. Meanwhile the business was expanding to include yet more warehouses, bottling halls, a cooperage and an extraordinary Gothic office in London's Holborn to handle the burgeoning export trade.

---

short, drunkenness is far from being the sin of our times,' the pamphlet concluded 'It is the drinking of tea among people in low stations … from which I pray that a good God may deliver us.' It is impossible to know whether consumption really increased because so much of the whisky drunk in the past had been flowing underground from illicit stills. John Stein of Kilbagie, the biggest distiller in Scotland, had told a House of Commons Select Committee in 1798 that over half the whisky consumed in Scotland was illegal, not that he could prove it of course. But once whisky crossed into legality, the temperance lobby now had figures to quote.

Although new distilleries were being built, like Dalmore in 1839 and Glen Grant the year after, the overall number fell from an all-time high of 230 in 1835, to 169 a decade later. Malt whisky had always struggled to reach new customers round the back of the Lowland industrialists, until the mid nineteenth-century railway boom. Suddenly you could travel to Aberdeen from London and thence by a web of local branch lines deep into Speyside. But the plight of remote distilleries can be illustrated by Talisker which

1899 Advertisement

While other whisky brands relied on images of heather-clad hills and swirling mists, James Buchanan could boast a string of Royal warrants and endorsement from the House of Commons in this.

was sold for £1000 in 1854 – a third of what it cost to build the previous year.

By the mid nineteenth century, whisky had become one of Scotland's biggest industries whose giant grain distilleries matched the mighty iron and coal works of William Baird & Co. in scale. Whisky was also still being made on farm distilleries like Grand Tully in Perthshire and in medium-sized operations from Orkney to the Mull of Kintyre. It was by then completely welded to Scottish agriculture, especially in the Lowlands, swallowing up mountains of barley and then spewing out great torrents of draff to feed the cattle. It had become a vital part of the Scottish economy and a major source of revenue to the government, yet if it ever dreamt this merited some kind of special treatment or even acknowledgement, the dream did not last long. From henceforth whisky would have to justify itself in the face of an increasingly shrill backlash against the dark forces of drink.

Until the big grain distillers could offer a smoother and more consistent drink, it would always be difficult to wean the English off their beloved port and brandy. The then Chancellor, William Gladstone, hardly helped by signing a commercial treaty with France which significantly cut the duty on imported wines and spirits, which led to a boom in brandy. At the same he upped the tax on whisky, causing an immediate drop in consumption by one-fifth. Important concessions were allowed to blenders

however, and the following year his 'Single Bottle Act' effectively created the off-licence trade allowing grocers to sell wines and spirits under their own label, one bottle at a time. Andrew Usher was perfectly placed – he was agent for Glenlivet and he had his own malt distillery in Edinburgh. With access to grain from the newly built Caledonian distillery, he had all the ingredients for a blend to capture the mainstream and even seduce the Sassenachs down south.

Help for these early whisky barons came in an unlikely form – a tiny eight-legged aphid with an insatiable appetite for vine roots. Phylloxera was first spotted in France in 1863, in the Rhône valley, and began slowly to munch its way through great swathes of Europe's vineyards. Brandy had always been more expensive, which was not entirely surprising given the quality of much of the whisky sent south fresh from the still. 'The effects of a debauch after drinking new whisky is a punishment long to be remembered,' it was reported in 1864. But as phylloxera spread into the region of Cognac, prices began to soar. In desperation, merchants resorted to fraud and a steady stream of fake spirit flowed into Britain, some of it quite undrinkable if not actually poisonous, causing brandy's reputation to plummet. The Victorian conversion to Scotch did not happen overnight, however. For the affluent middle classes who decamped to the Highlands in August to fish and stalk and be close to their Queen at Balmoral, whisky was a robust outdoor drink. It was fine for the river bank and the grouse moor, but hardly suitable for the Home Counties or the club surely? Besides, if whisky was to catch on, there was no guarantee it would be Scotch. One of the leading wine & spirit merchants of the time, W & A Gilbey, was selling well over twice as much 'Irish' as 'Scotch' in 1875, though how much of it actually came from the Emerald Isle is another matter. The massive Caledonian distillery was then happily pumping out 'the variety known as Irish… whisky precisely similar to that which is made in Dublin' from its five acre site in Edinburgh.

'The future of the wine trade is whisky', declared the *Wine Trade Review* in 1886, and though distilleries continued to fail and demand could fall short of supply, the early brands were on a roll. There was a growing crowd of speculators eager for a ride on the great whisky bandwagon and the banks were more relaxed than ever about lending – after all the spirit was now enjoying genuine, sustained growth. The result was an unprecedented boom in distillery building with no fewer than 33 firing up their stills for the first time during the 1890s. Two-thirds were on Speyside, attracted by the proximity of barley in Moray and Banffshire and the popularity of the region's smooth-tasting malts among the blenders. There was also a pool of locally skilled labour and off-the-shelf distilleries, complete with those distinctive pagoda shaped roofs available from specialist architect, Charles Doig of Elgin. Having installed the hardware and perhaps merged with others in the trade, the aim was to float the business as soon as possible and cash in. At the same time there was a spate of brewery conversions and distillery reconstructions such as Brora, Clynelish, Dalmore and Glen Scotia. And for those who didn't fancy building a distillery you could always invest in bulk whisky, reaping the rewards of maturation as it gained in value. If the late-Victorian whisky boom had echoes of the millennium dot.com bubble, so too did the crash. When it came, it came with terrifying speed.

Arthur Bell
Founder of Britain's best selling blend.

When the firm of R & W Pattison, blenders from Leith, became a public company in 1896, the shares were six times oversubscribed. This was a blue-chip company on a par with Dewar's and Buchanan's, having built a huge home trade with brands like Royal Gordon Whisky. These were promoted by a rip-roaring tirade of adverts packed with generals, cavalry charges and the whiff of grapeshot. In 1898 Robert and Walter Pattison decided to treble their advertising budget to an unprecedented £60,000 and launch a new blend called 'Morning Gallop'. That summer they were announcing record profits, and in November a senior firm of Edinburgh accountants scotched rumours that the business was in some kind of trouble. A month later, owing massive debts, the company collapsed pulling ten other firms down with it.

The survivors were quick to speak of their 'long-held' suspicions after Robert and Walter had been sent down for embezzlement and fraud. They left behind their palatial headquarters on Commercial Street that once proclaimed the fact that the Pattisons had 'arrived', but now stood to remind the world of the folly of speculating in drink. The truth was, it could have been anyone – by the end of the decade whisky stocks had reached 90 million proof gallons worth a cool £15 million, of which the Pattisons' share was a mere £144,000.

Whatever – it was one hell of a way to kiss the nineteenth century goodbye. The industry woke up on January 1, 1900 with the worst hangover of its life – one that took 50 years to cure.

Staff at Arthur Bell & Sons
Early 1900s.

MODERN TIMES

SCOTCH WHISKY 1900 – PRESENT

The Pattison collapse left an indelible impression on William Ross, the newly appointed managing director of the Distillers Company Limited (DCL). The company was founded in 1877 as an amalgamation of the big grain distillers like John Haig and was quickly swallowing up struggling distillers across Scotland. Their stills would often be run well below capacity and sometimes shut down and scrapped in a determined effort to learn the lessons of 1899 and bring production closer into line with consumption.

From a high of 36 million proof gallons, whisky production fell by a third and some 30 distilleries, including Jura, Benriach and Caperdonich, shut down supposedly for good. At least exports, led by Australia, followed by the US, Canada and South Africa, were on the rise, hitting 7.5 million proof gallons by 1909 and dominated by the big three – Dewars, Buchanans and Johnnie Walker. These were all blends of course, which was no great comfort to the malt distillers. During the Pattison trial it transpired that the brothers had been selling whisky as 'malt' when it was 99 per cent grain. If others were passing off their new patent spirit as something 'pure' and 'old', it was not only devious, it was not going to keep many malt distilleries in business.

To most people beyond Scotland, whisky was a very new vice and there was considerable confusion. Amidst the maelstrom of competing brand names there were venerable old malts and the meanest mouthwash fresh from the still. There were even whiskies made in London such as NSS or 'Never Seen Scotland' as the brand was soon dubbed. Matters came to a head in 1905 when, following a number of successful prosecutions against adulterated brandy, Islington Borough Council turned its gaze towards purveyors of 'so-called' whisky. But what was whisky? Should it come from a patent or only a pot still? No one seemed to know. The North London Police Court found for the Council, but on appeal the magistrates were split down the middle leaving the distillers in limbo to await the ponderous deliberations of a Royal Commission set up in 1908. While the two sides of the industry waited for an outcome, William Ross, MD of the Distillers

Company, launched a patent still whisky, called 'Cambus', to poke fun at the pot-still mafia in the Highlands. Adverts claimed it was 'mild and mellow... [a] wholesome stimulant' that promised 'not a headache in a gallon'.

In the end the Commission ducked the issue and proposed no minimum for the amount of malt to be used when they released their findings the following summer. Interestingly Alexander Walker had proposed a minimum of 50 per cent, which had the malt distillers backed it, could have changed the industry completely. It had transpired that the 'Fine Old Scotch' seized by Islington Council contained just 10 per cent malt putting it on a par with the cheapest own-label whisky today.

For the blenders there was no time to celebrate because Lloyd George, the Liberal Chancellor and later Prime Minister, had just raised the duty on spirits by a third, while keeping tax on wine and beer the same. Whisky had been taxed at 10s a gallon since 1860, the only change being a 1s rise in 1900. 'But what can one expect from a Welsh country solicitor being placed without any commercial training as Chancellor of the Exchequer in a large country like this?' declared the dyed-in-the-wool Tory, Peter Mackie of White Horse. But behind the venom lay fear. During the previous century roughly 30–40 per cent of government revenues came from duty on alcohol, far more than from income tax which had only reached five pence in the pound by the 1890s to help pay for the Boer War. Under the old regime you knew where you were, all that mattered was generating revenue – there was no great moral dimension when it came to tax and booze. With Lloyd George and his crusade 'to abolish thirst' there was no telling where it might end.

The 1909 Budget pushed the price of a standard blend of Scotch to over half a crown a bottle and many saw it as the beginning of the end. Consumption fell by a third and with it excise revenue by over £1 million which did not seem to phase the Liberals as it would have done the Tories. Peter Mackie knew whisky had to improve its image and believed the answer lay in maturation. 'What the

Early Marketing Placement

From being a 'robust outdoor drink', Scotch needed to establish its pedigree to have a place in the gentleman's club, as in this 1912 advert for Begg's – an Aberdeen blend from the owners of Lochnagar.

America's Uncle Sam

He watches his still run dry while that stern mistress, Prohibition, looks on (Emmett Watson in 'Judge' 9th October 1920).

of spirit sold, especially near munitions factories. The difficulties faced by the Highland distillers helped William Ross in his plans to consolidate the industry and bring as much whisky production as possible under the control of his Distillers Co. (DCL). For Tommy Dewar, who had joined up with Buchanan's, Ross was 'our new Moses to lead us out of the wilderness of strenuous competition and lead [us] into the land flowing with respectable dividends'.

Before the war was over, Talisker, Dailuaine and Royal Lochnagar were all in the fold, a trend that continued into the 1920s with Caol Ila, Craigellachie and Lagavulin. DCL were also buying up blending houses, including Andrew Usher & Co., distilleries in Ireland, and even toyed with a distilled substitute for petrol. In 1927, William Ross, now chairman of DCL, spelt out his philosophy:

'My conception of a combine [i.e. DCL] is that it should be strong enough to withstand the temptation to crush a weaker competitor who is striving by legitimate means to make an honest livelihood and at the same time strong enough to keep in check unscrupulous competitors'.

His self-appointed role as policeman to the trade was tied-in with the desire to cut supply to fit demand and end the cancer of overproduction. The only way to do this as far as he could see was to bring as many distilleries as possible under the same control and if necessary close them down. In the year of his pronouncement just 84 distilleries were licensed for production compared to 124 two years earlier. Much of the problem stemmed from American prohibition.

AMERICAN PROHIBITION

Oh, thou demon Drink, thou fell destroyer;
Thou curse of society, and its great annoyer.
What hast thou done to society, let me think?
I answer thou hast caused the most of ills,
thou demon Drink.

public wants is age and plenty of it'. It was an issue close to his heart. 'Experience teaches us that most of the riotous and obstreperous conduct of drunks comes from the young, fiery spirit which is sold. While men who may overindulge in old matured whisky become sleepy and stupid, but not in a fighting mood'. The law that spirit had to spend three years in cask to be called whisky was finally passed during the First World War in 1915.

That year Lloyd George claimed he knew something more damaging '...than all the German submarines put together...We are fighting Germany, Austria and drink; and as far as I can see the greatest of these deadly foes is drink'. All kinds of petty restrictions were introduced and for a while the spectre of complete prohibition loomed on the post-war horizon. As long as the fighting lasted there were unforeseen markets – such as surgical spirit for the field hospitals and fusel oil to 'dope' aircraft and varnish warships. It may not have been whisky, but it helped keep many distilleries afloat.

During hostilities, the authorities periodically banned all distilling and fought to lower the strength

Thus began an ode by the great William Topaz McGonagall, tragedian, teetotal poet and bard of Dundee. It was here that Neddy Scrymgeor, founder of the Prohibition Party of Great Britain, won a historic victory in the 1922 General Election over the local MP, Winston Churchill. Taunted as a 'WC without a seat', Churchill stormed off vowing never to return to the city of 'bestial drunkenness' leaving the country's one and only prohibitionist MP in his place. It proved to be the high-water mark of the anti-drink movement in Britain.

Over in the United States, domestic manufacture of alcoholic drinks was banned when the country entered the First World War in 1917, supposedly to

keep cereals and fruit in the food chain. By December, the powerful Anti-Saloon League had rammed through Congress a prohibition amendment that became law on 19th January 1920, prompting the American lyricist, Vaughan Miller, to write the following lines:

> There ain't going to be no more whisky
> There ain't going to be no more gin
> There ain't going to be no highballs
> to put the whisky in
> There ain't going to be no cigarettes
> to make folks pale and thin
> But you can't take away that tendency
> to sin, sin, sin.

Soon the gutters were running with confiscated liquor, and pictures of federal agents smashing casks appeared in newspapers across the country. Though US consumption of alcohol fell during prohibition, by as much as two-thirds some estimates claim, there was a seismic shift in drinking habits. When people gathered in the illicit bars and speakeasies, of which there were 100,000 in New York alone, they came not for beer or wine, but the hard stuff. The choice was between some local hooch, like bathtub gin, and imported spirits like whisky. Unfortunately, once the drinks trade was driven underground it spawned a whole new industry in counterfeit booze. It was said that for every genuine bottle that left Scotland, there were a dozen bottles of spurious Scotch being drunk. When the spirit was diluted with water, it did little worse than lessen the odd hangover, when it was cut

with wood alcohol it was leaving a trail of blindness, paralysis and death. And yet as the dangers of drinking bootlegged liquor increased so too did the demand for the real thing. After all, if you were sitting having a drink in, say, New York's Hotsy Totsy Club, you were already paying twice over the odds. There was the protection money paid to the local hood and the sweetener paid to the cops for not busting the joint. So why not pay that little bit extra if it meant a reduced risk of going blind?

Macallan 1917

Note the presence of women and boys with the men off fighting in France.

1904 Poster

Robertson's blend – note the top hat which became almost obligatory for whisky adverts at one time, perhaps inspired by the runaway success of Johnnie Walker. Dundee had a significant whisky business until the 1960's when Stewart's Cream of the Barley was bought out by Allied Distillers.

Whisky flooded into the States across the vast, unpatrolled border with Canada thanks to entrepreneurs like Sam Bronfman who built the giant Seagram's drinks empire on the back of US prohibition. Canadian tax revenue from alcohol quadrupled during the 13 year period despite a drop in domestic consumption. Scotch was also coming in through Nassau in the Bahamas where many British firms had their agents. The system went as follows: whisky was delivered into bond and then loaded onto British-registered vessels which sailed off to encircle New York; the ships would sit at anchor, just inside international waters in a 150 mile crescent known as Rum Row and wait for their US customers to show up. What happened thereafter, the machine-guns on the beach, the shoot-outs at the speakeasy, was something best left to the Americans.

There was no doubting the scale of the business however. You only had to see the clippers laden high with whisky by the waterfront and smell the spirity fumes wafting down Nassau's Bay Street whose warehouses held over US$10 million worth of liquor. It was after such a visit that Francis Berry, a partner of the blue-chip wine merchants, Berry Bros. & Rudd, decided there had to be an opportunity here for his newly launched blend – 'Cutty Sark'. Constructing a brand in a world of racketeers and bent politicians was never going to be easy. Sooner or later someone would be forging the labels and passing off something, quite possibly poisonous, as Cutty Sark. And being a market that officially did not exist,

Francis Berry could hardly check out the nightclubs and speakeasies to keep tabs on the brand's authenticity. Clearly it had to start clean, untainted and totally reliable. Berry needed someone who could take the drink into the US and somehow maintain its integrity to ensure that anyone who put their lips to a glass of Cutty Sark would be getting the 'Real McCoy'.

Sadly history doesn't relate the role played by Bill McCoy in giving Cutty Sark a head start in the American market. Anything discussed by the two men remained strictly confidential as they chatted along Bay Street or at The Lucerne, the hotel where the bootleggers met, swapped tales and occasionally traded bullets. Francis Berry was only 60 when he died, just three years after Franklin D Roosevelt repealed prohibition in 1933. In little more than a decade he had built the foundations for a world-beating brand. By the mid 1970s Cutty Sark had become the biggest-selling Scotch whisky in America – the biggest spirits market of all time.

The distillery closures of 1927 were as nothing compared to what was coming. Within five years the number of distilleries in production had halved and a year later had fallen to just 15. Throughout 1933 the only malt whisky made was at Glenlivet and Glen Grant from whose stills dribbled just 285,000 gallons – the lowest level for over a century. This was a deliberate attempt to turn off the tap and save what was left of the whisky industry in the midst of a worldwide recession precipitated by the Wall Street crash of 1929. It was not just whisky that was crippled. Shipbuilding on the Clyde had been literally decimated in the three years since 1930, causing chronic unemployment. In the country, distillery closures threatened over 1000 jobs as well as remote farms, which relied on the draff they supplied for winter feed.

With whisky there was at a least a glimmer of hope from across the Atlantic with the election of a new president who pledged to repeal prohibition. Franklin D Roosevelt did just that, but the effects took a while to work their way through. It was not as if Scotch whisky shipments had completely dried up during prohibition – either as legitimate imports as 'medicine' or bootlegged in from Nassau and across the Canadian border. But once the hefty US$5 a gallon extra import duty was dropped at the end of 1935, transatlantic shipments began to take off. By the outbreak of the Second World War the USA were importing 4.8 million gallons.

The economic slump had gone on too long for some and distilleries continued to change hands, often for very little money. In 1936

ROBERTSON'S Dundee Whisky

JOHN ROBERTSON & SON, Ltd
DUNDEE.

Arthur Bell & Sons were able to buy Inchgower on Speyside for just £1000 in the year the big Canadian distillers, Hiram Walker, bought Miltonduff and the blenders, George Ballantyne. A year earlier, William Ross, the so-called 'Abraham Lincoln of the Trade', retired, leaving a leaner but no doubt healthier industry to withstand the rigours of another war.

The U-boats returned, the Atlantic convoys were torpedoed, grain was restricted and once again production was cut dramatically, but at least this time the Prime Minister was on the side of drink. When down in his bunker plotting the war Winston Churchill may have occasionally reached for a bottle of Johnnie Walker Black Label, though his first choice was always brandy & soda or Champagne. Either way he was not about to 'abolish thirst' as his Welsh

**Canonmills' Cooperage
in Edinburgh**
The workforce at Wm.
Lindsay & Sons (1909).

predecessor fatuously declared. Churchill's famous minute written towards the end of the war is worth repeating: 'On no account reduce the barley for whisky. This takes years to mature and is an invaluable export and dollar producer. Having regard to all our other difficulties about export, it would be most improvident not to preserve this characteristic British element of ascendancy'. There is no way that could have come from the pen of Lloyd George.

Of course the distilleries were expected to do their bit. Sales were skewed towards exports, especially in the States, to help with the balance of payments. Meanwhile, restrictions and high tax which doubled the price of a bottle discouraged home sales and led to a brisk trade in black market Scotch. But compared to the First World War, many more distilleries managed to stay open if only to produce a few thousand gallons each year. And being expensive and hard to come by had its advantages – it certainly boosted the allure and desirability of Scotch. There was also the fact that by concentrating on the States, those Americans, only recently weaned onto whisky, never lost the taste for Scotch during the war. This was something that could be built on as soon as the fighting stopped.

The first half of the century had been a time of painful contraction for Scotch whisky, which had survived the terrible recession of the early 1930s and US prohibition. Along with the number of operating distilleries, which during the period, which halved during the period, there were many casualties among the blending houses. If you

wanted to be part of one big happy family and join the Distillers Co., and they were keen to have you, the future could be relatively safe. But if you wanted to control your fate and maintain an independence outside, life could be pretty tough. Those best placed to survive in the long run needed to look abroad. Overseas sales offered the best hope, since the high domestic taxes imposed during the 1930s and 1940s were hardly going to melt away as if by some peacetime gesture of goodwill. The trouble was, former big whisky drinking markets took a leaf out of Britain's book. Australia, Canada and South Africa all imposed hefty import tariffs to protect their own spirits industries.

POST-WAR WHISKY

The cash-strapped British economy urgently needed export earnings to restore the balance of trade after the war. Scotch whisky fitted the bill perfectly – it was a high-value commodity and it was something that no one else could produce. Just under six million gallons, around one third of the whisky produced, was shipped abroad, a half of it ending up in the US. The then Labour government was very interventionist, this being the age of rationing, and only released barley to distillers on the basis that two-thirds of the whisky produced was sold abroad. If you were a stay-at-home brand like Bells, that could make life very difficult, especially in 1950 when black market whisky accounted for an estimated one in

**1898 advert for
George Beer's blend**
Plenty of mixed messages in this ad. Note the 'comic' Scot with tam'o shanter, the army officers and the First Class carriage.

Early 1920's Advert
This advert shows a
different tack.

Who are the Scots?
For early admen, the Scots
were a curious muddle –
were they a race of noble
warriors or comic drunks?

new grain distilleries, such as Invergordon on the Cromarty Firth in 1961. Originally planned by the provost of Inverness and a local accountant, it was to provide employment in the region after the announcement that the Invergordon naval base was to be run down. By 1963 two more Coffey stills were added to boost production to a potential 10 million gallons, while William Grant & Sons (as in Glenfiddich), built their grain distillery at Girvan the same year.

In the 1960s the increased demand by blenders, led to a surge in malt whisky. Everywhere disused distilleries were dragged out of retirement and the stills fired-up after years lying cold and empty, or else rebuilt like Glenturret and Caperdonich. Many added extra stills – Glenfarclas, Bunnahabhain and Dalmore were all doubled, and five completely new distilleries were built, four from scratch and one, Deanston in Perthshire, converted from an old cotton mill. There were other 'new' malt distilleries like Ben Wyvis and Ladyburn which were bolted onto the side of existing grain distilleries such as Invergordon and Girvan.

For a symbol of the irrepressible self-confidence that gripped Scotch whisky at the time there is no better example than Tormore. Built by the architect Sir Albert Richardson, a past president of the Royal Academy, this palatial building of pale granite and massive arched windows was to be the spiritual home of the 'Long John' blend and was opened in 1960. The original plan had even included dressing up the obligatory chimney stack to look like a giant whisky bottle, but the idea was later abandoned as being impractical. Even so, to see Tormore looming up beside the A95 in Speyside is quite something – it certainly looks like no other distillery in Scotland. Whether it is particularly beautiful is hard to say, but it does appear solid and permanent, unlike many of the hastily erected glass and concrete sheds that passed for distillery designs in the 1960s.

By the end of the decade the amount of malt whisky produced had doubled. The industry had seen nothing like it since the twilight years of Queen Victoria. Of course the driving force then, even more than now, was coming from blended whisky which was taking the US market by storm. By 1968 American consumers were drinking around 160 million bottles of Scotch a year, up almost three times since the start of the 60s. Among the favoured brands were Dewars, Cutty Sark and J&B Rare.

The expansion paused to catch its breath and then continued into the seventies. In one year alone, Glenfiddich, Tomatin, Tomintoul, Tullibardine and Ardmore were rebuilt or extended. Again it was not a vintage period in distillery design, but then the aim was production not looks – it was not as if they were open to the public after all. When Glenfiddich

three bottles drunk in Britain. That said, a year earlier Bells felt sufficiently bullish to kick Blair Athol distillery back into life after a lengthy period in mothballs.

Once restrictions fell away, a mood of optimism began to descend on the trade. The 1950s proved to be a busy time for coppersmiths building stills as never before to expand whisky-making at Macallan, Ardmore and Ben Nevis to name but three. In 1957 Chivas Brothers, Seagram's Scottish subsidiary, began building Glen Keith on Speyside. This was highly significant – being the first new malt distillery to be built anywhere in Scotland, since the late Victorian whisky boom ended in tears some 60 years earlier.

It was the rise in patent still whisky that was even more dramatic. Between 1959 and 1966 the amount of grain whisky more than doubled to nearly 90 million gallons – an incredible, and ultimately unsustainable, figure. This was achieved by building

Whiskie – Whisk(e)y – Whishky

The definition of Scotch whisky, as a spirit made and matured for at least three years in Scotland, is set in stone. The Scotch Whisky Association has a battalion of lawyers and is not afraid to use them whenever someone elsewhere tries to pass off their local hooch as Scotch. But plain old 'whisky', which is usually but not always a grain-based spirit, can be made anywhere.

IRISH WHISKEY

If they really did invent whisky as they claim, the Irish must rue the day they taught the Scots how to make it. In the late eighteenth century there were an estimated 2000 stills operating in Ireland, and one hundred years later Irish whiskey was well-established in England and poised to overtake Scotch. Then came independence in 1916 which forced the Irish to look beyond Britain and the British empire. Over 400 brands were being sold into America, when disaster struck in the form of US prohibition. It was a body-blow from which the industry never recovered and one distillery after another closed down. By 1968 the five that remained, decided to form the Irish Distillers Group and concentrate production at the new Middleton distillery in Co. Cork. This is where all whiskey is now made apart from Bushmills in Co. Antrim and the independent Cooley distillery in Co. Louth. Along with the extra 'e', Irish whiskey employs an additional still in its production. Triple distillation is not an exclusively Irish phenomenom, but it does give a national style that tends to be lighter than Scotch whisky, especially since the malt is rarely peated. Another difference is the use of malted and unmalted barley together, the exception being Bushmills, whose single malt is correspondingly closer to what you would find on the other side of the Irish Sea.

BOURBON

It was eighteenth century Irish and Scots emigrants who founded the American whiskey industry in Pennsylvania and Kentucky. As the pioneers moved west, the basic ingredients changed from just rye to corn (maize) and rye, and was a mixture of malted and unmalted grains. Some distillers, like Jack Daniel's, evolved a sour mash style using cornmeal, malted barley and rye that is distilled in a column still and then filtered through vats of sugar maple charcoal. Bourbon develops its strong vanilla flavours from the years spent in freshly charred new oak barrels.

CANADA

During prohibition, the flow of Canadian whisky pouring over the US border turned into a flood. Then, as now, it was made principally from corn and rye using continuous stills followed by at least three years in a barrel. Its style was therefore close enough to the home-grown Bourbon the Americans were being denied. On the back of this lucrative trade, Sam Bronfman founded the mighty Seagram empire which played a big role in the whisky industry on both sides of the Atlantic, until the drinks side of the business was sold off for $8.15 billion in 2000.

JAPAN

On the other side of the Pacific, Shinjiro Torii began building the first Japanese whisky distillery in 1923 near the city of Kyoto to produce a malt whisky that became known as Suntory White. Today, the Suntory corporation dominates the market and has expanded abroad to Mexico, Thailand and Brazil, acquiring Morrison Bowmore and the Bowmore distillery on Islay along the way.

OTHER WHISKIES

All over the world you can buy local whisky that varies enormously in style and quality. Some Japanese whiskies taste remarkably similar to the Real McCoy, thanks to having a hefty dollop of Scotch whisky, that has been shipped over in bulk, in the blend. Cross over to India, which, depending on definition, is the biggest whisky drinking nation on the planet, and the staple raw ingredient is molasses, not grain. If the flavours seem foreign, the brand names and the imagery used on the labels are as Scottish as can be. Next time you are in Bombay ask for a 'Bagpiper' and you will see what I mean.

decided to build a visitor centre and let in the general public in 1969, most of their rivals thought they had gone soft in the head. Who on earth would want to look round what was essentially just a factory? Of course the industry has changed its mind since.

There were doubtless a few Cassandras even then pointing out that the boom couldn't last, that all good things have to come to an end one day, that the bubble would eventually burst, but no one was listening – the sales figures were simply too compelling. In the three decades since the war worldwide sales of Scotch whisky grew by about 9 per cent year on year – a rate higher than any other comparable major export. After such a prolonged period of sustained growth, the decline of the interwar years, when at one point production almost dribbled to a halt, all seemed something from another world. In 1978, exports reached their twentieth-century high – the equivalent of nearly a 100 million bottles of Scotch whisky. North American demand had peaked a few years earlier and was beginning to slip into slow, seemingly irreversible, decline. Scotch whisky was about to suffer from its past success.

The fact that whisky in the States was so widespread and had been around for such a long time meant recruiting new drinkers was that much harder. The next generation were looking to drink something

1930's Poster

No one believed in advertising like Dewar's – learning to relax by the seaside and shed its white tie for once.

DEWAR'S "White Label" SCOTCH WHISKY

never varies

Celebrate with the finest drink in the world

Dewar's Pipe Major

The Pipe Major has long been a standard bearer for Dewar's. What would this version from 1953 make of the admen's latest creation where the Pipe Major comes bare-chested, clutching a surf board?

new and not that old 'Doo-wers' the old man always drunk. Part of this fall from favour was inevitable given that the drink's image was bound to grow tired and get a little grey around the edges, in-line with its most loyal consumers.

Back in Britain, whisky was slowly being crucified by tax and, so its rivals would claim, by DCL's decision to hold prices down in an apparent attempt to snuff out all domestic competition. The situation was made worse in 1982 when whisky suffered a double whammy of increased duty and VAT at the same time which added £1.20 to the price of a bottle. Much more serious, however, was the issue of overproduction at the distilleries. Three decades of growth had taken warehoused stocks of whisky to unprecedented heights – by 1975 the figure was already over one billion gallons. The trade has always had to gaze into its crystal ball to somehow

anticipate what demand will be in the future. While the weathermen have trouble predicting tomorrow's weather, each distillery had to try and guess how thirsty people will be in three years time – this being the minimum age for whisky. Like steering a super tanker, it can take a long time for the industry to slow down. And to make things even more difficult there is not just one captain on the bridge but many, all in charge of their own whisky firms and each with their own vision of the future. The whisky loch was already full to overflowing when the recession hit in 1979.

Four years later on 31 May 1983 DCL were forced to close 11 of its 45 distilleries, of which only Benromach and Knockdhu survived. For some it was only a temporary measure and after a period in 'mothballs' they were brought back to life. Less than two years later, a further ten were shut down.

For a while it was assumed the remedy to depressed sales at home and in the States lay in the Far East where whisky drinking among Japanese increased by an incredible six times in the early 1970s to make Japan the second biggest importer of Scotch in the world. In the end the much less volatile markets of southern Europe have proved the real saviour of recent years, and nowhere more than in Spain, which is now the most valuable market for Scotch whisky in the world.

THE MALT WHISKY BOOM

If sex was an invention of the sixties, as the poet Philip Larkin famously maintained, then so it was with malt whisky. Prior to that date, with the exception of a few specialist outlets and close friends of the distillery manager, the world had never heard of single malts. Scotch whisky meant blended whisky and that was all there was to it.

But the world has a short memory, for malt whisky had always been around; it was the original Scotch whisky after all, and had existed for over three and a half centuries before blends were even thought of. The first little barrel of whisky ever produced would now be heralded as a highly prized single malt that was unfiltered and at cask-strength — words that would have meant nothing to the original distiller. Not even the word 'whisky' would have made any sense. As for laying it down in a cold, damp cellar for at least ten years, the idea would have been quite absurd; in fact the idea of using a cask at all would have been pretty unlikely. What was made in the morning would be drunk that night, for who knew what tomorrow might bring?

Gradually the benefits of maturing malt whisky were discovered. The appeal of illicit Glenlivet, apart from being forbidden fruit which always tastes sweeter, was to do with being 'long in wood' as contemporaries knew full well. But until the invention of blended whisky in the mid nineteenth century, malts tended to be very unreliable. This need for a consistent, dependable product was a crucial first step to building brands. If the label never varied, then nor should the contents – a fact hammered home in countless early whisky adverts. The 'What is Whisky?' case of 1909 did represent a last-ditch showdown between the big blending houses and the malt Mafia of the north, but the contest was hardly even. The public had proved beyond doubt that what they wanted were blends that would taste reassuringly the same wherever and whenever they were drunk.

So completely did blended Scotch win the day, that soon very few people knew what the words 'malt whisky' even meant. Like farms growing wheat to be ground into flour to make bread, malt whisky distilleries were producing a raw ingredient for processing further down the line. There were always exceptions of course – there were limited bottlings from the likes of Cardhu, Glenfarclas and Macallan. Laphroaig famously posed as a medicinal spirit to bypass US prohibition, but none were easy to come by, especially outside Scotland.

In 1965, having had some success in Scotland

To friends everywhere we send Greetings and all Best Wishes for
A MERRY CHRISTMAS AND A GOOD NEW YEAR
"BLACK & WHITE" SCOTCH WHISKY
JAMES BUCHANAN & CO. LTD., SCOTCH WHISKY DISTILLERS, GLASGOW & LONDON

with their Glenfiddich Pure Malt, William Grant & Sons decided to take on drinkers south of the border. To help the whisky stand out it was put into the famous triangular green bottle designed for Grant's Standfast some years earlier by Hans Schleger, a pre-war refugee from Nazi Germany. The idea behind the radical shape was to imbue the brand with personality, though others saw added and often unforeseen benefits. Businessmen admired how it fitted into the newly fashionable slimline attaché case, others for the way it stacked neatly in the cellar, while one woman praised it as the only bottle that didn't roll out of bed!

There were pros and cons of being completely unknown – initially shopkeepers and barmen were reluctant to take Glenfiddich for the simple fact that no one asked for it, but soon it was getting plenty of coverage in the press.

Magazines and newspapers fell over themselves to talk up this 'new' drink and explain how malt whisky was made. It hardly mattered whether they mentioned Glenfiddich or just the word 'malt' since the two were to all intents synonymous. By 1970, 24,000 cases of Glenfiddich were sold in the UK, much of it in England. This was sweetly ironic considering the Scotch Whisky Association had been questioning the wisdom of selling malt whisky to the Sassenachs only a year before.

Without the financial clout of some of their

The Modern Whisky Scene

Considering that Scotch whisky has been around for so long despite efforts to tax it out of existence, the drink remains remarkably popular in the UK even if sales have fallen since the peak of 1979, with consumption at around 4 bottles per head of the adult population. With the odd blip, whisky then began a slow, steady decline until 1995, when in November the Chancellor, Ken Clark, reduced the tax on Scotch for the first time anyone could remember. It appears the Treasury finally realised this particular cash cow had been milked dry. Since then consumption has remained static, and today we each drink between 2 to 3 bottles of whisky a year.

In its homeland, Scotch has become a slight victim of fashion with a 'pipe and slippers' image that's proved hard to dispel. As a result vodka has temporarily taken over as the country's 'national drink'. There is at least one compensation – the fact that most of it is made in Scotland. But who knows? – perhaps Smirnoff Ice will become the Babysham of tomorrow, and Glasgow's style bars will one day echo to cries of 'Black Bottle & Coke'.

Meanwhile two hours south by plane, Scotch whisky has been enjoying a terrific boom in Spain. After years of pent-up demand and tax discrimination, whisky suddenly took off like a rocket when Spain joined the EU in 1986. Suddenly Scotch was in and local brandy was very definitely out. In just three years imports doubled, and Spain went on to overtake first Britain, then the USA and now France to become the most valuable Scotch whisky market in the world - worth £299 million in 1999.

In Spain Scotch is definitely not an old man's drink for sipping by the fire-side. From the first, late evening cry of 'Vamos de copas!' – let's go for a drink – the streets begin to flow with Cutty Sark, Ballantines and 'Jota Be', or J&B. And, with an estimated two thirds of it drunk between midnight and sunrise, usually mixed with Coca-Cola, Scotch belongs to the country's youth.

Next-door the French still claim to drink more Scotch whisky than anyone else, though the Spaniards are catching up fast. Despite the fact 'Le Scotch' has been around for a long time it has retained a wide appeal, to be enjoyed by young and old of either sex with ice, water, soda and sometimes Coke.

Blessed with much lower taxes on drink, sales in other southern European markets remain strong, especially in Greece where per capita consumption is the highest in the world. Italy boomed on the back of Glen Grant 5 year old, making the country unique in having a malt as the most popular brand. Sadlly an economic recession, a powerful backlash from the health lobby and a fear that brown spirits were somehow fattening, have conspired to cut consumption by half since the late eighties.

The health lobby must also share some of the blame for whisky's decline in the USA, though more important has been the failure of the major brands to appeal to younger drinkers. During the nineties consumption fell from 153 to 107 million bottles a year, but there are some signs the fall has now levelled out. As the old generation of whiksy drinkers die off, a new generation of Americans may rediscover the delights of Scotch. Meanwhile, in the rest of the world, Scotch whisky has been on a roller-coaster ride of economic booms and busts in south-east Asia and Latin America. It has yet to catch on to any significant degree in China, but has high hopes for India. With a population now over a billion and a proven taste for 'whisky' – albeit the local variety made from molasses – the potential is enormous. If just half the population had just one dram a year, it could spark off the biggest distillery building spree Scotland has ever seen. Then again it won't happen tomorrow.

rivals, William Grant's had to use every trick up their sleeve to gain publicity. One brilliantly simple idea was to bottle a line of Glenfiddich with flat ginger ale and supply it free of charge to London's TV studios and theatres. In any production that required the drinking of whisky, this fake Glenfiddich became a popular substitute for that old theatrical standby – cold tea. Meanwhile Glenfiddich was beginning to spread overseas via airport duty-free shops and introduce people to their first ever taste of single malt whisky.

Other distillers began to see there was real potential here, but it took years to have sufficient stocks of suitably aged whisky to launch their own single malt on a serious scale. By the time Glenmorangie and The Macallan were ready in the mid-1970s Glenfiddich had established a lead it has never lost. Though, according to Glenmorangie, the most popular malt in Scotland, Glenfiddich's days of supremacy in the UK are strictly numbered. In the early 1980s DCL released their 'Classic Malts' range. These consist of Lagavulin, Talisker, Oban, Glenkinchie, Cragganmore and Dalwhinnie – reflecting all the great whisky regions of Scotland. With 27 distilleries to choose from, no other group has such a geographic spread.

Today it is hard to think of one malt distillery whose whisky is not being sold as a single malt, whether in the supermarket or via some obscure independent bottler who managed to secure a cask or two. In fact if you add in all the casks still lurking in some warehouse from some distillery that has gone silent or no longer exists, the choice of single malt is considerably wider than the number of distilleries would suggest. Whether all of it should have been bottled is another matter. There are some unbalanced monsters around.

HOW WHISKY IS MADE

———◆———

It may seem a bit perverse, but let's examine the whole business of making Scotch whisky in reverse. As far as I am aware every book on whisky approaches the subject in the tried and tested fashion of a cookery book — assembling the ingredients before describing the process. So just to be contrary let's pour ourselves a communal dram and do things back to front for a change. Actually there is method in this madness, because by tracing a fully matured Scotch whisky back to its roots we will encounter the most recent stages in its development first. The further we travel from the glass in our hand the less impact each part of the process has until we reach the raw ingredients themselves. In other words the type of cask chosen is far, far more important than the selected strain of barley. Certain malt whiskies are said to derive well over two-thirds of their flavour from the way they are matured, and when Bells moved from being a five-year-old to an eight-year-old blend it changed dramatically for the better. So let's leave those wavering fronds of barley in the field and peer into the bottom of the barrel.

For all the advances in technology no one has managed to come up with a better solution for maturing Scotch whisky than that of wooden casks. Originally the very first whisky made in Scotland would have been drunk pretty much as it came off the still. Soon a vessel, like a stone jar, was used to maintain a store of whisky after the distilling season ended in the spring. As whisky-making developed into a year-round activity and grew in scale something larger was required.

The answer was obvious — that age-old, multipurpose container, the oak barrel, used for storing everything from salt cod to iron nails. It just happens that oak is perfect for holding liquid, being hard, but pliable and above all watertight. Nobody knows when barrels of whisky began to appear — probably towards the end of the eighteenth century. The fact that the American whisky industry, founded by Scots and Irish emigrants, was using barrels from the very start implies prior use back home. But the issue was of storage rather than maturation — there is a very important difference.

At some point it was noticed that if you kept the spirit in the barrel long enough, the character of the whisky began to change. The most obvious example was colour — the fact that the clear spirit from the still picked up a golden tint from the wood. If oak could turn a colourless liquid into a brown spirit, what was it doing to the flavour? Oak contains high levels of extracts which the spirit can absorb as it matures in cask. It is also sufficiently porous to allow it to breathe, but not so much that all its aroma evaporates away. At first all this was just idle speculation, since all that really mattered was that the cask did not leak, but it has since become the subject of intense scrutiny. In fact it is now probably the biggest single obsession among whisky-makers.

The interaction between wood and whisky is a science in itself, and one that is not yet fully understood. There is still some mystery, for example, why seemingly identical casks filled with the exact same spirit from the same run off the still can result in noticeably different whiskies ten years down the line. Under the microscope every stave of every cask is different in how grainy and porous it is, and these differences are multiplied in the case of Scotch whisky by the age of the barrels and what was previously held in them. In fact the idea that every drop of Scotch whisky has passed through a rag-bag of hand-me-down wooden casks is pretty bizarre when you stop and think about it. It is the part of the process most subject to the whims of chance.

Though distillers talk of 'new' casks to refer to those barrels that have never previously held Scotch whisky they are in fact all second-hand. This is not just the Scots being canny and wishing to save on the cost of buying new timber to make their barrels. It is really because the taste of virgin oak would simply swamp the freshly made spirit, which despite its strength is actually quite delicate. The aim of ageing in wood is to shape the whisky's development, not dominate it. After all the taste of wood itself is not

The Water of Life

47

The Cooperage

Cooper's tools and a stencil, Fettercairn distillery, Kincardineshire.

particularly pleasant if you can remember sucking on the stick of an ice lolly once the lolly itself has gone.

To remove the intrusive flavours of new oak, the Scotch whisky industry has formed a remarkable symbiotic relationship with American distillers who need that sweet smack of vanilla to make Bourbon whisky what it is. Every year there are up to a million of these old barrels available, half of which end up in Scotland.

Today, nine out of ten whisky casks in circulation are made from American white oak *Quercus alba* and once held Bourbon. Every Bourbon barrel is assembled from new wood and then held over a furnace to catch fire. This leaves a blackened, charred layer on the inside, about an eighth of an inch deep, which helps the wood release flavour compounds into the drink. It is believed that the combination of new oak and a heavy char gives Bourbon its distinctive aroma of caramel, honey and vanilla. Every year there are up to a million such barrels available, and the Scotch whisky industry requires around half of them. The majority of these are shipped across the Atlantic as staves and reassembled into hogsheads – 250 litre casks. Once they have already been used to age one lot of whisky they become known as 'refilled hoggies' in

the trade and can be used up to six times. Not bad for a second hand cask that only cost around $50. There have been fears that the supply may be under threat as the peaks and troughs in demand for Bourbon do not necessarily coincide with those for Scotch, and that other spirits, notably rum, are also in the market for used barrels.

One idea to solve this potential supply problem is a radical idea dreamt up by the whisky scientist, Dr Jim Swann of the consultants Tatlock & Thomson. In a three-year project involving trials at the Tamdhu distillery on Speyside, Dr Swann and his team invented a system that takes new wood and transforms it into old wood. Using radio frequency technology new oak staves are microwaved and then toasted with infrared light to give them all the characteristics of a ten-year-old Bourbon barrel in just ten minutes. 'Like Bourbon,' says Swann, 'the process has a washing effect – it removes the intrusive flavours of new oak'.

The other main source of second-hand barrels is Jerez, southern Spain, in the form of 500 litre sherry butts. Because they are twice the size and can be reused more often, proportionately more whisky is matured in them than the numbers suggest. Impregnated with the rich, nutty flavours of, say, Oloroso sherry, the casks

Maturing Stocks of Balvenie
Outside the distillery at Dufftown on Speyside.

slowly release these back into the maturing spirit adding an extra dimension to the whisky. These barrels are made from European Oak or *Quercus robur* and are toasted rather than charred, being placed over a fire which is quickly drenched with water.

Another difference between the two types of cask stems from the fact that Bourbon is at least twice as strong as sherry. The stronger the alcohol the deeper it penetrates into the wood and the more of those primary flavours of new wood it manages to suck out. In other words, all things being equal, there should be a lot more extract left in sherry wood for the next occupant, i.e. whisky, to enjoy. Macallan are great believers in sherry casks, and maintain that the resinous, spicy character of their whisky can be traced all the way back to Jerez. Curiously a number of the top blenders say that Macallan is a much more interesting dram when it has been matured in something else.

FINISHING SCHOOL

Beyond the mainstream of the barrels mentioned above which account for the vast majority of Scotch whisky, there are some weird and wonderful experiments going on. Today you can find limited editions of malt whisky matured in casks that previously held Madeira, Port, wine from Burgundy and even Chardonnay. The last sounds like someone's been reading too much Bridget Jones. Often the word 'finished' is used – this means the whisky spent its last x number of months in such a cask before it was bottled.

The current fixation with wood finishes has spread to blended whisky, a move pioneered by William Grant with its 'Sherry' and 'Ale cask' version, and Famous Grouse which came out in a 'Port wood' finish and one using 'Islay wood'. So far no one is finishing off their whisky in a barrel that previously held Brent Crude, but it could just be a matter of time.

Casks of Bunnahabhain
Beside Loch Indaal on Islay, waiting shipment to the mainland.

Dalmore Distillery
To speed up condensation
of the spirit produced by
the Dalmore distillery near
Inverness, the lyne arms are
swaddled in giant copper
cooling jackets.

TIME

Since 1916 all maturing spirit must spend at least three years in oak to be called whisky. This is true of spirit destined to be some venerable single malt and priced accordingly, as it is for the cheapest grain whisky. In fact watching how fast grain is converted into alcohol at a grain distillery – a matter of about three days – it is pretty striking when you consider it is then left to slumber for the next three years. For the bean counters of the industry it must all seem like a sin it is so indulgent, after all vodka is drunk and paid for within a week of being distilled.

How much longer whisky then stays in cask has a profound effect on its final character as it slowly breathes in air through the pores in the wood and breathes out whisky fumes – the so-called 'Angel's Share'. Whisky evaporates at a rate of two per cent per annum on average, which if you multiply by all the spirit slumbering in Scotland's warehouses works out at something like 150 million bottles a year. It seems the Angels are having one hell of a party!

For the industry the only consolation while waiting for each cask to reach maturity, is that none of the lost spirit is taxed. The amount of time depends on the individual whisky – as a general rule lighter whiskies mature faster than those that are heavier. But it is not simply a case of the older the better – some whiskies continue improving in cask for 20 or 30 years, others would be dried out and dominated by the taste of wood well before then. Also the ability of

each cask to influence the spirit declines each time it is used. A whisky that has spent five years in a cask that is on its third time around, might taste hopelessly immature because the wood has nothing left to give.

And of course time is money – for standard blends, most malts are drawn off and mixed with three-year-old grain whisky relatively early. If it is to be a single malt or part of a deluxe blend they are left until they are ten or twelve years old and often longer. The exception being five-year-old Glen Grant, Italy's favourite malt.

PLACE

The type of warehouse and where it's located also helps determine how quickly a whisky will mature. A stone built vault with an earthen floor, like that of Bowmore on Islay, is noticeably humid with its wonderful dank smell. As a result evaporation is less than in a modern, temperature controlled warehouse, but the alcoholic strength of the whisky declines faster. If left too long there is a danger that a cask will slip below 40 per cent abv and have to have racked with other casks to be legally called whisky. They say that traditional vaults make for a more mellow spirit, and that whiskies matured on site at the distillery enjoy a greater sense of provenance. A cask of Islay malt lying at the place it was conceived is bound to inherit something from ten years of inhaling the ozone rich breeze blowing in off the sea. If nothing else there will be that lingering salty tang

in the taste. And yet the great majority of whisky is tankered south from the Highlands and Islands to be stored in casks close to the big bottling lines in the Lowlands.

DISTILLATION

Leaving the barrels to slumber in peace, let's slip into the still room and discover the secret of distillation. This is the heart of the distillery, a room that appeals to all the senses at the same time with its mass of brightly polished copper, its heat and its

wonderful spirity aroma. There is nothing quite like visiting a distillery when the weather is dreich, when the rain is lashing down outside and the last coach tour left months ago. To stand beside those towering stills radiating warmth and whisky is to get one step closer to understanding the drink's magical allure. As every distillery cat knows, there is simply no better place to be than curled up right here when the rest of Scotland is caught in the icy grip of winter.

The first thing to learn about distilling is how little the process has changed over the years. If an eighteenth-century Highlander who knew how to operate a small pot still could somehow travel through time he would not feel completely thrown by life in a modern malt distillery. The size of the stills and the odd flashing light from a computer might alarm him, but essentially the business of making whisky remains as it always has. In its simplest terms a distillery converts a flat, moderately strong beer, known as wash, into malt whisky by heating it up and collecting the vapours. The system works because the component parts of the wash including the good and bad alcohols have different boiling points. As each of these turns to steam and rises up the neck of the still, the stillman can capture those vapours he wants to keep and reject the rest.

To turn wash into whisky and jump from a barley brew of 6-8 per cent alcohol to a spirit eight times stronger is a two-step process, with every malt distillery having at least two stills – the wash and the spirit still. The easiest way to think of a still is as a

Fresh from the Still
Assessing the clear,
new-make spirit at Balvenie.

large copper kettle. As the wash is pumped into the first still until it is between a half and two-thirds full, the heat is turned up. Originally this would have been by lighting a fire underneath, until it was discovered by the Victorians that it was easier to control the heat by inserting a copper coil inside the still and filling it with steam. Thinking of the analogy above, these are like electric kettles.

One or two traditionalists remain, however, like Macallan and Glenfiddich who continue to use gas fires beneath the stills and swear their whisky is all the better for it. This necessitates the use of rummagers or rotating arms that scour the inside of the still with heavy chain mail made of copper to stop a burnt deposit building-up.

After about half an hour boiling away, the stillman turns down the heat to prevent the wash getting too frothy and foaming up the neck of the still. To keep an eye on the process he can peer through a pair of port holes, or sight glasses, set one above the other in the side of the still. In the past before stills came complete with little windows the stillman had a wooden ball suspended on a chain to bang against the still and depending on the sound he could judge the level of the wash. Another trick to dampen down the frothing was to use soap – quite what it did to the whisky is anyone's guess.

Nowadays by carefully lowering and raising the heat while keeping the wash between the two sight glasses the run continues until all that remains is the pot ale, which is siphoned off and reduced to a syrup

which goes to make a high protein cattle cake. What interests the distiller, however, are the so-called 'low wines', collected by the condenser at a strength of around 21 per cent abv.

The low wines are still not strong enough to separate out into the ethers needed to produce whisky, so they are first diverted to the low wines charger and mixed with the alcoholic residue from the second distillation to raise the strength to 28 per cent abv. Then it is pumped into the spirit still and again brought to the boil. To use a musical analogy it is like a symphony in three movements. The first being the foreshots, which start to vaporise and climb up the neck of the still once the temperature reaches 90° C. At this stage the stillman has a quick glance at the spirit safe, a small padlocked box of glass and polished brass, through which everything distilled has had to flow since 1823.

Condensed back into liquid the foreshots flow through the spirit safe and off to the low wines and feints receiver to await the next run off the wash still. The foreshots are highly alcoholic when they start coming off the still, and gradually reduce in strength. They are also pungent and full of impurities or 'congeners' as they are known.

Like bacteria in the body, some impurities are welcome and some are not. A spirit distilled and distilled until it was virtually 100 per cent pure, would just be neutral grain spirit. If redistilled with botanicals like juniper, coriander and orange peel it might make a good gin, but it would never make

Some Good Old-Fashioned Plumbing
At the Glengoyne distillery in the Campsie Fells.

whisky. In some malt whiskies and red wines as many as 400 different congeners have been identified. The average gin meanwhile, has just three.

The art of distilling whisky is to know when to make the cut, when to judge that the 'impurities' are worth collecting. To help him pick the right moment the stillman can perform the demisting test. He can mix a little of the spirit flowing through the spout in the spirit safe with water, if it goes cloudy the foreshots have yet to finish. When clear, the spout is redirected and 'the cut' begins. A further check can be made using the hydrometer – a glass instrument that looks like a large thermometer kept inside the spirit safe. This measures the level of alcohol.

The cut starts running at about 75 per cent abv and continues to decline in strength until the feints begin to flow perhaps half an hour later. At first the feints smell quite sweet and wholesome and are therefore well worth keeping, but gradually they degenerate into off-notes and begin to smell slightly rank and sweaty. Before this happens the stillman has to end the cut by redirecting the spout in the spirit safe so that the feints flow off to join the foreshots. This is the critical moment in distilling whisky and varies from one distillery to the next. The decision of when to stop collecting the spirit depends on the type of spirit sought – whether light and delicate, heavy and robust or somewhere in between. If it is to be a gentle Speyside for example, the stillman might end

the cut at 69 per cent abv, whereas if we are talking something big and beefy from the west coast, the strength might be allowed to drop as low as 60 per cent abv.

Of course, the idea of the stillman frantically checking and re-checking the spirit safe as the spirit comes spurting out the spout is not quite how it is in real-life. Some distilleries simply run the cut for a specific time and don't bother with doing any tests. Besides, not only will our stillman have done it thousands of times before, but he has centuries of experience behind him.

What is critically important is the shape of the still, which can vary dramatically. Today there are almost as many different-shaped stills as there are distilleries in Scotland. In every case there would have been a prolonged period of trial and error before the distiller found the exact style of whisky he was looking for. Some stills are fat and dumpy, others tall and graceful, some seem to have been squashed to fit the stillroom, others were used for making gin as at Glenmorangie. But not one distiller would dare play around with the design and risk losing the unique character of their whisky for ever. The original shape of a still may have been by accident, but it is nonetheless faithfully copied by the coppersmith whenever it needs replacing.

But why copper? Well that is another happy accident, because if the first distillers had chosen some other metal they would have quickly given up and Scotch whisky simply would not exist. Copper is crucial in the way it reacts with the spirit and helps to cleanse it of heavy, sulphurous compounds that would otherwise make whisky undrinkable. As the hot vapours rise up the neck of the still they condense on contact with the copper and trickle back down into the pot. This re-condensation is known as reflux and increases in proportion to the height of the still and if the lyne arm, the pipe that connects the still to the condenser, is angled upwards. The more of this reflux you have the lighter and cleaner the whisky will be. Too much and you would have something as clean as a whistle, but not brimming with personality. Too little and you would know about it the next morning. Those congeners mentioned above can really do your head in, which is one reason why gin drinkers suffer gentler hangovers, or so they claim.

Because of all this reflux going on, the average distillery probably loses several kilograms of copper a week and the various panels that make up the still may have to be replaced every 10 to 15 years. How long it lasts – this 'conversation with the copper', as some distillers call it, depends on more than just the shape of the still. Other things to consider are the amount of liquid in relation to the surface area of metal, how fast the stills are run, and whether one is using worms or condensers. The latter are made of copper rods inside a tube cooled by water and should give a cleaner spirit than a worm.

FERMENTATION

Leaving behind the warmth of the stillroom with all its brightly polished copper, we travel back through the distillery and into what smells like a brewery. Instead of those sweet, spirity aromas, we get the fug of yeast and ale of the tun room.

The fermentation process to produce the wash for the stills all happens in large containers called washbacks. In a typical distillery there might be half a dozen circular washbacks some 12 feet in diameter, each big enough to hold thousands of litres of what is basically beer.

At this point one can speculate about when it was those early monks in their pre-Reformation monasteries decided to abandon their beloved ale for something stronger. Perhaps it was a brew that had turned sour and become undrinkable that persuaded some erstwhile brewer to cook it up and see what happened. By making it stronger and more concentrated he would be 'adding value', to use the current business jargon, and could therefore charge more money. Who knows?

A syrupy, non-alcoholic liquid called worts, which we will come to shortly, is pumped into the washbacks until they are two-thirds full. Then a sprinkling of fresh yeast is tipped in and the lid closed down. As a living organism yeast needs oxygen as surely as you and I. Once denied it they start to feed on the sugar in the wash creating carbon dioxide in the process which, being heavier than air, sits on top of the wash like a

Checking the Wooden Washbacks
At Highland Park during fermentation.

blanket. Peer too closely into the washback and it will literally take your breath away.

At first all is calm for a couple of hours and then suddenly the liquid begins to bubble and froth like some demented cauldron on a witch's fire. Only of course there is no fire, all the energy, and there is plenty of it, comes solely from the chemical reaction going on between the sugar and the yeast. If not properly bolted to the floor, the washback can begin to rock on its moorings. If made of wood – usually pitch pine or larch – the staves can be heard to groan as the fermentation grows more violent, at which point the brewer will turn on the switchers. These are metal rods that spin round to beat back the froth. In the past this job was done by young boys armed with brooms made of heather. Without switchers the washbacks would overflow like a badly poured pint of beer.

During fermentation which is usually completed in about 44 hours the temperature of the wash rises by about 15 degrees to around 35° C, at which point things begin to calm down. This final stage lasts around 12 hours and belongs to bacteria which take over from the poor exhausted yeast cells to begin what is almost a secondary fermentation. This is where the process differs from making beer, because the wash used for making whisky is not sterile and therefore unstable. If it was left to ferment for days on end it would turn quite sour and ultimately to vinegar.

The finished wash is perfectly drinkable though it plays havoc with your bladder apparently. Besides it would be a shame not to wait – in a few hours this flat, murky brew will be beautiful, new-make spirit.

The only real debate going on among brewers in the whisky business is between those who insist that traditional wooden washbacks are best and the modernists who favour stainless steel. It used to be that wood was harder to scrub clean between washes which matters because too much bacteria can render the yeast useless, but modern cleaning methods have meant there is now little difference. On the other hand wooden washbacks help insulate the wash against cold draughts which might give the yeast a bit of a chill. They certainly look nicer, though whether some expert 'nose' could pin a particular flavour on the use of Oregon pine in the tun room is pretty doubtful.

What is noticeable is whether the wash was made on the Thursday and left over the weekend before distillation on the Monday or whether it went to still straight away. The former can give the whisky a touch more complexity.

MAKING THE MASH

On our way round the tun room we met a syrupy liquid called worts – this is the product of mashing which happens in another circular vessel called a mash tun which is usually made of stainless steel and covered with a gleaming copper lid. As with brewing this is the preliminary step to prepare the raw ingredients – in this case just malted barley and water – for fermentation.

The Mash Tun Rakes
Stirring up the worts to
help maximise the
conversion of starch into
soluble sugar, Auchentoshan
near Glasgow.

First the malt has to be ground-up in a mill hopper which operates rather like a coffee grinder. Inside are two rollers first to crack the husk and then to pulverise the grain, after which it is tipped into the mash tun and mixed with water from the previous mashing. The hopper can be adjusted to produce anything from a light, powdery grist to one that is coarse and rough – the ideal being somewhere in between to allow the greatest possible extraction without clogging up the works. This might happen if the grist was too fine.

Sticking with the coffee analogy, the mash tun is like a percolator using the hot water to extract all the goodness, in this case soluble sugars, out of the grain. At first the liquid is heated to around 64° C, which is the maximum temperature the enzymes in the grist can stand. These enzymes then get to work breaking down the sugars, known as maltose, while special mechanical rakes, fitted inside the mashtun, help stir things up. After about half an hour, the perforated plates in the bottom of the tun are opened up and the worts drain through into the underback below. The porridge-like substance left behind still has plenty of soluble sugars in it, so two further extractions are made using progressively hotter water. The last, called 'spargeing', brings the temperature up to 85 degrees and last about a quarter of an hour. This is then drained off to become the first water of the next mashing while the solids left in the mash tun are mixed with the pot ale residue from the wash and turned into dark grains – a rich, protein-packed cattle-cake.

MALTING THE BARLEY

To make malt whisky you first need to malt the barley. After the harvest the grains of barley are stored in giant silos and kept dry. Without moisture the grain is still alive but fast asleep until it is woken up, literally with a cold bath, in a process called steeping. By plunging the barley into water two things happen – the grain swells in size as it absorbs moisture and a tiny enzyme is suddenly triggered into life. Each grain contains its own source of energy in the form of starch which allows it to germinate and grow. But before this can happen the enzyme has to break down the cell wall to get at the starch.

The barley is steeped for a few days until each grain is almost half water. If it were then left it would begin spouting and putting out roots which would start to use up that precious supply of starch, and leave less for turning into whisky. For our purposes the grain has to be allowed to germinate but no more, which means that having begun the process the maltster must be able to put the grain back to sleep. This is how it works.

Originally all distilleries carried out their own maltings in a malt barn, usually on the first floor where it was drier. Here the steeped barley was evenly spread across a stone floor to a depth of about six inches and was then left for a week, or maybe more in winter. As the damp grains began to dry they would start putting out little rootlets which created a certain amount of heat especially close to the floor. To spread

Knee-Deep in Barley
Highland Park.

a better whisky is hard to say – those that have them swear it does, though admit that their existence is not wholly unconnected with having a visitor centre. Compared to industrial maltings which employ huge rotating drums, the floormaltings are less reliable. It is obviously more labour intensive even if the rhythm of the shiels has given way to the whirr of a mechanised plough, but it is more romantic especially the next stage when the green malt is sent to the kiln.

At Bowmore the malt is spread 18 inches thick on a fine, wire mesh floor suspended 12 feet over the kiln. The idea is not just to dry the malt but to let it soak up the dense blue smoke wafting up from the furnace below. This is the famous peat reek – a mixture of molasses, damp tweed and the sweet smell of burning rubber. It is strange and pungent, but not unpleasant. The smoke is drawn into the thick blanket of malt, up through the tapering chimney and out through the slats in the pagoda roof. This bizarre oriental effect, invented by the Victorian architect, Charles Doig of Elgin, to help improve the draw of the chimney soon became the trademark design for distilleries right across Scotland. Those that remain are preserved with pride and no one would dream of knocking them down even though most are now redundant. Only those handful of distilleries that malt their own barley still have smoke drifting out of their pagoda roofs.

To stand behind the furnace at Bowmore and watch the sparks crash into the spark plate as the smoke is funnelled upwards is an unforgettable experience and one which puts the standard distillery tour in the shade. For there is no smoke without maltings and without maltings the tour invariably begins with the grist hopper, and believe me when you have seen one grist hopper you've seen them all.

Watching barley being malted is certainly memorable, but what effect if any does it have on the whisky? The answer lies with our old friend peat.

PEAT

Peat is partially decomposed vegetable matter in the first stages of becoming coal. It comes not from trees but from grass, heather, gorse and sphagnum moss, among other things, compacted into a hard black layer since the last Ice Age 10,000 years ago. If you hold a brick of peat to your nose, it smells of nothing as if the aroma has been locked in, frozen for thousands of years. Only on the fire are these released as the peat begins to smoulder. These different smells depend on where the peat was cut. If from Orkney, the smoke can have a slightly sweetish fragrance from the decomposed heather, if from Islay it can give off the scent of seaweed and perhaps the bitter-sweet aroma of bog myrtle.

this warmth around and prevent the roots matting together, the 'piece', as it was known, had to be regularly turned. Wearing soft canvas shoes, the men would slowly work their way across the floor scooping up barley with wooden shovels, or 'shiels' and tossing it over their shoulders. Some distilleries preferred to use rakes which were towed behind like a plough. To ensure an even germination the piece had to be kept nice and flat – any hillocks could seriously wind up the distillery manager.

Today there are about half a dozen distilleries, including such famous names as Laphroaig, Bowmore and Highland Park, which still malt their own barley. None are self-sufficient and typically have to buy in two-thirds of their malt from the big maltsters who supply everyone else. Whether floor maltings make for

In the wet, cold barren landscape of the Highlands and Islands, peat bogs are relatively common and for centuries provided the only real source of fuel. It is less efficient than coal, but what it lacks in heat it makes up for in smoke. Scottish homes were traditionally built with an open hearth in the kitchen from which the dense blue peat smoke escaped through a hole in the roof. Since none of the internal walls reached up to the ceiling, any foodstuffs like mutton or fish, not to mention clothes and bedding, would have been permanently impregnated like an over-smoked kipper. Given the circumstances, the idea of unpeated whisky… well it just wouldn't have been whisky.

If you only have peat to malt the barley, it would have taken longer and resulted in a pretty pokey brew by the time it dribbled off the still — one that caked the tongue with tar and blistered the tonsils on its way down the throat. After all most of the whisky would have been denied the soothing influence of age. Today, even the most pungent single malts are made using peat only for its smoke in the kiln, and rely on the heat from other fuels to actually dry the grain.

The peat cutting season lasts from April to September, though ideally you want to cut it in the spring and leave it stacked up in the open air to dry until late summer. The best peat is not too near the sea where it can be too sandy, or low-lying where it can be too wet. Nowadays it is nearly all cut by machine, though one or two traditionalists like Bowmore like to crumble a little hand-cut peat on top

of their furnace just to give that little extra something. They say it produces a better smoke.

BARLEY

This is the raw ingredient for making malt whisky. As such you might imagine it would have a huge impact on the flavour, with individual strains of barley promoted by distillers with all the fervour of wine makers discussing the different grape varieties. But the general view is that distillation is just too strong a process for any variation to survive the transformation from grain to distilled spirit. If there were any

Smoke From the Kiln Below

Rising up through the malt on the drying floor at Highland Park.

differences to start with, they are simply blown away at these high levels of alcohol. The varietal approach to tasting wine may make perfect sense, but not when it comes to whisky. Not even the best 'nose' in the business can pick up a dram, sniff deeply, and declare with confidence 'Mmm… yes… I'm definitely getting Golden Promise here', this being the type of barley demanded by Macallan, who believe quite the contrary – that the particular strain does have a subtle bearing on the quality of the spirit produced; in this case helping to give The Macallan some of its characteristic oily richness.

Golden Promise was introduced in the 1960s as the new high-yielding variety for Scotland. It soon became the leading strain, popular among farmers because it harvested early and popular among brewers and distillers for its yields. But fashions come and go, and as new even more productive strains of barley were invented, Golden Promise began to lose its shine. Today only a handful of Scotland's east coast farmers have stayed loyal to the variety – which means there is now only enough to meet a quarter of the distillery's needs. To secure its supply, The Macallan have taken out long-term contracts with farmers, hoping the knowledge that their barley is being used to make such

a whisky will inspire them. Ideally, they would like to rely completely on Golden Promise even if it means paying the farmers a slight premium and having to use ten per cent more barley to achieve the same yield. They insist that it does make a difference and point to tests in the early nineties where other, more modern, varieties produced a noticeably flatter, less effervescent spirit. Macallan is certainly a fine single malt, so perhaps they are right.

What is beyond doubt, is that whisky does require high-quality grain. Among the nine grades of barley only the top 20 per cent is suitable for malting. The grain needs to be well-ripened, plump and dry – if it has too high a moisture content it might go mouldy in storage. Of crucial importance is that the great majority will germinate successfully, for it is this which kick-starts the complicated chemical reaction that breaks down the starch into something more soluble. In general the barley needs to be high in starch, but low in protein and nitrogen – which means the farmer has to be careful not to use too much fertilizer.

Beyond that, distillers are naturally keen to get the best value – which means the highest possible yields for the best possible price. There has been some concern that if you pursue high yields to the exclusion of all else, some of the flavour may be lost along the way. There is a clear logic to this, after all it is happening with other crops such a coffee beans, but so far the latest types of barley do not seem to have noticeably damaged the quality of Scotch. Nor is there any great issue over genetically modified grain for whisky, as yet at least.

OTHER GRAINS

What is heartening, at least in terms of Scotch whisky being an integral part of Scotland, is that much of the grain is sourced locally from the fertile strip of land that runs along the east coast of the Moray Firth to the Borders. Since a failed attempt in 1909 to restrict the definition of Scotch to being the product of just Scottish barley, whisky distillers have been free to import grain from anywhere in the world. It now seems there is a general and by no means sentimental belief, that local grain is best. This has been a boon to Scotland's farmers, but not just those growing barley.

Before Britain joined the EU, most grain distillers used maize shipped in from South Africa and the United States. Since then they have switched almost completely to wheat and swear that there is absolutely no difference in terms of flavour in the whisky produced. They have worked with agricultural colleges in Scotland to develop new strains of spring and winter wheat adapted to the climate and for conversion into spirits. In contrast to the sort that is

ground into flour for bread, distilleries look for wheat with a nice fluffy endosperm, high in starch and low in protein. The fact that well over half the wheat and barley is now home-grown in Scotland has been one of the whisky industry's lesser known success stories.

YEAST

If mother nature had never intended us to discover the joys of drink, then why did she give us yeast blowing freely in the wind waiting for the right conditions to burst into life? OK, there is bread I suppose, but the truth is fermentation of grape and grain happens pretty well spontaneously. Given the right conditions — somewhere warm, damp and enclosed with the right food, i.e. sugar, the dormant microscopic yeast cells indulge in a feeding frenzy that would make a piranha blush. As anyone who has ever mixed a little yeast and flour together in a cup will know, the energy in terms of heat released by this little organism is quite extraordinary. When tipped into the washback, the reaction happens fast — it takes just a couple of hours to get things going after which yeast cells start doubling again and again until their job is done, at which point they die. 'What kills them off?' I once asked a distillery manager 'Well,' he replied, 'there's the temperature, the strength of the alcohol and, to use a technical term, the fact they're buggered.'

Each cell is on a 48-hour suicide trip — just two days to gorge on sugar and transform it into copious

The Peat-Fuelled Furnace of the Kiln

quantities of CO_2 and alcohol. It is a remarkably selfless contribution when you stop and think about it.

Though the wind-borne variety was relied on by the earliest distillers, it was soon realised that different types of yeast are better suited for different jobs. For example if brewer's yeast was used for baking it would give the bread a bitter taste while if used for making whisky it would have trouble producing a sufficiently alcoholic wash. Some distilleries use a combination of brewer's yeast for flavour and distiller's yeast for strength, others use just the latter.

Yeast does play a role, albeit minor, in adding to the complexity of whisky by creating small quantities of esters, aldehydes and acids which eventually end up in the glass.

WATER

Without water there would be no water of life. Having a source of clean, pure water has been an essential prerequisite for anyone wanting to make whisky since the word go. First you need cold water to steep the barley and prepare it for malting. Then you need hot water for mixing with the ground up grain or grist to produce the wash which in turn produces the spirit. It is then needed to cool the hot, alcoholic vapours rising up the neck of the still and condense them back into a liquid. The earliest distillers relied on cold air to do this, but the yield would have been a fraction of what you can achieve with cold water, either in a condenser or a worm tub.

De-mineralised water is also used to reduce the strength of the spirit to 63.5 per cent alcohol by volume, before it is poured into its cask. Some time ago it was discovered that this was the optimum strength for maturing whisky which is slightly less than what it comes off the still. Any higher and you slow down the ageing process, any lower and you risk the whisky in the cask dropping beneath 40 per cent abv by the time you come to bottle it. Below this it can no longer be called whisky.

This legal minimum strength is what most Scotch is bottled at nowadays and again de-mineralised water is used to dilute the whisky before it is pumped into the waiting bottles and despatched to the shops and bars to be drunk. This tends to happen miles away from where it was made, usually in some vast bottling hall in Scotland's central belt. The exception to the above is with cask-strength whiskies and at rare distilleries like Glenfiddich which have their own filling lines and can therefore boast that their whiskies are 'château-bottled'. There is also the case of Bruichladdich on Islay which now goes to the trouble of taking spring water from the island and tankering it over to the mainland for bottling.

One can imagine that it was the sound of running water that would have attracted the first distillers to a particular site. The sacks of grain would be steeped in the burn, while a channel would be built to divert some of the water to a tub for cooling the worm. Over the years the source of the water would be jealously

Château-Bottled Glenfiddich

Where the whisky is filled on site at the distillery.

Famous Grouse
Scotland's favourite blend,
flying down the bottling
line at Drumchapel.

guarded. History is littered with examples of neighbouring distilleries sharing the same spring or burn who have fallen out over who owns the rights and have had to have their differences resolved in courts. Even now distillers will often go to considerable lengths, such as buying up the surrounding land to ensure their source of water is kept safe.

It is true that today the vast majority of grain arrives at the distillery already steeped and malted. Even at the few that have retained their own floor maltings, the majority of the malt will come from outside. But the issue of water is as important today as it has ever been – in fact probably more so. If you think that distilling was originally a seasonal affair that was carried out after the harvest and was over by spring. Today it is a non-stop operation requiring water 365 days a year come rain or shine. If there is a prolonged drought, which is not completely unknown in Scotland, distilleries can and do find themselves shutting down for the whole summer whether they like it or not. At those like Dalwhinnie which still have their own worm tubs, it is not just the volume but the temperature of the water that counts. If this begins to rise then less vapour is condensed in the worm, and the only way to maintain the same quality is to run the stills at a slower rate.

Modern whisky-making can demonstrate an incredible thirst for water. In Fife, the massive Cameronbridge grain distillery requires up to 50 million litres of the stuff each week, and if one of its four bore holes dried up it would be a disaster. That said, much of this is 'borrowed' for cooling purposes and is then returned to the land.

So no one would dispute the importance of water; the question is, what effect does it have on the quality of the whisky produced? Here its real impact on flavour is felt at the fermentation stage, when it is added to the grist for mashing. The importance attached to water by each individual distiller depends on what they feel makes their whisky so unique, and here it can be hard sometimes disentangling the truth from the marketing-speak. The oft-repeated quote that the best whisky comes from 'soft water, through peat, over granite' probably only applies to a fifth of all Scotland's distilleries. In any case there are plenty who would disagree – Glenmorangie and Highland Park to name but two. The fact is no one really knows for sure – of all the factors that go into making whisky, the effect of different types of water is the most mysterious and least understood.

Obviously most water used falls from the sky in the form of rain, but what happens to it then? If it runs quickly down the side of the hill over hard, crystalline rock there will be little chance of picking up much in the way of minerals before it tips into the lochs, burns and rivers. Such water will be soft and acidic. But if it falls on something more permeable or slips through the cracks in the rock its mineral content will be considerably higher. In the case of limestone it will be hard and alkaline. Some distilleries will make great play of their particularly hard or soft water, others will tell you it has very little effect and will prefer

Staves from Kentucky

Most casks used for maturing Scotch whisky are ex-Bourbon barrels shipped over and reassembled in Scotland as 250 litre 'hoggies'.

to talk of their weird-shaped stills.

Up in the far north-east at Glenmorangie they make a virtue out of both. The distillery's water comes from the local springs in the Tarlogie hills and bubbles up from the depths through 250 million-year-old red sandstone to emerge unusually hard and rich in minerals. This contributes to the spicy character of the finished whisky, or so they claim.

To give another example from the other side of the country, the man-made channel or lade, that connects Bowmore on Islay to its source of water,

travels across a real cross-section of the island. On its 5 mile journey from the River Laggan to the distillery, it comes into contact with heather, limestone, peat and grey sandstone. With a drop of just 80 feet the slow-flowing water has plenty of time to absorb the different elements on the way. Precisely what it does to the whisky is hard to quantify, but it is all part of what makes Bowmore special. For Jim McEwan, who was distillery manager here for over a decade, the water of Islay is second to none. Now manager at Bruichladdich on the other side of Loch Indaal, his long-held dream to bottle the stuff commercially may yet happen. On the same note – there is something undeniably satisfying about drinking Glen Grant at its distillery with water from the same burn that was used to make it.

WHISKY AND WATER

The Base of a Copper Pot Still for Making Malt Whisky

Beaten into shape and welded by hand.

For anyone who lives in the Highlands and Islands, or who has stayed for just one night the effect of peat on water is immediately obvious – you only need to fill a bath with what looks like stewed tea to see that. Before visiting my first ever distillery, I reckoned that this must be how whisky got its colour – I am sure I am not the only one. The truth is of course, that peat has no effect on this at all, because what gives whisky its golden brown tint is the time spent in wood and the tiny drop of caramel added at the end just prior to bottling to ensure a consistent colour.

Talk of bottles, brings us back to the start, for perhaps the greatest influence of water is when you pour a dram and dilute it to taste. The reason why this is often a good idea is not just because it prolongs the drink. Water helps wake up the spirit – it opens up the esters and aromas that have been locked up in the whisky for years and sets them free. Undiluted Scotch tends to burn the tongue and anaesthetise the nose, though some swear that an after-dinner malt sipped slowly, tastes all the better for being neat.

Some people get incredibly precious about the subject, especially when it comes to malt whisky – expressing dismay if you dare to dilute the spirit with soda water and ice. This turns to horror and cries of 'Rape!' when the subject of blended Scotch and fizzy drinks comes up.

Of course there is nothing new about whisky being a mixable spirit – in fact the British Empire was built on Scotch and soda as much as gin and tonic. In Glasgow, up until the 1960s, bottles of lemonade would be left out on the bar to mix with your dram, as opposed to Scotland's east coast where orange squash was the preferred mixer. Meanwhile in Paris, whisky and Orangina was one of the more popular if less sophisticated cocktails on offer at the Crazy Horse.

But it was never the accepted way to drink Scotch, and looking back the whisky industry has certainly appeared rather stuffy about people wanting to drink it with anything other than water, preferably still. That was OK when sales were booming after the war, but not any more. If people want to mix whisky with Irn-Bru or Red Bull or even pop it in their milk-shake the current view is that's fine just so long as they buy the stuff.

Yet one can sympathise at least from the production side of the whisky business. Unlike vodka, which can be made in the morning and sold in the afternoon, it takes three years to create a bottle of Scotch – three years of choosing the casks, selecting the malts and marrying them into a balanced blend. With all that carefully nurtured complexity, it's only human to be a little wistful at seeing it drowned under a splash of Coke from a spray gun at a bar.

Personally I am not mad about whisky and coke, and would rather stick with sparkling water or ginger ale. Because the CO_2 tickles a little valve in the stomach wall, the alcohol enters the blood stream that much quicker – something the makers of champagne have known for a long time. Bottled water, flat or fizzy, is certainly a lot more palatable than the over-chlorinated water in London, which according to popular urban folklore passes through nine bladders in its life cycle.

The Scots are much luckier than that and have always taken their plentiful supplies of mainly soft water for granted. This is not so surprising when it accounts for a fair proportion of the climate, especially in the west. It is claimed that some 900 billion litres of rain falls in Scotland each year and that from this nine million litres of whisky is produced. Alternatively bathed or pelted with rain depending on the season, the country's burns, lochs and rivers barely have time to stagnate, and any impurities like the occasional dead sheep soon get washed away. With all that pure water, and with barley growing out of its ears – is it any wonder that Scotland and whisky was a marriage made in heaven from the start?

Charring the Inside of the Casks with Fire
Allows the maturing whisky to penetrate the wood and extract flavour from it.

Ensuring Consistent Blends

The daily task of sniffing or 'nosing' dozens of samples goes on day after day.

THE ART OF BLENDING

The chances of you or I winning the National Lottery jackpot are not high – over 20 million to one against. Yet such is the size of the prize and the fact that somebody somewhere does win every week, millions of us are prepared to give it a go. Whatever this says about human nature and its inherent optimism, it is extraordinary that from just half a dozen balls each marked with a two digit number, you can achieve such a fantastically rare, random number.

Of course the answer to this lies in the almost endless combinations that can be created, and so it is with blended whisky. Not all blended whisky of course. Some blends have few component parts of any interest, are barely a day older than the legal minimum age of three years and have been matured in barrels used so often they have nothing left to give. The result will be depressingly one-dimensional – at best, bland and boring, at worst thin and insipid. A decent bottle of blended Scotch on the other hand, can be extremely complex.

Imagine yourself as a master blender for a moment. To start you must assemble your ingredients in sample bottles on a large table. You might have two or three grain whiskies and perhaps as many as 30 or 40 different malts. First think of the overall mix of malt to grain, and then the individual proportion of each separate whisky that will go into your blend. Take that feisty Highland malt, are you going to use a good measure of the stuff or just a drop? And how will it marry with the pungent aroma of smoked fish wafting out of that sample from Islay? Will it swamp the sweet, heathery flavour of that Speyside? … and so on until you have assessed how every single one will react en masse. Then consider all the different ages the whiskies could be, all the different casks that could have been used from a first-fill sherry butt to a fifth-hand Bourbon cask. When you stop and think about all the possible permutations, creating a good quality blend is not so far removed from a game of

Taking a Cask Sample

Warehouse at Bruichladdich on Islay.

chance like the Lottery.

Not so long ago, individual malt whiskies were considered like musical instruments or paints on an artist's palette. They might make a sweet sound or a bold colour on their own, but it was how they mixed and matched, whether they clashed or complemented one another that mattered. The idea being that any composer or artist needs the widest possible range of notes or colours to choose from.

Now that all sounds a bit far fetched when you apply the analogy to your average bog-standard blend that rattles off the shelf at £9.99 on special offer. We are talking mass-market brands after all, not some priceless work of art. Mercifully the Scotch whisky industry, at least the production end of it, is pretty down to earth for the most part. This is just as well – the thought of the prima donna of the blending room, would not go down well in Scotland's central belt where most blends are assembled. As it happens most blenders are rather shy, modest creatures who shun the limelight. If pressed they might mumble something about blending being all down to teamwork and experience. And yet for all that, even pretty humble blends are conceived on the same simple pretext as the best recipes – namely that the whole should be greater than the sum of its parts.

Before looking at what happens in the blending lab, there are a couple of interesting 'what if'

scenarios to consider. When whisky burst out of its homeland in the late nineteenth century to conquer first England and then the world, there was no saying that it would be Scotch. Irish whiskey was actually more popular. Scotch had a reputation for being fiery and inconsistent at the time, its malts would have been more oily and peaty than they are now, whereas whiskey was lighter because Irish distillers tended to use a mix of malted and unmalted barley and often preferred to fire their kilns with coal rather than peat. On top of that their whiskies are triple distilled. If Ireland had gone the blended route, which would have given them the necessary quantity, Irish whiskey might be as big as Guinness.

The second scenario, concerns the 1909 'What is Whisky?' case – this was the last time the malt distillers were pitched head to head with the big blenders. If the Royal Commission employed to answer this vexed question had decided that from then on all whisky had to be made from malted barley from a pot still it would have had dramatic consequences. Scotch whisky would be nothing like the size it is today. It would be a small, niche industry needing far fewer distilleries to sustain it as the Highland Malt Mafia would have quickly discovered. Besides nowadays, all the major whisky companies are involved in every aspect of the trade from buying and making grain spirit, to selling bulk spirit to marketing their most exclusive single malts.

Whisky Casks Disgorging
Rows of whisky casks disgorging their contents before being 'married' in a blending vat, prior to bottling.

A Master Blender Lost in Concentration
Nosing samples of malt whisky to check on their development.

HOW IT WORKS IN PRACTICE

'Meet our blender,' said the man from Diageo, 'I think he's on Johnnie Walker Black at the moment', and with that I was shown into a small, windowless room. Instead of a technician in a white coat with clipboard and half-moon specs, there was a small white box on the wall about two foot square with various different coloured lights on it. As robots go, it looked positively pre-war. It seemed to work like a paint mixer at a DIY shop, squirting pre-set quantities of dye to obtain the desired colour. Next door four lines of barrels with their bungs off were being rolled along tracks disgorging their contents into a narrow trough cut into the floor. There was a wire mesh on top, presumably to stop the odd splinter, but that was about it.

The real blending room is a secret world, sealed behind closed doors to the public who traipse round distilleries in their thousands. It resembles a library, spotlessly clean and hushed, where endless rows of 50cl bottles in various shades of gold, amber and straw have replaced the books. Because whisky barely alters once it is in a bottle, each sample represents a snap-shot of the spirit's precise evolution at the point of bottling. Each sample bottle is labelled with the name of the distillery, the date it was distilled, the type of cask and where it was matured. Thus the blender can track the best moment for a particular whisky to be used in a particular blend.

Most of the work is in checks and balances to ensure consistency. Every morning the blender is faced with dozens of whiskies in small, tulip-shaped glasses. By sniffing or 'nosing' each one and giving it a short-hand description of two or three words like 'green/oily and metallic' or 'meaty and sulphury' the aim is to ensure that a bottle of Bells or Famous Grouse never varies from one year to the next. Given that a big firm like Diageo has over seven million casks maturing in its warehouses, it is obviously impossible for a sample to be drawn from every one of them. However, the system needs to be as watertight as possible because there will always be the odd rogue cask waiting to catch the blender unawares and unbalance a particular blend. If not weeded out in time, it could ruin an entire vatting.

The concept of 'consistency' may not sound exciting, but trying to achieve it is almost an art in itself. One firm's blend might contain a dozen malts bought in from outside. What if one of the distilleries involved closes down, or cuts back production or starts using inferior casks... all of which can happen. For a blend of many different whiskies, where the blender has good stocks to rely on, it is fairly easy to phase out a particular malt over a five year period and replace it with one or two malts without anyone noticing.

But blends do change, they can be aged longer as with Bells when it went to an eight year old, or they can be 'dumbed down'. Sometimes you can almost taste the result of an internal battle where the company

bean-counter has triumphed over the blender. It can easily be the other way round, since those responsible for the firm's blends are pretty crucial to its success or failure. When the blender responsible for Teachers told his bosses that keeping the coal-fired stills at the Ardmore distillery mattered to the blend and had the samples to prove it, he got his way.

The real excitement, though, is when a new blend is commissioned – nowadays that happens all too rarely and the chances are it will be a supermarket own-label where price is going to be the dominant factor. That said, a number of 'reserve' own-label whiskies with a little bit of age, can put some of the long-established blends to shame. In deciding which malts and grains should go into this new creation, the blender needs to be aware of their availability now and in the future. Predicting the future is always the hardest part. In fact like the captain on the bridge of a super tanker the whole industry spends its time staring into the middle distance trying to predict where it will be in years to come. With wars and recessions and suicide bombers it can be an inexact science to say the least.

Having discovered what materials there are to play with, the blender needs to split the malts into those that will provide bulk and those known as the 'top dressings' that will really determine the character of the blend. These top quality malts need to be used sparingly – too much of a pungent, peat-smoked Islay malt like Caol Ila could easily knock a blend off balance. This is especially true with a lighter blend like 'J&B Rare' or 'Cutty Sark'. There have been various attempts to give malt whisky distilleries a rating such as 'Top, 1st, 2nd and 3rd class', but most modern blenders prefer to rely on experience. The trouble with any classification is that things change especially when distilleries are regularly bought and sold, or brought back to life after years in mothballs.

Having decided on the blend, the whiskies are tipped into a blending vat of up to 25,000 gallons and compressed air is pumped in to thoroughly mix up the contents. Some blenders like Richard Paterson, responsible for such stalwarts as 'Whyte & Mackay', believes in vatting the malts and the grains separately, and leaving them to 'marry' properly, before mixing them altogether. Others introduce all the component parts to each other right at the end. Then, just before bottling, it is chilled and filtered to precipitate out any solid oils that could turn the whisky cloudy. Also a tiny amount of caramel is often added for no other reason than to ensure a consistent colour.

If Scotch whisky could be bottled straight from the still it would certainly make life a lot easier, blending could be like following a recipe or mixing paint. But having to hang around in a cask for at least three years before it can be bottled, somehow protects the whisky business from itself. It is almost as though the company accountant had admitted defeat and accepted the fact that if you have to wait that long anyway, what's another few years going to matter.

THE WHISKY REGIONS OF SCOTLAND

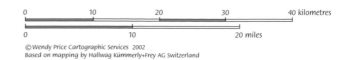
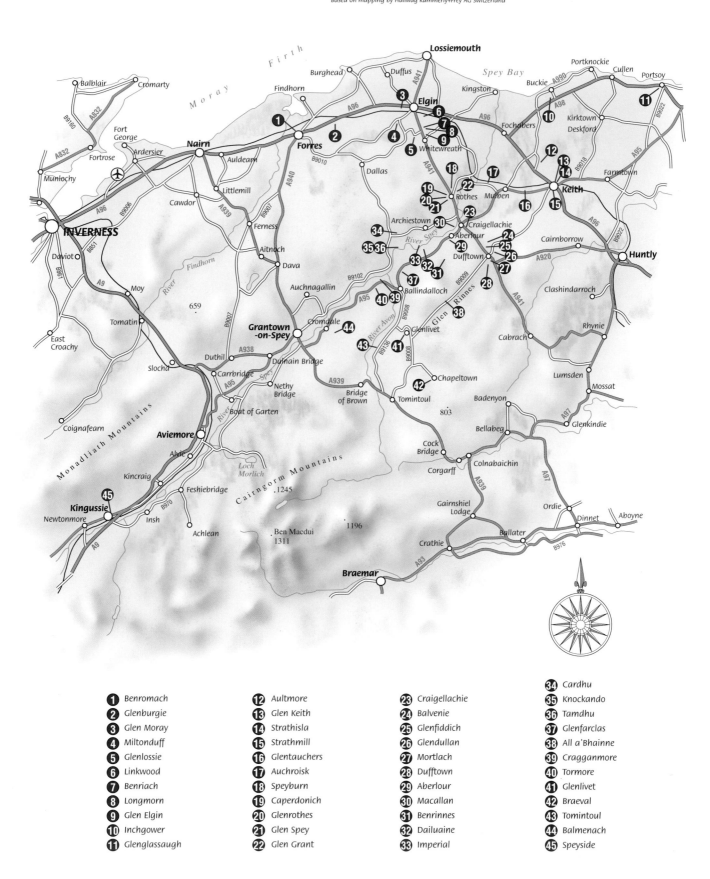

SPEYSIDE DISTILLERIES

The river Spey rises in the Monadhliath mountains, south of Loch Ness and flows in a straightish north-easterly line for a hundred miles before disgorging its contents into the Moray Firth at Spey Bay. It is one of the three great rivers that split Scotland west to east and yet despite its length the Spey feels much smaller than the Tay and the Forth, especially as they approach the sea and open up into great gaping firths or estuaries. By contrast the Spey is rarely much over 100 yards wide. There is something unique and magical about this crystal clear river nonetheless. As it clatters past, seldom still, it manages to capture a little of the untamed beauty of the Grampian Highlands. The Spey is one of the fastest flowing rivers in Britain. Its cuts a swathe through Banff and Moray and has helped to fashion the landscape, especially in the middle sections, through periodic flooding and changing course in its headlong rush to reach the sea. Time has been the main factor – some 400 million years of bad weather and the Ice Age have smoothed peaks that were once as high as the Himalayas and exposed rock at one point miles beneath the surface. Today the river's tributaries are fed by melting snow and rain that cascade down the steep slopes and impenetrable granite. The water is as pure and pristine as you could wish for – one reason why the Spey is one of the greatest salmon rivers in the world, with a catch of salmon and grilse that averages almost 10,000 a year.

No one could really dispute its beauty, but why has Speyside become so synonymous with whisky such that there are, depending on where you set the limits, as many as 59 distilleries in the region? Not all of them are working right now – some are 'mothballed', probably for good, but the great majority are producing whisky and have been, on and off, for over a hundred years. The answer lies first and foremost in the landscape itself – something easier to grasp if you come here in the winter months when the whole of Speyside begins to close in on itself behind the vast granite bulk of the Cairngorms. Even now some of the smaller routes into the region quickly become blocked after a heavy dump of snow. If conditions can be bad now, just imagine what they were like in the eighteenth century when the invention of tarmac and modern snow-ploughs was a long way off. If isolation provides one clue, the weather provides another. The poor soil in the scattered high glens that feed into the main valley of the Spey have been whipped by the wind, and battered by driving rain and hail seemingly forever. For anyone living off the land, this was subsistence farming. There was little point taking one's meagre crop of grain down to the markets by the coast, for how could it compete with the bountiful harvest grown on these fertile flatlands. Here the Laich of Moray forms part of the great barley belt that sweeps round Scotland's east coast from Inverness, to Dundee and beyond. Better to keep the withered stems and try and extract some goodness from them in the form of whisky.

There was an ancient monastic tradition of brewing beer and an even older one of heather ale to provide some knowledge in the first stages of whisky making. There were peat bogs on the moors to provide fuel, and there was an abundance of pure water. Finally, there was the added attraction of what they were doing was illegal. To the warming, life-giving properties of whisky was added the glorious, sweet taste of defiance. The fact that every drop denied the oppressive regime down south some of its revenue must have improved its flavour no end. And there was good cause to be defiant and raise a toast to the 'king o'er the water', for the authorities had sought to snuff out Highland culture in the aftermath of the Jacobite revolt.

Towards the end of the eighteenth century, there was moonshine being made right across Scotland, but in Speyside as well as the knowledge and the inclination, the smugglers had time and space. Given that the glens would become impassable through mud and snow for months on end, each small pot still could be set up and allowed to run at its own pace.

Second-hand Barrels –
waiting a new home on
Speyside.

appreciative audience. Faced with such demand, the authorities had little choice but to bow to pressure and temper the laws accordingly. As the US Government discovered a century later with prohibition, trying to impose from above without the people behind you is ultimately self-defeating.

At first the whisky makers had all the trump cards over the early excise men who would arrive in Strathspey from outside, poorly paid and demoralised before they had even started trying to track down the odd illicit stills. For the smugglers the hard part was getting the spirit to market, especially if you were heading over the hills to Aberdeen and ran into Malcolm Gillespie, Scotland's most notorious 'gauger'. In his 28 year reign of terror Gillespie impounded 6535 gallons of whisky, 62,400 gallons of barley wash, 407 stills, 165 horses and 85 carts. Along with his heavily armed band of fellow excise men, his secret weapon was his dog which he had trained to grab horses by the nose and make them stumble and throw the load of kegs they were carrying on their backs. In 1827 Gillespie finally fell foul of his masters for issuing forged bills [cheating on his expenses?] and was condemned to death. As he was led to the scaffold he showed the crowd the 42 wounds he had sustained in his long career.

Though the real boom in Speyside whisky had a lot more to do with the coming of the railway in the second half of the nineteenth century than any romantic notions of smuggling, the early underground history of whisky making did lay the foundations. As on Islay the art of distillation was too deeply bred in the bone to ever disappear when the laws were relaxed and legal distilling took off. The original Glenlivet-style whiskies were defined when Glenlivet was still on the wrong side of the law. Without these factors, distilling on Speyside could have slipped into irreversible decline after 1824. Until the first trains pulled into Dufftown and Keith thirty years later, there were plenty of other regions, notably Campbeltown and Perthshire, that were appreciably closer to the main markets in the central belt. In time the romance of Glenlivet and others was itself an important factor. It chimed so well with the whole mystique of the Highlands, the swirling mists, the clans, the noble savage in his kilt... all the things that appealed to the deeply sentimental side of the Victorian psyche. With all those etchings of smoke snaking upwards in the moonlight from a smuggler's bothy, all those ripping yarns of battles won and lost with the gaugers, visitors from the south soon succumbed to whisky's spell.

In the 1870s, there were still only sixteen distilleries in the region, and in Dufftown, the future 'whisky capital of Speyside', there was just one – Mortlach. Whereas in Campbeltown there were

Today this would be called something like 'trickle distillation', then it was just the only way people knew. Once a good, reliable source of water had been found, and a suitable bothy or cave close by, the still and the worm could be established almost permanently. There were plenty of suitable hiding places and it was not until the late 1820s that the excise men, backed up by squadrons of armed dragoons, managed to flush out the last smugglers from the Speyside glens. Well before then, whisky had become a form of currency and a way of paying rent, which is why many of the landowners were sympathetic if any of their tenants came up before them on the magistrate's bench.

Besides it was already known that 'Glenlivet', which one suspects meant most of Speyside, produced good whisky for which there was a highly twenty-one, though most had been built back in the 1820s and 30s. The great distillery-building boom on Speyside happened fifty years later, inspired by the railway, particularly the Strathspey line which opened in 1867. The first to take advantage of this was John Smith at Cragganmore, built just beyond Ballindalloch station, with its own siding linking it to the track as if by umbilical cord. It was not just grain and whisky that steamed in and out of the distillery, Smith himself always travelled by train and always in the guard's van on account of his size. If the Cragganmore label has something of the 'wild west' about it with its heavy script and puffing steam train, it may almost be intentional. Distilleries in this part of the world sprung up like American homesteads beside the track as the 'West' was opened up.

The Strathspey line shut down in the 1960s and forms a part of the sixty mile 'Speyside Way' that links Keith with Boat of Garten. Between the two lay a string of 'whisky stations': as well as Ballindalloch, there were Aberlour, Craigellachie and Knockando. As it puffed its way down to join the various branch lines on its route south, the train must have taken forever, but what a journey! Especially that first stretch beside the Spey.

With the lines of communication in place, Speyside was all ready to supply the Lowland blenders with what they required. With Glenlivet, there was a well-established 'house-style' which other distilleries were keen to emulate. It famously became the longest glen in Scotland with countless distilleries bolting the suffix 'Glenlivet' onto their name in the hope of some reflected glory. With all that good quality barley growing close by, peat from the Faemussach Moss and no shortage of water, the distillers were well set up.

For their part the blenders made a bee-line for the region, because it produced complex, elegant malts that work supremely well in blends. Speysides tend to be noticeably lighter and more floral than West Coast malts and therefore take less time to mature. Initially

they would have been a lot heavier than today on account of the peat, but soon blenders were calling for malts that were less assertive. The region responded by switching their kilns to coal which was no problem, now that they had their railway. Between 1886 and 1899 no less than 23 distilleries were built on Speyside, all of them still standing and most with their neat little pagoda roofs still proudly in place.

The triumph of Speyside to become the biggest, most important whisky region in Scotland, is partly down to that simple truth that nothing succeeds like success. A hundred years on and the prospects for some Speyside distilleries is less enticing. Those without strong personalities, sold as just another blending malt and easily swapped, may be facing an uncertain future, whereas those strung out on the islands, so long penalised for being so remote, now have a clear point of difference to tell the world about.

If there is still a Speyside style it is safer to say it has evolved over time, rather than being a product of its place. It is perfectly possible to make atypical Speyside whiskies and people do, but for the most part they share a sweet, gentle fruitiness, often with floral, heathery notes, and sometimes the scent of pear drops. Some distillers swear by the special quality of the water, its hardness or high mineral content, but the climate probably plays a more decisive factor. As the earliest distillers knew, when winter catches Speyside in its long icy grip, there is no better weather in the world for making whisky.

The Whisky Capital of Speyside

A wall of barrels greet visitors to Dufftown.

Benromach Distillery
The previously Mothballed Speyside distillery is now back in production with the old established family firm of Gordon & Macphail.

BENROMACH

Pronunciation: ben**roam**akh

Founded: 1898

Founder: Duncan McCallum & F. W. Brickman

Region: Speyside

Production Capacity: 500,000 litres

Address: Forres, Morayshire IV36 3EB

Tel: 01309 675 968

website: www.benromach.com

Parent Company: Gordon and Macphail

Visitor Centre: April–September, Mon–Sat, 9.30am–5pm.

June, July and August also Sun, 12–4pm.

October–March (excl. Christmas & New Year), Mon–Fri, 10am–4pm.

Last tour 45 minutes before closing.

No. I Cask
Signed by Prince Charles on the reopening of Benromach in 1998.

Set up in 1898 in the ancient town of Forres, Benromach is some distance from the River Spey and the main concentration of Speyside distilleries. But the fact that it had a chequered career and has changed hands six times in its first 100 years, was nothing to do with location. It was always just a wee bit small, with its two stills capable of producing a fraction under one million litres of alcohol a year.

Benromach began as a partnership between a distiller from Campbeltown and a merchant from Leith and produced its first run of spirit in 1900, only to close before the year was up. The stills were fired up in earnest after the First World War, but went cold with the Great Depression of the 1930s. In 1938 Benromach found itself in a stable of such Kentucky thoroughbreds as Old Crow and Old Grand-Dad Bourbon, having been bought up by National Distillers of America.

Then came the war and another bout of inactivity, which was repeated in 1983 when the distillery was 'mothballed' by United Distillers. The stills were ripped out, the warehouses knocked down and it looked increasingly unlikely that any more whisky would ever be made here until Gordon & MacPhail, an old family firm of whisky bottlers in Elgin, made a bid.

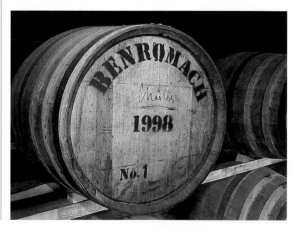

New stills were installed, and Benromach was expected to be in production by 1994, but due to various technical problems, especially the supply of spring water which meant digging up most of Forres to repair the pipe, it took a lot longer. Finally the distillery was re-opened by Prince Charles and the first spirit ran in August 1998, exactly one hundred years after its birth.

GLENBURGIE

Pronunciation: glen**burg**ee

Founded: 1829 As Kinflat distillery

Region: Speyside

Production Capacity: 2,300,000 litres

Address: Forres, Morayshire IV36 0QU

Tel: 01343 850 258

website: www.allieddomecqplc.com

Parent Company: Allied Domecq

Visitor Centre:

Contact distillery for details

If you leave aside Benromach, whose production of just 150,000 litres of spirit a year puts it firmly in the boutique distillery camp, and Dallas Dhu which is now a museum, Glenburgie is the last survivor of Speyside's western fringe. There used to be plenty more, but for some reason the action shifted north at some point, as if to be closer to the Spey.

Glenburgie lies between Forres and Elgin, surrounded by the Monaughty forest, and was first established as the Kilnflat distillery by 1829, though an unconfirmed reference puts the date as early as 1810. The fact that it did not survive in its original form may have had something to do with its size. If the stillroom really was below ground in the curious stone hut beside what is now the manager's office, little more than a trickle of Scotch can have been produced.

The trickle had already dried up by the time it was sub-let to Charles Hay, who renamed it Glenburgie and built the distillery into more-or-less what you see today. It then passed through various hands until being acquired by the blender, George Ballantine. Now owned by Allied Distillers, a significant part of the whisky produced is still used in the Ballantine's blends. For a while a secondary malt was produced, called Glencraig, quite unlike the light, apple-scented Glenburgie. Anyone hunting for this hidden glen was directed to Willie Craig in Dumbarton, head of Allied Distillers' malt distilleries – one of the few people ever to have a malt named after them.

GLEN MORAY

Pronunciation: glen**murr**ay

Founded: 1897

Founder: Henry Arnot

Region: Speyside

Production capacity: 1,850,000 litres

Address: Bruceland Road, Elgin, Morayshire IV30 1YE

Tel: 01343 542 577

website: www.glenmoray.com

Parent Company: Glenmorangie

Visitor Centre: All year, Mon–Fri, 9am–5pm.

Tours available all day by appointment.

Pre-booking advisable.

Another of the many late nineteenth century hopefuls that sprung up around Elgin to feed the flood of whisky flowing out of Speyside, only to suffer the drought that followed. Like Glenmorangie, its sister distillery on the Dornoch Firth, Glen Moray was also a brewery conversion, this time of Henry Arnot & Co.'s West Brewery in Elgin. In 1910 it closed down, and despite periodic bursts of activity was in the hands of the liquidators after the First World War. The distillery was bought for £12,000, 'less £700 for repairs to the roof' by the famous Leith-based whisky firm of Macdonald & Muir in 1920. M&M had been buying Glen Moray for some while for their blends, notably 'Highland Queen'.

Benromach

With its solitary pair of stills and an annual production of 150,000 litres, Benromach gets by with a combined staff of two.

Production was doubled with the addition of two new stills when the distillery was modernised in the late 1950s. A few years later, before anyone – not Glenfiddich still less Glenmorangie – had even considered the idea of selling single malts on a commercial scale, little old Glen Moray sold three vintages in a row to 'All Nippon Airways'. Later ventures into special expressions of Glen Moray aged in 'Chardonnay wood' have a slight air of desperation about them, though the owners insist their motives were entirely pure. It was to sweeten the dry-ish, grassy flavours of Glen Moray, and was not merely an attempt to ride on the back of the most popular grape variety the world has ever known – of course not.

But Glen Moray's greatest role is in the superb blend Bailie Nicol Jarvie, which has just been relaunched by the parent company and still deserves far greater recognition.

MILTONDUFF

Pronunciation: milton**duff**

Founded: 1824

Founder: Andrew Pearey and Robert Bain

Region: Speyside

Production capacity: 5,240,000 litres

Address: Elgin, Morayshire IV30 3TQ

Tel: 01343 547 433

website: www.allieddomecqplc.com

Parent Company: Allied Domecq

Visitor Centre: September–June, Mon–Thurs, 10am–2pm. All visits by appointment only.

On the same theme that behind every great distillery lies a great blend (or is it the other way round?) Miltonduff and Ballantine's Finest had been joined at the hip ever since Hiram Walker took over the distillery in 1936. Twice in the second half of the twentieth century Ballantine's managed to ride the Scotch whisky boom, first in the States where the foundations for the brand had been well laid during prohibition, and then in Spain. That second wave of popularity has yet to break, making Spain the biggest market for Scotch in the world, with Ballantine's in second place behind J&B. The distillery cannot take all the credit, since Allied Distillers who now own Ballantine's, claim that 57 malts go into the blend, though admit that Miltonduff does play a pivotal role.

If whisky evolved out of beer and if the roots of

distilling lie in the monastery, then the two come neatly together at Miltonduff. It was built beside the ancient Pluscarden Priory near Elgin and first licensed in 1824. The stills were installed inside the old brewhouse where the monks used to make ale of such sublime quality 'that it filled the abbey with unutterable bliss.' No doubt it helped that the water of the Black Burn used to make the ale had been blessed by an Abbot way back in the fifteenth century. With heavenly beer and a source of sacred water, Miltonduff could hardly go wrong. A little of the two million gallons that spurt from its six stills is allowed to be bottled as a single malt, but most goes to make Ballantine's the excellent blend that it is.

GLENLOSSIE & MANNOCHMORE

Glenlossie

Pronunciation: glen**loss**ee

Founded: 1876

Founder: John Duff

Region: Speyside

Production capacity: 1,100,000 litres

Address: Thornshill, Elgin, Morayshire IV30 3SS

Tel: 01343 862 000

website: www.diageo.com

Parent Company: Diageo

Visitor Centre: Contact distillery for details

Mannochmore

Pronunciation: mannokh**more**

Founded: 1971

Founder: John Haig & Co

Region: Speyside

Production capacity: 1,300,000 litres

Address: Thornshill, Elgin, Morayshire IV30 3SS

Tel: 01343 862 300

website: www.diageo.com

Parent Company: Diageo

Visitor Centre: Contact distillery for details

In 1876, John Duff decided that after his years as distillery manager at Glendronach it was time to branch out on his own. The site he chose to build, at Glenlossie was just a few miles west of Lhanbryde, near Elgin, where he had once been an innkeeper. It had its own reservoir fed from water from the Mannoch hills, which in turn fed a small channel used to cool the worms and supply the power via a

waterwheel. To take advantage of the main railway line south of Elgin that ran close by, he quickly installed his own siding so that the freshly filled casks could be dispatched directly to the leading blenders in Perth. Duff also built houses for his staff of 20 employed in the distillery and also to look after his herd of 50 cattle fed on all the draff created in making whisky.

DCL gained a controlling share in 1919, and took complete control after a bad fire at the distillery in 1927. By then DCL was fully confirmed in its role as the great whale of the whisky trade, 'hoovering up' distressed distilleries like so much plankton. Then, as if to celebrate the arrival of electricity, which finally replaced the waterwheel as the chief source of power in 1960, another pair of stills were added to bring the total to six. What makes them highly unusual is the use of purifiers on the three spirit stills which cause a lighter distillation.

The following decade, Glenlossie had to make room for Mannochmore, a new distillery built alongside to share the same workforce but a different source of water. Thanks to the purifiers, Glenlossie's malt is more fragile than its fresh, fulsome neighbour. Mannochmore was mothballed for the second half of the eighties, but came back to unleash the first black whisky called 'Loch Dhu'. As dark as Coca-Cola, the colour comes from using heavily charred barrels and not caramel as some feared.

LINKWOOD

> **Pronunciation: link**wood
>
> **Founded:** 1820
>
> **Founder:** Peter Brown
>
> **Region:** Speyside
>
> **Production capacity:** 3,000,000 litres
>
> **Address:** Elgin, Morayshire IV30 8RD
>
> **Tel:** 01343 553 800
>
> **website:** www.diageo.com
>
> **Parent Company:** Diageo
>
> **Visitor Centre:** Contact distillery for details

The cluster of distilleries in the lower Spey valley that lie in a triangle between Elgin, Rothes and Fochabers, have never quite received the attention they deserve. Some of the finest malt whisky on Speyside is made here, yet far more interest is focussed on the distilleries further up the Spey, like Macallan, Cragganmore and Glenlivet.

Linkwood has been quietly distilling away since 1820, in what was once open country southeast of Elgin. It was established by a prominent local farmer, Peter Brown, who appears to have run a pretty self-sufficient operation, growing most, if not all, the barley needed by the distillery. The draff spat out as a by-product was hoovered up by Brown's herd of cattle.

Some 20 years later, James Walker, who had been manager at Aberlour, was brought in to run Linkwood. At the time production was running at about 20,000 gallons a year. Then, having rebuilt the distillery in the early 1870s and raised output to 50,000 gallons, the company was floated by William Brown.

The Linkwood-Glenlivet Distillery Co. stayed independent for longer than most before selling out to the mighty DCL for £80,000 in 1933. In recent times it has been expanded twice, adding four extra stills housed in a new building next door, while the original Victorian stillhouse was closed down in 1985. Five years later its solitary pair of stills was fired up again, effectively creating two distilleries whose spirit is vatted together to produce a complex single malt, with a burst of initial sweetness finishing quite savoury.

LONGMORN

Pronunciation: longmorn
Founded: 1894
Founder: John Duff
Region: Speyside
Production capacity: 3,300,000 litres
Address: Longmorn, Elgin, Morayshire IV30 3SJ
Tel: 01542 783 400
website: www.pernod-ricard.com
Parent Company: Pernod Ricard
Visitor Centre: Contact distillery for details

Just beyond Linkwood, on the road back to Rothes from Elgin, stand Benriach and Longmorn, a distillery double-act that has worked in tandem since 1970 when they became part of Glenlivet Distilleries. Though Longmorn is just four years older, having been built by John Duff in 1894, it towers above its younger brother in size and reputation. Under the four-tier classification system used by blenders, there was never much dispute that this was a 'top-class' distillery, and, throughout Benriach's 65 painful years of non-production, Longmorn was running pretty well non-stop.

Though it was more than able to stand on its own two feet, and even though it was stretching a geographical point, the early partners involved in Longmorn felt their baby needed that little extra magic that only the suffix '-Glenlivet' could deliver. This was only dropped from the title when Seagram took over in 1977. By this stage, Longmorn had undergone two expansions in quick succession to increase the number of stills to eight, enough to make

around a million gallons of alcohol each year.

The wash stills and spirit stills were kept in adjoining buildings and fired by coal fires underneath. This method of heating the stills was changed to internal steam coils in 1993, which, say the traditionalists, risks losing some of Longmorn's cherished complexity. At first this seems far-fetched, like debating whether heating the water on a stove or in an electric kettle effects the taste of tea. But some of the malt-drinking cognoscenti insist there is more to it than that, because direct-firing means using rummagers – copper chains that scour the inside of the still to stop scorching – and this could affect the end result. The result will be known any day now, when the new coil-heated 12 year-old appears in 2005.

BENRIACH

Pronunciation: benreeakh
Founded: 1898
Founder: John Duff
Region: Speyside
Production Capacity: 2,600,000 litres
Address: Longmorn, Elgin, Morayshire IV3 3SJ
Tel: 01542 783 400
website: www.pernod-ricard.com
Parent Company: Pernod Ricard
Visitor Centre: Contact distillery for details

Of all the Speyside distilleries built on the crest of the great speculative wave that completed the story of whisky-making in the nineteenth century, few crashed so badly as Benriach. Built by John Duff in 1898 it ran for just three seasons and then fell silent for the next 65 years. The fact that it was still standing at all when Glenlivet Distilleries took it over in the mid 1960s was fairly astonishing. They had to rebuild it from scratch and create a whole new whisky, since those who could remember the taste of the original Benriach were pretty thin on the ground by then. The reason it survived the intervening years was probably because of its floor maltings which had been used from time to time to supply malted barley to Longmorn, Benriach's sister distillery which was also set up by Duff and others in the 1890s.

The fact that the whiskies they both produce are decidedly different demonstrates once again that being next door to one another and sharing the same water supply is no guarantee of similarity in the end result. While Benriach single malt is light and flowery, Longmorn is in a different class - altogether richer and more complex.

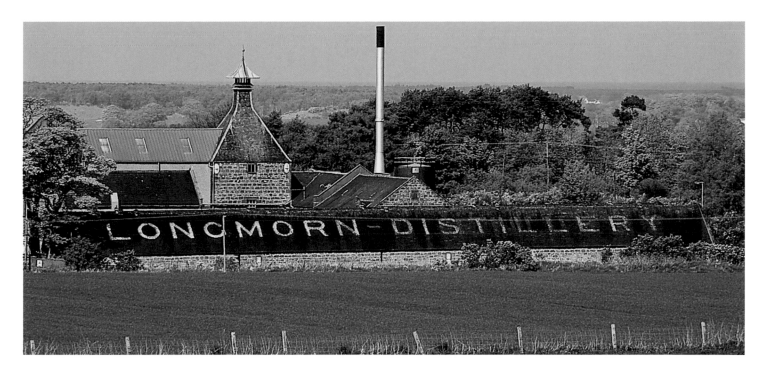

GLEN ELGIN

Pronunciation: glenelgin

Founded: 1900

Founder: William Simpson

Region: Speyside

Production Capacity: 1,600,000 litres

Address: Longmorn, Elgin, Morayshire IV30 8SL

Tel: 01343 862 100

website: www.diageo.com

Parent Company: Diageo

Visitor Centre: Contact distillery for details

If people had their doubts about Glendullan, at Glen Elgin even the architect, Charles Doig, had his doubts. When William Simpson, a former manager at Glenfarclas, hired Doig to build him a distillery on the road between Elgin and Rothes, the epic rise of Scotch whisky had already peaked. The construction of Glen Elgin was still in progress when Pattisons, the firm of Leith blenders, went broke. The Pattison crash shook the entire industry to its core, and it would be over 50 years before anyone on Speyside dreamt of building another distillery there.

The trouble with Simpson was he got there too late, the credits had already begun to roll by the time he leapt on stage. The original design was modified and contractors not paid in full, apart from the steeplejack who threatened to rip down the chimney

if Simpson defaulted, but the total venture still cost £13,000. It went into production on 1 May 1900 and was on the market six months later, to be sold early the next year for just £4000.

It limped along under various owners, its stills more often cold than hot, until rescued by DCL in 1936. Part of the trouble was that it shared the same water source as Coleburn. Being a mile upstream, Coleburn had first pick, which sometimes left Glen Elgin short. A new source was found and slowly the distillery was dragged into the twentieth century and hitched up to the National Grid in 1964. At the same time the number of stills was tripled to six. It was licensed to White Horse, where it can usually be found in the blend, and occasionally appears as a 12 year-old, honeyed floral single malt. Meanwhile Coleburn shut down for good in 1985.

INCHGOWER

Pronunciation: inshgower

Founded: 1913

Founder: Alexander Wilson

Region: Speyside

Production capacity: 2,200,000 litres

Address: Buckie, Banffshire AB56 5AB

Tel: 01542 831 161

website: www.diageo.com

Parent Company: Diageo

Visitor Centre: Contact distillery for details

Longmorn

This distillery has been cherished by blenders for over a century as a source of delightfully complex Speyside malt, and has rarely been out of production as a result.

The label of Inchgower 14 year-old, a dense, creamy vanilla malt whose sweetness fades on the tongue, states that the distillery was founded in 1824, which is stretching a point. There was a distillery called Tochineal nearby at Cullen, which was set up by John Wilson, but it closed in 1867 when the lease ran out. Given that Wilson's landlady, the Countess of Seafield, had doubled the rent, apparently because she did not approve of distilleries, his son Alex quite naturally decided to move and make his whisky elsewhere. The site he choose was a few miles west along Spey Bay, near Buckie, with water from the Letter Burn, plentiful supplies of peat and some of the richest barley to be found on the east coast. With its massive maltings, 400 ft long, and ample warehouses, the distillery prospered under the firm of Alexander Wilson & Co, set up in 1913. In its early days the distillery had its own 200-acre farm and employed a staff of 20.

Then, hit by the war and the ensuing depression, the business folded. After six years lying idle, the distillery was bought by Buckie Town Council for the princely sum of just £1000 in 1936, only to sell it on for £3000 two years later. Even with this 200 per cent mark-up the new owner, Arthur Bell & Sons, was hardly being ripped off. Today part of Diageo, Inchgower's main role is to provide a little edge to the gentler Speyside and Perthshire malts that go to make up Bell's 8 year-old, Britain's best-selling Scotch.

GLENGLASSAUGH

Pronunciation: glen**glass**aw

Founded: 1875

Founder: James Moir, Alexander Morrison, William Morrison and Thomas Wilson

Region: Speyside

Address: Portsoy, Banffshire AB54 2SQ

Tel: 01261 842 367

website: www.edringtongroup.com

Parent Company: Edrington Group

Visitor Centre:

Contact distillery for details

Among the partners behind the Glenglassaugh distillery in 1875 was a local coppersmith called Thomas Wilson. Having supplied countless stills, as had his father, Wilson presumably decided there was more money to be made in what came out of them.

This is one of the very few Speyside distilleries that sits right by the coast, inhaling the damp, salt-laden air blowing in off the North Sea. The inspiration for building here beside the fishing village of Portsoy, whose pretty pinkish-green stone crops up in Versailles, was two-fold. First there were all those nearby fields of barley, and second there was the fast-flowing River Glassaugh which provided all the power from day one. In the 1890s Glenglassaugh slipped into the fold of Highland Distilleries where it remains. During the following century it was to suffer long periods of neglect, only producing whisky for five years at most between 1907 and 1960, at which point it was completely rebuilt. Rarely seen as a single malt, its main role is behind the scenes in such blends as Famous Grouse and Cutty Sark, though even here its job is not guaranteed, and the smell of mothballs is never far away.

AULTMORE

Pronunciation: a**wlt**more

Founded: 1896

Founder: Alexander Edward of Forres

Region: Speyside

Production Capacity: 1,800,000 litres

Address: Keith, Banffshire

Tel: 01542 882 762

website: www.dewars.com

Parent Company: Bacardi

Visitor Centre: By appointment only

This was one of the many distilleries to spring up on Speyside during the 1890s, this time on the flatlands between Keith and the sea. It was a region that had known its fair share of moonshine in the heyday of illicit distillation. It was built by Alexander Edward, a well-known figure among the local distillers who had previously taken over Benrinnes and was a joint partner in Craigellachie. Just before the Pattison crash which brought the late nineteenth century whisky boom to an abrupt end, Edward was also involved with Oban and Dallas Dhu.

Aultmore never quite recovered from the crash and was sold to John Dewar & Sons in 1923 for £20,000 and from there to what is now Diageo. A second pair of stills was added to double the capacity in 1970, when many of the original buildings were replaced. In its present form, Aultmore represents the standard box-shaped unit that passed for distillery design in the 1970s – perfectly functional, but nothing to look at. The distillery now belongs to Bacardi, and its malts are only occasionally available from independent bottlers.

GLEN KEITH

Pronunciation: glen**keith**

Founded: 1958

Founder: Seagram

Region: Speyside

Address: Station Road, Keith, Banffshire

Tel: 01542 860 333

website: www.pernod-ricard.com

Parent Company: Pernod Ricard

Visitor Centre:

Contact distillery for details

As post-war austerity began to fade, a growing sense of optimism emerged in the late 1950s. Rationing had ended four years earlier and exports, especially to the United States, were beginning to boom. Seagram decided that 1958 was the right time to build a new distillery in Scotland, just across the road from its recently acquired flagship – Strathisla in Keith.

As the country's first fully fledged malt distillery for nigh on 60 years, the event was highly significant. The Glen Keith Glenlivet distillery was built out of an old mill that had been grinding flour and oatmeal for as long as Strathisla had been making whisky. Little was retained of the original building, but by using local stone and popping a decorative pagoda on the roof it was a sympathetic conversion. At first its solitary wash still was connected to a pair of spirit stills to achieve a form of triple distillation, common in Ireland and the Lowlands, but virtually unheard of in the Highlands. This was later dropped as more stills were added. In 1970 the distillery became the first in Scotland to employ gas-fired stills, before converting to internal steam coils three years later. Further expansion has brought the total number of stills to six.

Once Seagram had swallowed up Glenlivet, the old affix was quietly dropped and 'Glen Keith' even started to appear in a bottle under its own name as part of Seagram's 'Heritage Selection'. Having created something of a whisky loch of its own, the Seagram's distilleries went a bit quiet before being sold to the French group Pernod Ricard a week before Christmas 2000.

All the whisky made here is tankered a short distance to the other side of Keith to be filled into casks, from where all but a drop goes into blends, notably Chivas Regal and Passport. Provided these big export brands continue to thrive Glen Keith has little to fear.

STRATHISLA

Strathisla in Keith
From the far bank
of the River Isla.

Pronunciation: strath**eye**la

Founded: 1786 as Milltown Distillery

Founder: George Taylor and Alexander Milne

Region: Speyside

Production Capacity: 2, 00,000 litres

Address: Seafield Avenue, Keith, Banffshire AB55 3BS

Tel: 01542 783 044

website: www.chivas.com

Parent Company: Pernod Ricard

Visitor Centre: April–October, Mon–Fri, 10am–4pm. Sun, 12.30–4pm.

'No it's just not possible, I can't do it,' muttered a photographer as he emerged from the trees across the road from Strathisla, shaking his head in disappointment. He had discovered the simple fact

The Twin Pagodas of Strathisla

One of the prettiest distilleries on Speyside add an oriental note to the town of Keith.

that however hard you try, from whatever angle you like, Strathisla remains unbelievably photogenic. With its squat, speckled stone walls like nougat, beneath long sloping slate roofs topped with a pair of twin pagodas, it is as pretty a place for making whisky as you could wish for. There is an old-world charm about the place and a sense of longevity being the oldest surviving distillery in the Highlands and fourth oldest in Scotland. It is however, largely late Victorian in its present form, and though it is clearly well cared for now, it has suffered its fair share of neglect in the past.

It was founded as the Milltown distillery in 1786 by George Taylor and Alexander Milne. Taylor had made his money in banking and the flax trade and was keen to get out of the ailing textile industry and try his hand at something new. By building this small-scale distillery with just one 40-gallon still he could also take advantage of the Wash Act passed two years earlier. We know he did have some experience having been caught with an illicit still and fined a token £2. 2 shillings. Not much else is known about George Taylor except that he ended his days as something of a hermit in a little cottage outside Keith, having been

dashed against a tree when his horse bolted.

The distillery was built beside the Fons Bulliens Well, which is still used to this day. Way back in the eleventh century the same well was being used by monks to brew a potent heather ale. Whether the distillery somehow evolved out of a brewery no one is quite sure, but clearly both needed a reliable source of good clear water. The source was the Broomhill spring which flows down the hill to collect in a reservoir behind the distillery. One Victorian visitor noted, 'the water is so bright and clear that a pebble dropped into it seemed magnified into a huge crystal boulder.' Later the water was mixed with some from the River Isla itself which gave its name to first the whisky and then eventually the distillery itself.

During the nineteenth century the distillery passed to William Longmore, a local banker and grain merchant who was also something of a philanthropist, giving Keith its town hall and bowling green. Luckily he had the financial resources to survive a bad fire in 1876, which killed thirty cows, and destroyed a threshing machine and steam engine. Then, just three years later a stone clipped the side of the mill, sending off a spark which ignited the fine,

**The Upper Tun Room –
Strathisla**

powdery residue from the milled grain and set Strathisla ablaze yet again. It was time to re-build the distillery in something less flammable – hence the stone of today.

By the 1880s production from the two stills was running at 90,000 gallons a year. The local trade was supplied in 5 gallon stone jars bearing the name 'Wm. Longmore'. Grocers would sell it on by the bottle, while bars would dispense it via a tap from elegant glass decanters etched with the words 'Strathisla Whisky'. Some whisky was being sent south to England and some was shipped to the colonies.

To rebuild the distillery, Longmore's son-in-law, John Geddes-Brown, who had taken over by this stage, set up the firm of William Longmore & Co. and offered the public 7000 shares at £5 each. This was apparently one of the first flotations the whisky trade had seen.

Unfortunately letting in outside investors eventually led to the family losing control to a notoriously crooked financier and theatrical impresario called Jay Pomeroy in 1942. Having built up his stake until he was the main shareholder, Pomeroy became chairman of Wm. Longmore & Co. With no experience of distilling people must have wondered why on earth he was interested in a distillery, especially when a government order had recently limited whisky firms to a quarter of the barley they had been using before the war. But Pomeroy knew exactly what he was doing, the squeeze on supply had a dramatic effect on price, and on the London black-market whisky was trading at £20-25 a

gallon. Not bad when it cost just 16 shillings (80p) a gallon to make. The first priority was to cease all local trade in bottled Strathisla and have it all sent south. If the people of Keith were anything like the islanders in 'Whisky Galore' this must have caused huge resentment and may have prompted one of the locals to grass on him. When Pomeroy was arrested in 1949 the fraud squad unearthed tax evasion on a grand scale. It was an elaborate scam involving a room in London full of telephone kiosks, each marked with the name of a fictitious company. Pomeroy was sent down owing £111,000 in tax or just under £2 million in today's money.

Strathisla was in a bad way when Jimmy Barclay paid £71,000 for it in 1951 on behalf of Seagram, who had recently bought Chivas Brothers in Aberdeen. Barclay was one of the last great whisky barons, who began his working life earning 2s 6d a week as an office boy in Benrinnes in 1902 and died in the 1960s leaving an estate worth around £7.5 million in today's money, and hotels in Scotland and the Bahamas. Along the way he trained with Sir Peter Mackie of White Horse, and met Sam Bronfman, the man behind Seagram out in Canada when both were doing a spot of bootlegging. When he bought Strathisla he used a church organist from Aberdeen to do his bidding, presumably to dampen speculation that Seagram was interested. Either way, the distillery's future was secure, especially as the heart of the mighty Chivas Regal – the world's top-selling deluxe blend.

**Strathisla and
Chivas Regal**

As the sign on the distillery gate shows – the fate of Strathisla and Chivas Regal are welded together. Each depends on the other for their continued success.

85

STRATHMILL

Pronunciation: strathmill

Founded: 1891

Founder: A Keith consortium

Region: Speyside

Production capacity: 1,700,000 litres

Address: Keith, Banffshire AB55 3DQ

Tel: 01542 882 295

website: www.diageo.com

Parent Company: Diageo

Visitor Centre: Contact distillery for details

If you did not want to build your distillery from scratch, you needed to find a building to convert, the most obvious candidates being a redundant brewery and a grain mill. A group in Keith chose the second option in 1891, and turned the Strathisla mill into the Glenisla-Glenlivet distillery, nearly 70 years before Seagram did the same with Glen Keith. As well as grinding flour and oatmeal, it was rumoured the Strathisla mill had been producing something a little stronger on the side for well over a generation.

In 1895 the new distillery was sold for £9500 to Gilbey's, the London wine & spirits merchants, to add to Glen Spey which they had bought eight years earlier. Gilbey's merged with Justerini & Brooks to form IDV in 1962, which gave Strathmill a notable range of blended whiskies to influence, including Dunhill's 'Old Master and 'Gentleman's Speyside Blend'. It also plays a supporting role to Knockando in J&B.

Apart from a second pair of stills, added shortly after, Strathmill has been preserved pretty much intact – a pretty, late Victorian distillery with its twin pagoda roofs firmly in place. The stills are cooled by the River Isla, with water for the wash coming from a spring within the grounds. But for the occasional independent bottling of the whisky as a single malt, the entire production goes into blends.

GLENTAUCHERS

Pronunciation: glen**tawkh**ers

Founded: 1897

Founder: W. P. Lowrie and James Buchanan

Region: Speyside

Production capacity: 3,250,000 litres

Address: Mulben, Keith, Banffshire AB55 6YL

Tel: 01542 860 272

website: www.allieddomecqplc.com

Parent Company: Allied Domecq

Visitor Centre: Contact distillery for details

The cobbled Courtyard at Strathisla.

Some distilleries evolved out of the farmyard or sprung up in the vague hope that someone might be around to drink the produce. This was not the case with Glentauchers, built three miles beyond Keith in 1897, close to the main east coast line that connected Aberdeen with Inverness. It had two malting barns whose pagoda roofs still stand, two stills and a supply of water to mash the grain, condense the spirit and even power the machinery.

From the word 'go' the Glentauchers Distillery Co., a partnership between the Glasgow-based whisky brokers, W.P. Lowrie, and James Buchanan, knew exactly where its malt whisky was destined. It was to go into 'Buchanan's Blend', later registered as 'Black & White', a massive brand that competed head to head with Dewar's 'White Label' to be the world's most popular Scotch. The distillery was fully taken over by James Buchanan in 1906 and became part of a portfolio of five distilleries, of which only Dalwhinnie survives. Buchanan went on to merge with his arch rival Tommy Dewar in 1915, and together they both joined DCL after the war.

As long as people's thirst for Black & White did not slacken, Glentauchers had little to fear. In the mid 1960s a major refit saw the number of stills increased from two to six and installed behind the tall windows of a new, rather prefab-looking stillhouse. By then DCL had, strangely, begun to regard Dalwhinnie as the true spiritual home of 'Black &

White' and when drastic measures were needed to drain the early 1980s whisky loch, Glentauchers found itself struck off. Luckily a buyer was soon found in the shape of Allied Distillers who have so far left the bottling of any single malt to Gordon & Macphail of Elgin.

AUCHROISK

Pronunciation: awkh**roshk**

Founded: 1986

Founder: Justerini & Brooks

Region: Speyside

Production Capacity: 3,100,000 litres

Address: Mulben, Banffshire

Tel: 01542 860 333

website: www.diageo.com

Parent Company: Diageo

Visitor Centre: Open all year, Monday–Friday, 10am–4pm. All visits by appointment only.

Auchroisk was built by IDV before Allt'A Bhainne, again with blends in mind, this time for J&B Rare, which slipped badly in the States, but has now become the biggest selling Scotch whisky in Spain.

SPEYBURN

ESTABLISHED 1897

SINGLE

HIGHLAND MALT

Scotch Whisky

OFFICE
&
ENQUIRIES

The design is clean-cut and modern, though it does have more of the look of a distillery than Allt'A Bainne. In front is a curious, small turret where the yeast is stored which pokes up through the ground like the head of a rocket.

The distillery sits on a hill above Rothes beside the Mulben burn which flows into the Spey. Like every distillery there has ever been, the location was dictated by having a good, reliable source of water – in this case the beautifully soft spring water from Dorries' well. The Gaelic name translates as 'ford across the red stream'. It was bottled as a single malt for the first time in 1986, under the name 'The Singleton of Auchroisk'. Apparently it was felt that 'Auchroisk' on its own might be tricky for malt whisky aficionados to get their tongues round. With just a few thousand cases available, this toffee flavoured mellow malt is relatively rare.

The little set aside for bottling is aged partly in sherry butts and is sold as a vintage. For the most part its current owners, Diageo, recognise it for what it is – classic Speyside blending material. The interior of the distillery is spotless and sparkles with stainless steel, while the still-room is laid out for possible expansion should J&B ever re-conquer America.

SPEYBURN

Pronunciation: **spay**burn	
Founded: 1897	
Founder: John Hopkins & Co	
Region: Speyside	
Production capacity: 1,000,000 litres	
Address: Rothes, Near Aberlour, Aberdeenshire AB38 7AG	
Tel: 01340 831 213	
website: www.inverhouse.com	
Parent Company: Inver House	
Visitor Centre: Contact distillery for details	

Rumour has it that United Distillers might have lived to regret selling off Speyburn in 1991, and that the purchasers, Inver House Distillers, walked away with rather a bargain, there not being too many buyers around at the time. Either way, the new owners were soon winning awards for Speyburn as a 10 year-old single malt.

Speyburn was still being built as 1897 was drawing to a close. The windows and doors to the stillhouse had yet to be fitted and with snow swirling in from outside, the distillery manager ordered the stills to be fired up – all to have some spirit to celebrate Queen Victoria's diamond jubilee.

Tucked among the trees of the Glen of Rothes, almost wedged in by the steep slopes, Speyburn is as classically Speyside as the day it was built. The only dark note to this dreamy setting just on the edge of Rothes on the road out to Elgin, is that this was the site of the old gibbet where the town's criminals were strung up. Whether or not ghosts haunt the stillroom at night, the whisky is as fresh and innocent as can be. What it lacks in length and muscle, it makes up for in feminine charm.

CAPERDONICH

Pronunciation: caper**don**akh	
Founded: 1897	
Founder: James & John Grant	
Region: Speyside	
Production Capacity: 2,100,000 litres	
Address: Rothes, Morayshire AB38 7BS	
Tel: 01542 783 300	
website: www.pernod-ricard.com	
Parent Company: Pernod Ricard	
Visitor Centre: Contact distillery for details	

As anyone with a precocious older sibling knows, it can get a bit tedious always being introduced or referred to as 'brother of the more famous…'. And so it was with Caperdonich which has spent its entire life under the shadow of Glen Grant. The story is remarkably similar to that of Benriach and Longmorn, though in this instance, it seems that Major James Grant really did believe he could produce a replica of his proven success next door. So with Glen Grant approaching its sixtieth birthday and already one of the biggest distilleries on Speyside, the Major decided to build 'Glen Grant No. 2'. By using the same-shaped stills, the same source of grain, it was bound to work – surely?

The authorities insisted that what was produced by the new distillery had to go through the same spirit safe as Glen Grant, so a pipe was rigged up to pump the spirit over the road for vatting as 'Glen Grant'. Somehow it never worked out, and within three years of being set up, what became Caperdonich shut down as if forever.

Then, with worldwide demand for Scotch apparently insatiable, Glenlivet Distillers rebuilt and rechristened the distillery in 1965, adding another pair of stills two years later. It was swallowed up by Seagram along with Glen Grant in the 1970s and now belongs to Pernod Ricard.

Glenrothes

Despite having a cemetery for a neighbour, Glenrothes did not slip into an early grave and has continued to prosper thanks to its popularity among blenders.

GLENROTHES

Pronunciation: glen**roth**es

Founded: 1878

Founder: W. Grant & Co

Region: Speyside

Production capacity: 5,600,000 litres

Address: Rothes, Morayshire IV33 7AA

Tel: 01340 831 248

website: www.edringtongroup.com

Parent Company: Edrington Group

Visitor Centre: Contact distillery for details

The year James Stuart of Macallan and his various partners began building their new distillery in the centre of Rothes, happened to coincide with one of the worst bouts of economic recession to hit the nineteenth century. In 1878 the Caledonian Bank who were funding the project through a couple of agents on Speyside, was forced to suspend trading. The partnership collapsed, Stuart scurried back to Macallan to lick his wounds, and the two agents, Willie Grant and Robert Dick, were left to pick up the pieces. One can imagine the two men gazing out at the town cemetery next door, and wondering whether their venture would survive or slip into an early grave. In the end, by frantically borrowing money from anyone, including £600 from a local Presbyterian minister, Glenrothes managed to cling on. Together with Bunnahabhain on Islay, it helped lay the shaky foundations for Highland Distilleries, formed in 1887 and still going strong as part of Edrington – the largest private sector group in the industry.

Today Glenrothes stands out for its massive smooth-flanked, pink, granite stillroom constructed in the 1980s to share five pairs of big copper stills which can pump out some 5 million litres of alcohol in a good year. It has always been popular among blenders, partly because it comes round so quickly. It reaches a balance and complexity at five years that a robust Islay malt could only dream of at that age. It plays a starring role in the Famous Grouse and Cutty Sark, whose parents, the blue-chip London wine merchant, Berry Bros. & Rudd, do bottle a vintage version. Sweeter on the nose than in the mouth, it develops into a long, creamy, seriously smooth dram on the tongue.

GLEN SPEY

Pronunciation: glen**pay**

Founded: 1884

Founder: James Stuart & Co

Region: Speyside

Production capacity: 1,400,000 litres

Address: Rothes, Banffshire AB38 AU

Tel: 01340 832 000

website: www.diageo.com

Parent Company: Diageo

Visitor Centre: Contact distillery for details

James Stuart knew all about the good-quality water in the Rothes burn, when he decided to convert his Mills of Rothes, where he had been grinding oatmeal, into a fully-fledged distillery to add to his production at Macallan. Having been denied the chance to build Glenrothes in 1878, he got his revenge on his former partners by building Glen Spey on the other side of the burn soon after. This sparked off an inevitable tussle over who owned the water rights. In 1887 Stuart sold out to Gilbey, the London-based drinks company best known for its gin. This was one of the earliest cross-border raids from the south, and meant that whisky, once thought suitable for only the grouse moor or the river bank, was now becoming almost respectable even in the salons and clubs of London society.

Much later Gilbey's merged into IDV with Justerini & Brooks, whose predominantly Speyside blend, J&B, was soon keeping Glen Spey in business. Thanks to the great post-war surge in demand in the States, where David Niven made a small contribution as one of the brand's early salesmen, J&B became the second most popular whisky on the planet. As a result Glen Spey was rebuilt and given an extra pair of stills in the 1970s, though care was evidently taken to preserve as much of the original Victorian feel of the distillery as possible.

Now that IDV is part of Diageo, who have over two dozen malt distilleries to choose from, Glen Spey only appears as a single malt on the lists of independent bottlers as an occasional oddity.

Glen Spey in Rothes
Has retained some of its Victorian charm despite rebuilding in the 1970s.

Maturing Whisky –
under lock and key at Glen Grant.

GLEN GRANT

Pronunciation: glen**grant**

Founded: 1840

Founder: James & John Grant

Region: Speyside

Production Capacity: 5,400,000 litres

Address: Rothes, Morayshire AB38 7BS

Tel: 01542 783 318

website: www.pernod-ricard.com

Parent Company: Pernod Ricard

Visitor Centre: April–October, Mon–Sat, 10am–4pm. Sun, 12.30–4pm.

Group bookings by appointment.

John and James Grant were proud members of clan Grant, part of one of the oldest and most powerful clans in the Spey valley whose power-base was twenty miles up-stream at Castle Grant. Born in Inveravon, eight miles from Rothes, John worked on his father's farm before becoming a local grain merchant, while James set up as a solicitor in Elgin. In 1840 they decided to establish a distillery at Rothes, apparently using John's knowledge of making- whisky from his earlier experience supplying grain to illicit stills. The position of the new venture was well chosen. It was relatively close to Garmouth on the Spey from where supplies could be shipped in and whisky shipped out to the world beyond. It was also near to the barley fields of Moray and had the Glen Grant burn to provide water for the mash and power for the machinery. In 1858 Rothes was finally connected by rail to Elgin, as part of the Moray railway of which James Grant was a founding member.

Rothes, a busy place of 1500 souls, was to become a major whisky town where distilleries outnumbered the churches three to two. But for the first forty years, Glen Grant stood alone until the arrival of the first newcomer – Glenrothes. By 1861 it was sufficiently successful to become not just the first distillery, but the first industrial premises of any kind in the Scottish Highlands to install electric light. When James Grant died in 1872, leaving the distillery to his son, James, he bequeathed a business perfectly placed to ride the great whisky boom that was about to take Scotland's national spirit to undreamt of heights down south. Per capita consumption in England stood at just seven pints a year – less than a third the amount in Scotland, but it was already rising fast.

The young James Grant, or 'the Major' as he came to be known, was the quintessential Victorian gent. It was almost as though he was born in thick tweeds, already sporting his magnificent walrus moustache, so perfectly did he slip into the role of Highland laird. And naturally he was a keen fisherman and fine shot, bringing back strange stuffed animals from his visits to the 'Dark Continent' to hang on the walls of Glen Grant house. These used to arouse considerable curiosity among the locals and fear among his more timid servants. On one trip to what is now Zimbabwe, he found a small Matabele boy abandoned by the roadside. It seemed the boy's parents had been slaughtered in a tribal feud, so the Major decided to christen him Biawa and bring him back to Speyside. Biawa was sent to the local school where he picked up a broad Rothes accent and a lifelong devotion to the town's football team. After school he became the

Major's butler and lived well into his eighties. One local historian recorded in 1954 that 'everyone loves Biawa and Biawa loves Rothes and all its inhabitants.' He died in 1972 leaving his gun, fishing rod and wood saw to Rothes Football Club, and his clothes to the Aberlour Orphanage.

Back in 1898, Glen Grant was already one of the biggest distilleries in the area, whose four stills, including the 5000 gallon 'Wee Geordie', were pumping out over 200,000 gallons of malt whisky a year. But such was the demand from blenders, it was decided to build Glen Grant No. 2 just across the road. By using the same shaped stills and the same source of barley, the end result would be just the same... surely? Sadly not, and for some reason it never lived up to the fame and fortune achieved by the original Glen Grant. One curiosity was the so-called whisky pipe built on the insistence of Customs & Excise in 1898 to connect the younger distillery to its big brother across the road as if by umbilical cord. For years cars and people passed beneath it, though the pipe ran dry in 1901, when the Grants were forced to close down No. 2. It remained mothballed for the next sixty-four years, until miraculously brought back to life as Caperdonich, named after one of the springs feeding the Glen Grant burn.

James died in 1931, at the age of 84, having outlived all but one of his eight children. His grandson, Douglas MacKessack, took over and years later recalled the old man ordering him and his mother to fish his beat of the Spey every day even though the ghillie had told them there were no fish in the river. By 1977, MacKessack, one of the last 'gentleman distillers' bowed to commercial pressure and sold out to Seagram, whose Chivas Regal blend swallowed up most of whisky produced by Glen Grant.

Today the distillery teems with visitors especially Italians, curious to discover the source of their country's favourite malt. In fact Glen Grant 5 year old is the biggest selling whisky in Italy full stop. What is now the distillery's main office is a substantial, no-nonsense piece of Victorian architecture in granite embellished with a touch of

Scots baronial flair in the form of two pepper-pot turrets on either side, each adorned with a gold cock.

But the best reason for coming here, at least in spring and summer, is to see the gardens, which have been beautifully restored to their former glory by Seagram. It was here that Major Grant used to bring his guests after dinner. They would follow him past greenhouses full of orchids and exotic fruits, past the copper beech tree, past orchards and banks of rhododendrons tended by his fifteen gardeners and along the path beside the Glen Grant Burn. Then, when he reached a little ravine, he would turn to his guests and unlock a small safe embedded in the rock to produce glasses and a bottle of Glen Grant. And if anyone required water they merely had to dip their glass in the burn as it sparkled past in the moonlight. Now you would really have to loathe whisky to turn down a dram like that.

The Still-room
Glen Grant – home of Italy's favourite Scotch whisky.

Glen Grant
Over 160 years old and still going strong.

Craigellachie

The modern chimney of the Craigellachie distillery rises high above the rooftops of the town like a silver mast.

CRAIGELLACHIE

Pronunciation: craigelakhee

Founded: 1891

Founder: Peter Mackie & Alexander Edward

Region: Speyside

Production Capacity: 2,300,000 litres

Address: Craigellachie, Banffshire

Tel: 0141 551 4000

website: www.dewars.com

Parent Company: Bacardi

Visitor Centre: Contact distillery for details

The village of Craigellachie, named after a crag above the Spey, grew to five times its size during the course of Speyside's late Victorian rise to fame as the pre-eminent whisky region in Scotland. On an individual basis some distilleries on the Western Isles may have more cachet, but as a region nothing compares with the tens of millions of gallons of spirit that flow through the stills of Speyside. With distilleries all around it is strange that the village itself, which sits beside the River Fiddich where it feeds into the Spey, only has one. Today the metal chimney of the Craigellachie distillery rises high above the rooftops like a silver mast. In its present

form it is very much a product of the 1960s when it was enlarged and effectively rebuilt. All that remains of its Victorian roots are parts of two of the original warehouses.

The Craigellachie distillery was built in 1891 by a partnership of blenders, including the early whisky baron, Peter Mackie, and led by one of Speyside's leading distillers – Alexander Edward already involved with Aultmore and Benrinnes. Mackie bought the distillery outright after the First World War, though not all of it's production disappeared into his White Horse blend. It seems that, like the other directors of the Craigellachie Distillery Co., he recognised the quality of this whisky allowed it to stand on its own two feet. Almost from the start it was available by the bottle as a single malt. It is now owned by Bacardi and occassionally appears as a luscious, lightly smoked rarity.

Craigellachie's Main Role in Life

Now part of the Bacardi empire, Craigellachie supplies malt to the Dewar's White Label blend.

BALVENIE

Pronunciation: bal**ven**ee

Founded: 1892

Founder: William Grant

Region: Speyside

Production Capacity: 5,600,000 litres

Address: Dufftown, Banffshire AB55 4BB

Tel: 01698 843 843

website: www.thebalvenie.co.uk

Parent Company: William Grant

Visitor Centre: Contact distillery for details

For the thousands who visit Glenfiddich each week, the name of Balvenie is mentioned at the start of each tour as it sets off from the visitor centre. For

those on a coach trip with two more castles and Loch Ness to fit in before lunch, the bus driver will be tooting his horn if anyone so much as wanders back for a second glance. But for those not on a whistle-stop tour 'O'er the Hielands' or tempted to jump ship and leave Nessie for another day, a trip round Balvenie is well worth the experience. For a start you can peer beneath its smoking pagoda roof to see and smell the barley being malted on site – this being one of the very few distilleries with its own maltings still in operation, and certainly the only one on Speyside.

Built within the grounds of Glenfiddich in 1892, Balvenie now appears almost buried by the sheer scale of its more famous older brother whose modern corrugated iron warehouses stretch out in all directions. For a cautious man like William Grant, the decision to double his capacity and construct Balvenie just five years after Glenfiddich, was almost spontaneous. In fact there were various factors behind his decision to invest £2000 in a second operation, beyond the proven knowledge that this was a good place to make whisky. A local man from Ben Rinnes had been making enquiries about taking a lease on land next to Glenfiddich and possibly erecting a distillery there. Had he been successful he would have been entitled to a half share in Glenfiddich's precious water supply.

At the same time, William Grant had been passed a valuable customer by Glenlivet who had been temporarily forced out of production due to a fire. This customer, a blender from Aberdeen, required 400 gallons a week – almost the entire run from

95

One Serious Hangover
Counting the barrels is one
way to assess the health
of the whisky industry. If
full of maturing stock it
could suggest a serious
hangover.

Glenfiddich's stills. Rather than be held to ransom by one powerful customer, it made sense for Grant to have a second string to his bow. So he quickly bought the land, including Balvenie House, and began enquiring among his trade contacts for any second-hand equipment going cheap and for an agent to handle the spirit produced. One firm replied that they might have a spare mash-tun for sale though it was deeper than what he was looking for. On the back of the letter Grant scribbled a note to his son – 'Don't be afraid of the depth of the mash-tun if otherwise suitable – a man does not need to piss his pot full unless he likes.' The original stills, which have been faithfully copied ever since, came from Lagavulin and Glen Albyn, and have much taller necks than those at Glenfiddich.

Congratulations poured in about this romantic idea of turning a castle, actually a derelict Georgian manor house, into a distillery that was first known as Glen Gordon. One jarring note did arrive however, from a merchant in Liverpool who criticised the venture for merely adding to the overproduction of whisky and hastening another crash in the trade. In view of what happened just seven years later, the merchant clearly had a point, not that William Grant appears to have been fazed. With the maltings set up in Balvenie House and the basement cleared as a warehouse, the first spirit flowed fifteen months later.

When it came, at the turn of the century, the crash in the whisky industry must have hit the Grant family pretty hard. With their main customer, Pattisons of Leith, in gaol for fraud, the only solution was to get into blending themselves. Thus was born 'William Grant's Finest Scotch Whisky', 'Best Procurable' and 'Standfast' as in 'Stand fast Craigellachie' – the battle cry of the Clan Grant. By the start of the First World War, the company had set up an office in Glasgow and established over 60 agencies in 30 countries world-wide. William Grant was starting to lose his sight and spent the last twenty years of his life blind, but remained involved with the running of the distillery right up until he died in 1923 aged 83.

Some time afterwards comes an evocative description of Balvenie by night, written by the widow of one of his five sons.

'We would go to the still-house first. There Alfie

**More barrels
at Balvenie**

Mackray, the night still-man, would be making his supper — not a carried 'piece' but a nice, yellow haddock grilled to a turn on a shovel over a clean fire — the furnace fire; and a can, not a flask, of tea ... And then on to the malt barns, beautifully whitewashed and dimly lit with paraffin lights at intervals round them; and the golden grain on the floors and the sweet small of the grain and the way the night malt-men worked the malt shovels and scattered the grain as level as a table top; and the swishing noises it made in the stillness of the night. I thought it was one of the loveliest sights I have ever seen.'

The paraffin lamps and fish suppers cooked on a shovel may have gone, but the distillery retains its old-world, backwoods feel — something perhaps highlighted by having Glenfiddich for a neighbour. Apart from doubling the number of stills in the 1950s little has changed. While Glenfiddich was off to convert the world to single malt, Balvenie stayed at home quietly distilling away, its barley supplied in part from the surrounding fields. Most of the production goes into blends as it always has done, though a little of Balvenie has been available as a single malt since 1973. Quite who it was first aimed at one can only guess — the original bottles were packaged in black leatherette with gold lettering. There is nothing kinky about today's packaging however, and sold as a ten and twelve year old, Balvenie is a smooth, luxuriant dram, full of honeyed sweetness, nuts and the faint scent of orange blossom.

GLENFIDDICH

Pronunciation: glen**fid**eekh

Founded: 1887

Founder: William Grant

Region: Speyside

Production Capacity: 10,000,000 litres

Address: Dufftown, Keith, Banffshire AB55 4DH

Tel: 01340 820 373

website: www.glenfiddich.com

Parent Company: William Grant

Visitor Centre: Mid-October–Easter, Mon–Fri, 9.30am–4.30pm. Easter–Mid-October, Mon–Sat, 9.30am–4.30pm. Sun, 12–4.30pm.

The world's biggest selling single malt — the brand that reinvented the category and taught the world that there was more to whisky than blended Scotch — was a child in the 1960s. Before then, Glenfiddich — a name that few had ever heard of — was just another Speyside distillery whose spirit disappeared into blended Scotch. It was no more than a factory dealing with one part of the process that takes barley from the field and converts it into whisky to be bottled up and sold in bars and liquor stores around the globe. Then having created a single malt for the mass market — something that most of those

Just some of Glenfiddich's 29 Stills

involved in whisky thought at best bizarre, Glenfiddich went one further and flung open its doors to the public in 1969. Why anyone outside the industry should be that interested to want to look round an actual working distillery, was beyond most right-thinking folk in the trade. After all most people who are keen about cars have no burning desire to look round the works where the engines are assembled. All that has changed, however, and today virtually any distillery actively bottling its own malt now has some kind of visitor centre, a few tour guides and the inevitable shop. But for most of its history Glenfiddich was simply one among many of the distilleries conceived at the start of the late-Victorian whisky boom.

It was no overnight conception, but rather the result of a great many years careful planning by William Grant and the frugal house-keeping of his wife, Elizabeth. For a lesser man with nine children to support on an annual salary of £100, plus the £7 he received as the precentor of the Free Church of Dufftown, the dream of building one's own distillery would remain just that – a dream.

Born in 1839, William Grant left school to become an apprentice to one of the twelve cobblers in Dufftown, a town with no less than twelve of them, before going on to work at a lime quarry nearby. He

married and settled down to live in a Highland cottage with a clay floor that was made firm in the customary manner of having the locals in for a dance. There was some kind of dispute at the quarry and William was out on his ear three years later. As fate would have it, the town's solitary distillery of Mortlach was looking for a bookkeeper and took him on. After a few years he was promoted to distillery manager, yet still saw the job as a temporary blip in a life's ambition to open his own lime works, something he nearly achieved in 1871. A last minute change of mind by the landowner saw his hopes crumble into dust and himself back at Mortlach. Gradually a new dream took shape, that of making his own whisky.

He began to take an interest in the whole business of distilling, from how to malt the barley to what temperature to run the stills at. He also began saving, and after another sixteen years at Mortlach finally had enough to start his 'Great Adventure'. Hearing that Elizabeth Cumming, the lady distiller at what is now Cardhu, was about to replace her equipment, he bought the old copper stills, the tuns, worm and water-mill for £120. Then for another £650 he managed to construct a distillery with the help of his six sons out of stones from the bed of the river Fiddich. The chosen site of Glenfiddich' – the valley of the deer, was a small field below the Robbie Dhu spring which has been the distillery's source of water ever since. Beside it lay a burn which could be damned and diverted to power the malt mill, and the effluent could run off into the river below. The first spirit flowed on Christmas day, 1887.

The 'Great Adventure' sailed on through the whisky crash of 1899, the pernicious taxes of Lloyd George and the First World War. By the time of William's death in 1923, it was supplying much of the malt for the company's key blends which were being sold as far afield as Adelaide and Vancouver. William Grant & Sons survived American prohibition and began to thrive in the post-war boom when a five year-old bottling of Glenfiddich Pure Malt became the brand leader among single malts in Scotland. It was still a small market and one that hardly existed beyond the country's borders. So it was a brave decision in 1964 when William's descendants decided to replace it with a more expensive eight year-old version and roll it out nation-wide. It was decided to use a triangular, green bottle designed by Hans Schleger, a pre-war refugee from Nazi Germany. The idea behind the radical shape was to make the brand stand out on the shelf, but others saw added and often unforeseen benefits. Businessmen admired the way it fitted into the slim-line attaché case then fashionable, others, the way it stacked more efficiently in the cellar and one woman, for being the only bottle that didn't roll out of bed!

Among clever marketing tricks, it was decided to bottle a line of Glenfiddich with flat ginger-beer and supply it to theatres in London's West-End. It tasted

a lot better than that other theatrical stand in for whisky, cold tea, and won the drink plenty of free publicity. Abroad, duty-free sales at airports greatly helped spread the word and get people to try it for the first time.

Glenfiddich has since become a 12 year-old and continues to sell well over twice its nearest rival – Glenlivet. To cope with the demand there are now 29 stills, all modelled on the original cast-off from Cardhu. With its pale straw colour, this medium-bodied malt with a refreshing fruitiness and dry finish may not be the last word in complexity, but it still accounts for one in six bottles of malt whisky drunk in the world.

Checking the Spirit Safe Glenfiddich

Traditional wooden washbacks of Glenfiddich

**Glenfiddich –
Water Supply**

A distillery the size of Glenfiddich needs an abundant supply of cold water to cool the vapours as they come of the stills.

GLENDULLAN

Pronunciation: glen**dull**an

Founded: 1897

Founder: Williams & Sons

Region: Speyside

Production Capacity: 3,700,000 litres

Address: Dufftown, Banffshire AB55 4DJ

Tel: 01340 822 100

website: www.diageo.com

Parent Company: Diageo

Visitor Centre: Contact distillery for details

With six distilleries already, some may have felt Dufftown was already saturated, when William Williams, a firm of Aberdeenshire blenders, began to build Glendullan in 1897. It was the last distillery to be built in the town, but fared better than most, since it has only stopped working during the Second World War. It was well planned, getting its power for free from the River Fiddich via a giant waterwheel and sharing the private railway siding of its neighbour, Mortlach, which connected directly to the main line at Dufftown. More importantly it always made good-quality malt whisky, and won a Royal Appointment from Edward VII in its fifth year of production. From the start it was used in a couple of popular blends, Three Star and Strathdon. Meanwhile the Williams brothers were soon in partnership with the big blending house, Macdonald Greenlees, which eventually took them over in 1919 before being swallowed up by DCL. The Macdonald Greenlees connection lives on in 'Old Parr' blend, named after Thomas Parr, who died in 1635 aged 152, or so it was claimed.

Having rebuilt the distillery in 1962, it was decided to build a 'New' Glendullan next door a decade later. For the next 13 years the two distilleries worked side by side, mashing their own malt and producing their own wash. The spirit was then vatted together in casks and used for blending. In 1985, the original Glendullan was quietly dismantled. As a straw-coloured 12 year-old it has a medium rich malty character with the sweet smack of oak. How closely it resembles the original is another matter.

MORTLACH

Pronunciation: mortlakh

Founded: 1824

Founder: James Findlater

Region: Speyside

Production capacity: 2,800,000 litres

Address: Dufftown, Keith, Banffshire AB5 4AQ

Tel: 01340 822 100

website: www.diageo.com

Parent Company: Diageo

Visitor Centre: Contact distillery for details

By the time Dufftown had eclipsed Campbeltown as the pre-eminent whisky town of Scotland, Mortlach had been making Scotch here for the best part of a century. There had been a few early teething problems, it is true. James Findlater, who took out the original licence in 1824, was forced to sell seven years later for just £270. The stills fell silent and for a brief period the Dufftown Free Church moved into Mortlach's disused granary, before it was converted into a brewery. But, by the mid-nineteenth century, the stills were back, fired up and ready to go, since when it has never really looked back.

For the next 60 odd years it was in the hands of the Cowie family who doubled the number of stills to six in 1897, making it one of the biggest malt distilleries in the Highlands. It was here that William Grant served his 20 year apprenticeship as Mortlach's book-keeper before finally taking the plunge to set up on his own and build Glenfiddich.

Assuming the character of the whisky has not changed, and there is no good reason to think it has given the industry's innate resistance to change for the sake of change, Mortlach was as beguiling and perfumed a malt as it is today. Blenders loved the way it seemed to encompass all that floral-scented complexity and grace that is the very best of Speyside. In the 1920's the distillery passed via Johnnie Walker into the fold of DCL who found they had a substantial operation on their hands, all powered by a single steam engine. The buildings straddled both sides of the road and housed a monster mashtun and no less than four malt floors. Despite rebuilding in the 1960s it kept its pagoda and much of its Victorian charm.

Pagodas Jostle for Space

Above the roof-tops of Dufftown, the whisky capital of Speyside.

Dufftown Distillery

The Dufftown-Glenlivet Distillery Co. was founded in 1896. Like a number of other distilleries in the district it was a conversion of an old mill, this time one making oatmeal.

DUFFTOWN

> **Pronunciation: duff**town
>
> **Founded:** 1896
>
> **Founder:** Peter Mackenzie & Richard Stackpole
>
> **Region:** Speyside
>
> **Production Capacity:** 4,000,000 litres
>
> **Address:** Dufftown, Keith
>
> **Tel:** 01340 822 100
>
> **website:** www.diageo.com
>
> **Parent Company:** Diageo
>
> **Visitor Centre:** Contact distillery for details

The Speyside town that eventually took over from Campbeltown as Scotland's whisky metropolis, already had five distilleries when the Dufftown-Glenlivet Distillery Co. was founded in 1896. The company was a partnership of two Liverpudlians, a local solicitor and a farmer who owned the Pittyvaich farm on the edge of Dufftown. Like a number of other distilleries in the district it was a conversion of an old mill, this time one making oatmeal. The original mill owners, like the mass of small, illicit stills owners, had been attracted by the quality and reliability of the local water. It provided a regular flow to power the waterwheels for the mills and its pristine coldness was ideal for distilling whisky.

The town itself was founded in 1817 and named

after James Duff, the fourth Earl of Fife. It sits on the confluence of the River Fiddich and the Dullan Water.

Using barley from the Pittyvaich farm and water from 'Jock's Well' in the Conval hills, the first spirit dribbled from the still in November 1896, and the partners declared it was of 'excellent quality'. The neighbouring Mortlach, which had been going since 1824, was less impressed, especially with the way this parvenu had the nerve to use its water. Thus began yet another wrangle between two distilleries over water rights, this time involving the heated

Macallan Sherry Cask

One of Macallan's famous sherry casks disgorging its contents prior to bottling.

exchange of letters by day and the diverting and re-divirting of water courses by night.

In its second year, Dufftown was acquired outright by one of the Liverpudlians, Peter Mackenzie, who also owned Blair Athol. Mackenzie had been selling Blair Athol malt to Arthur Bell for some time, so it was only natural that Dufftown soon became a key filling in the Bell's blend. The connection has never been lost, and in 1932 Bell's bought out P. Mackenzie & Co. and its two distilleries. When not performing for Britain's best-selling blend, Dufftown does make an occasional guest appearance as a green, herbal, slightly oily single malt.

ABERLOUR

Pronunciation: aberlowr

Founded: 1879

Founder: James Fleming

Region: Speyside

Production Capacity: 3,200,000 litres

Address: Aberlour, Banffshire AB38 9PJ

Tel: 01340 871 204

website: www.aberlour.co.uk

Parent Company: Pernod Ricard

Visitor Centre: Contact distillery for details

Visitors are welcomed by appointment during the Speyside Whisky Festival.

Aberlour on Speyside
Home of France's most popular single malt.

The village of Aberlour had only recently been established a few hundred yards from the river Spey when a distillery known as Aberlour-Glenlivet sprung up on its main street. It was built by James Gordon in 1826 who quickly disappeared off the scene and it passed through various hands until the site was bought by a local banker, James Fleming. Having rebuilt the distillery in 1879 Fleming soon found himself up before the High Court in London along with half the distillers on Speyside defending the use of the suffix '-Glenlivet', a case they eventually

The stillhouse at Macallan
Radiating warmth and whisky.

MACALLAN

One of the Direct Fired Spirit Stills at Macallan

These are unusually small and work in tandem, each pair fed by a single wash still.

Pronunciation: macallan

Founded: 1824

Founder: Alexander Reid

Region: Speyside

Production Capacity: 6,000,000 litres

Address: Easter Elchies, Craigellachie, Banffshire AB38 9RX

Tel: 01340 872 280

website: www.themacallan.co.uk

Parent Company: Edrington Group

Visitor Centre: Easter–October, Mon–Sat, 9am–6pm.

November–Easter, Mon–Fri, 9am–5pm.

Last guided tour 3.30pm.

The Macallan lies a mile beyond Craigellachie, on the west bank of the Spey, well beyond the bustle of Dufftown and the 'malt whisky trail'. No tour buses pull in here to bag a distillery on their break-neck tour of Scotland, though visitors are welcomed. The Macallan, which once clung to the tag-line – Glenlivet, now stands firmly on its own two feet, a little aloof perhaps, but confident of being one of the finest malts in Speyside, if not Scotland. It was not a reputation built overnight however, far from it.

Easter Elchies farm had probably been making whisky on the side for some time when Alexander Reid, the tenant farmer, decided to open a licensed distillery here in 1824. The farm had long been a staging post on the old droving routes that led from the Morayshire plains to the markets of Falkirk and the central belt. It was a place to hold cattle, before crossing the Spey at the nearby ford and beginning the long journey south. And it was no doubt somewhere to pick up a cask or two of whisky.

The Elchies distillery, as it was then called, was a typical farm distillery whose production had slowly climbed to around 40,000 gallons by the 1880s. At this point it had changed hands twice and now belonged to James Stuart, the son of a shoemaker from Rothiemurchus. Stuart soon realised he needed funds to expand the distillery and so went into partnership with three local men. His partners included Robert Dick and William Grant, who later became two of the first directors of Highland Distillers, the company which eventually bought The Macallan in 1996 for £180 million.

Funnily enough, Highland Distillers had tried to buy the distillery once before. In 1898 they made an

won. In 1892 Fleming sold out to his agent R. Thorne & Sons of Greenock who rebuilt and extended the distillery six years later after a bad fire. This is much as it remains today, at least on the outside.

At first Aberlour sourced its water from the ancient well in the distillery's grounds, used a thousand years before by St Dunstan to baptise his flock before he went on to become Archbishop of Canterbury. The distillery now relies on spring water from Ben Rinnes.

After World War II, Aberlour became part of Campbell Distillers which was bought by the French drinks group Pernod Ricard in the 1970s. Not surprisingly the malt plays a leading role in Clan Campbell, France's most popular Scotch whisky. As a single malt it has won praise and a number of awards for being a supple, creamy and faintly spicy 10 year old.

unsolicited bid of £80,000 which was turned down by Rodney Kemp, who had bought out James Stuart six years earlier. It seems Stuart had become over-stretched in his plans to build the larger Glen Rothes distillery nearby, and had let things slip at the Macallan, something Rodney Kemp was determined to put right. Kemp was a self-made man with plenty of experience in business as a wine merchant in Elgin and as a distiller, having previously turned round the fortunes of Talisker on Skye. No doubt part of his determination to make the most of the Macallan sprang from his bitter disappointment at being forced to sell his interests in Talisker which he had part-owned since 1879.

He sold off his wine business to concentrate on the distillery, restoring the buildings, improving the equipment and generally upping the production. By the time of his death in 1909, the Macallan malt was becoming increasingly well-regarded among blenders, though it was many years before bottles of the single malt began to appear.

The Macallan remained in family hands and managed to survive the grim inter-war years when weekly production at the distillery barely climbed above 3,000 gallons, having been 2,500 gallons in the last years of Rodney Kemp. But for a new pair of bonded warehouses the distillery remained exactly as it had been in 1896, until after the war. A little Macallan slipped past prohibition into the States, but the home market fell by a third, thanks to heavy taxes, recession and the success of the temperance lobby. Yet apart from the 1932-33 season and during 1943, the distillery kept in production, under Kemp's two sons-in-law, first Alexander Harbison, who was succeeded by his wife, Janet, and then Samuel Shiach in 1938. He was succeeded by his son Gordon, who was tragically killed in a road accident in 1948, having survived the war as an Intelligence officer and the Nuremberg trials where he had helped interrogate Herman Goering. The distillery was finally rebuilt in the 1950s allowing production to treble from post-war levels to pass one million proof gallons in 1970. There was a completely new stillhouse and a succession of new warehouses, with one built every year, to start laying down stock which would eventually be bottled as Macallan 10 year-old. This was finally launched in 1978. At first the company was a little coy in proclaiming its single malt to the world. In 1974, just £25 was spent on advertising and promotion – a budget that had passed £1 million by 1990.

Anyone visiting Macallan in midsummer drives through a field of ripe barley down the distillery's own drive. A sign in the field declares the barley to be 'Golden Promise' – a new, high-yielding strain when introduced in the 1960s, that has long since been superseded by other varieties. The distillery has stayed loyal, despite the additional costs involved, and swears that using Golden Promise makes a difference to the end result, whatever the sceptics say. For their part the few farmers still prepared to grow the variety are paid a little extra and given the odd case of Macallan to keep them sweet. Another factor in making Macallan unique are the unusually small stills of which there are currently five wash stills each feeding a pair of spirit stills, making fifteen in total. Because of their size and the fact they are all direct fired which requires the use of rummagers to scour the inside of the stills to prevent scorching, the

**Towering Chimney
Stack –**

Ben Rinnes distillery near
Aberlour.

Dailuaine
One of Diageo's bigger distilleries whose six stills are mainly used to supply the company's wide portfolio of blends.

contact between the liquid and the copper is relatively high. This leads to a more refined, less oily spirit. Finally there is the insistence on sherry casks. The wood is bought 'on the tree' in northern Spain, transported south to Jerez, seasoned, turned into butts and filled with Oloroso sherry for a few years before being shipped to Speyside and filled with Macallan. The result is a dark, almost mahogany coloured malt, with a rich, spicy nose and smooth and sumptuous in the mouth.

BENRINNES

Pronunciation: ben**rin**is

Founded: 1834

Founder: John Innes

Region: Speyside

Production Capacity: 2,600,000 litres

Address: Aberlour, Banffshire AB38 9NN

Tel: 01340 871 215

website: www.diageo.com

Parent Company: Diageo

Visitor Centre: Contact distillery for details

Anyone who does the Speyside whisky trail will sooner or later come face to face with the formidable bulk of Ben Rinnes, heather-clad by summer, bare and bleak-looking by winter. A few hundred feet short of a Munro, Ben Rinnes stands at the heart of Speyside whisky. Today, around a dozen distilleries still draw their water from the network of springs that percolate through the granite flank of the mountain whose summit can be seen for miles. It was once used by fishermen out in the Moray Firth to fix their bearings.

The distillery was originally called Lyne of Ruthrie when it was licensed by John Innes in 1834, though it may have been distilling for some years before. Having changed to its present name, it passed into the hands of David Edward 30 years later, who doubtless benefited from the new railway line, with Aultmore station just three miles away. Then having been hit hard by the Pattison Crash along with its sister distillery, Oban, it became part of the Dewar's stable which was amalgamated into DCL in the 1920s.

At 700 ft up on the north-facing slope of Ben Rinnes, it shares that remote, isolated feel of Glenlivet and Glenfarclas, being set back from the Spey and the main centres of whisky making like Dufftown and Rothes. Its point of difference come from having its six stills work in pairs of three to produce its own unique variation on triple distillation. The result as a relatively rare 15 year-old is a full-medium bodied, sweetish after dinner malt.

DAILUAINE

Pronunciation: dalewan

Founded: 1851

Founder: William Mackenzie

Region: Speyside

Production Capacity: 3,200,000 litres

Address: Carron, Aberlour, Morayshire

Tel: 01340 810 361

website: www.diageo.com

Parent Company: Diageo

Visitor Centre: Contact distillery for details

Established in 1851 and greatly extended 45 years later, this hefty Speyside distillery was clearly built to last. A bad fire in 1917 gutted the interior but left much of the Victorian stone still standing as you can see as you drive into the small village of Carron halfway between Ben Rinnes and the River Spey. Lining the steep approach road into the village are row upon row of the distillery's gabled, mould-blackened warehouses.

It was founded by a local farmer, William Mackenzie, whose son Thomas formed a partnership with James Fleming of Aberlour and then teamed up with another distillery on the other side of the country, to form Dailuaine-Talisker Distilleries Ltd in 1898.

The ground around the distillery was flattened to make room for a railway siding. This allowed barley and empty casks to be delivered right to the front door by Dailuaine's own steam-train, or puggy, which would then chug back to join the main line at Carron station carrying full casks of whisky. The distillery could even ring the station master to let them know the puggy was on its way.

After such a promising start in the race to embrace the white heat of technology, Dailuaine appeared to falter and was only hitched up to the National Grid in 1950.

Most of what spurts off its six stills slips into Diageo's wide portfolio of blends, but the company does bottle a certain amount as a single malt under its Distillery Malts range.

Crow-step Gabled Warehouses
Lining the roadside at Dailuaine.

Cardhu

Showing Elizabeth Cumming's 'new' distillery of the 1890s and the refurbishment of the still house, mash-room and tun-room of 1960.

IMPERIAL

Pronunciation: imperial

Founded: 1897

Founder: Thomas Mackenzie

Region: Speyside

Address: Carron, Aberlour, Morayshire AB38 7QP

Tel: 01340 810 276

website: www.allieddomecqplc.com

Parent Company: Allied Domecq

Visitor Centre: Contact distillery for details

In 1897, with the British Empire in ascendance, and two thirds of the world map pink, it seemed only right and proper that Thomas Mackenzie should christen his new distillery beside the Upper Spey, Imperial. Besides, it was Queen Victoria's Diamond Jubilee, which had provoked a patriotic fervour throughout the land. Scotland had never felt so British, its industries humming away to supply, via Clyde-built ships, the Queen's loyal subjects abroad. At Imperial there was even a gilded model of the Imperial crown above the roof of the kiln.

Born to the sound of trumpets, this red-brick fortress was quietly made redundant six months later and was not to produce whisky for another 20 years.

Imperial began life linked with Talisker and Dailuaine, the neighbouring distillery founded by Thomas's father, William Mackenzie, in 1865. Its saviour in 1919 was our old friend DCL, who soon discovered that the massive 8000 gallon stills, the biggest in the business, simply produced too much draff. Unable to dispose of it all, distilling stopped, though the maltings continued for the next 30 years. It was only the discovery of how to make that form of cattle cake known as dark grains at Aultmore in the 1950s, that brought Imperial back to life. Such a symbol of big scale production did not fit in with the need to cut back supply in the mid 1980s and the distillery shut down again, until Allied Distillers fired up those big stills once more in 1989. Its malt is used for blending which, according to at least one distiller is no bad thing.

CARDHU

Pronunciation: car**doo**

Founded: 1824

Founder: John Cumming

Region: Speyside

Production Capacity: 2,300,000 litres

Address: Knockando, Aberlour, Banffshire AB38 7RY

Tel: 01340 872 555

website: www.diageo.com

Parent Company: Diageo

Visitor Centre: March–November, Mon–Fri,
9.30am–4.30pm.

July–September, Sat, 9.30am–4.30pm.

Sunday, 11am–4pm.

December–February by appointment.

John Cumming had been busted for smuggling whisky many times and had a string of convictions to prove it. But when he decided to go straight and apply for a licence for a distillery in Upper Knockando in 1824 it was duly granted. In these parts being up before the magistrate for illicit distillation appears to have been almost akin to unpaid parking fines today.

The son of a hill farmer and grazier, Cumming took the lease of Cardow (pronounced 'Car-doo') farm some time around 1810. It seems he began making whisky straight away. From the outset this was very much a farm distillery which operated on a seasonal basis once the harvest was gathered in and the water was cold enough to condense the spirit.

His wife, Helen, took care of the mashing and fermenting side of the process and used to sell bottles of whisky through their farmhouse kitchen window. To disguise the smell of fermenting barley she would be forever baking bannocks, it was claimed – something to offer the exciseman if ever he called in. And while he was tucking into his tea, Helen could quickly run into the yard and hoist a red flag to warn her neighbours that the gaugers were about.

On becoming licensed in 1824 little if anything changed – whisky making continued to be as rustic and home-made an affair as it had always been, but that was the way Cumming and his wife liked it. The only difference was that instead of having to smuggle the fruit of their labours over the Mannoch Hill to Elgin and Forres, it could now be taken by horse and cart to Burghead and shipped to Leith. His son and daughter-in-law, Elizabeth, carried on in the same artisan fashion until the mid-1880s when it became clear a new distillery was long overdue. This was built on land leased by Elizabeth Cumming who was now widowed. The old equipment was scrapped or sold off, including a pair of badly worn and patched up stills, for £120. These were bought by a local man called William Grant who was no doubt hoping that a little of the old Cardhu magic would rub off on his

new distillery – Glenfiddich.

Plans for the new Cardhu had already been drawn up when Alfred Barnard, who was compiling his great book on distilleries, called by in the mid 1880s. He wrote that the buildings were 'of the most straggling and primitive description and although water power existed, a great part of the work was done by manual labour.' Production was set to increase to 60,000 gallons and much was ear-marked for John Walker & Sons to be the heart and soul of their increasingly popular blend. However, some was bottled as single malt known as 'Cardow' for which adverts boasted that this was one of the few whiskies on Speyside which had never needed to affix the word '-Glenlivet'.

In 1893 Elizabeth, dubbed 'the Queen of the whisky trade', sold out to Walker's for £20,500 on the condition her family could continue the day-to-day running of the distillery. By a curious twist of fate her grandson, Sir Ronald Cumming, was to become chairman of DCL seventy years later. His father, John, had been in charge of Cardhu back in the 1920s when he ensured that all distillery workers' cottages had running water, electric light and even indoor toilets, long before it was the norm in the countryside. Hot water was provided by a cask left outside the boiler room for the families to help themselves each morning.

Production was interrupted during the Second World War owing to war-time restrictions on the use of barley for distilling, but picked up thereafter with all incoming supplies arriving by rail to Knockando station. From there it would be collected by the distillery's two eight-ton lorries which then returned with filled casks of whisky to be loaded on to the train. This continued until 1967, the year before the Strathspey line closed.

In 1960 the stillhouse, mash-house and tun-room were rebuilt. The first priority was obviously to preserve the innate character of the whisky, but the conversion to modern times also preserved the office, malt-barns and twin pagoda roofs of the late Victorian distillery. If Elizabeth Cumming, who lived to the ripe old age of 95, came back from the grave she would find her 'new Cardhu' pretty much intact.

The distillery had flirted with the idea of inserting a prototype steam coil into its two wash stills as early as 1924, which was way ahead of its time, but decided it was all too expensive. Steam-coils were eventually introduced in the 1970s when the number of stills were increased to six.

Meanwhile the water is still piped from the springs on the Mannoch hill which was once a source of peat in the dim, distant past. It is topped up from the Lynne burn which also supplies cooling water. Today the distillery is in full production supplying the heart of Johnnie Walker and a burgeoning market for Cardhu 12 year-old single. The Spanish, who have done more than anyone to revive the flagging fortunes of blended Scotch after the downturn in American demand, seem particularly fond of the sweet, silky smooth, unpeated flavours of Cardhu.

KNOCKANDO

Pronunciation: nokando

Founded: 1898

Founder: John Thomson

Region: Speyside

Production capacity: 1,300,000 litres

Address: Knockando, Banffshire AB35 7RP

Tel: 01340 882 000

website: www.diageo.com

Parent Company: Diageo

Visitor Centre: All year, Mon–Fri, 10am–4pm. No visitor centre, all visits by appointment only.

Cnoc-an-Dhu is Gaelic for the 'the dark hillock', which in this case stands guarding a bend in the Spey. The distillery, built by John Thomson in 1898, appears almost hidden until you see its pagoda roof poking above the trees. It lies tantalisingly close to the Spey, but not quite in sight of it, and, like all Speyside distilleries, does not actually draw its water from the river. With the next-door distillery of Tamdhu, built just a year earlier, Thomson knew that he had to secure his own source of spring water before he could start. Once this was achieved, he established a small distillery to produce whisky on a seasonal basis after the harvest. This seemed to hark back to the days when whisky-making was a cottage industry. In other respects however, Thomson was ahead of his times and was the first distiller to install electric light.

Unfortunately Knockando got caught up in the speculative bubble that burst a year later, and was quickly forced to close. It was bought in 1904 by Gilbey's for £3500, and but for occasional interruptions like war, has worked non-stop ever since. A large part of its success must be down to Justerini & Brooks, whose J&B was launched in the USA after prohibition and enjoyed spectacular growth for the next 30 years. As a key filling from the start, J&B brought Gilbey's and Justerini & Brooks into eventual marriage as IDV, now part of Diageo. As a single malt, released as a vintage, Knockando is ripe and flowery on the nose, quite sweet and creamy in the mouth, drying a little on the tail.

The Distillery Office at Knockando

A Decorative Still Stands Guard Over Glenfarclas

TAMDHU

Pronunciation: tam**doo**

Founded: 1897

Founder: Tamdhu Distillery Company Ltd

Region: Speyside

Production capacity: 4,000,000 litres

Address: Knockando, Aberlour, Banffshire AB38 7RP

Tel: 01340 810 486

website: www.edringtongroup.com

Parent Company: Edrington Group

Visitor Centre: Contact distillery for details

The best way to see Tamdhu is on foot from the Speyside Way, the long-distance footpath that follows the river inland from the coast for 60 miles. Part of the route is along the old, now dismantled, Strathspey railway that ran from Craigellachie to Boat of Garten and was closed in 1968. The line opened in 1863, and soon after, distilleries began to settle beside the track like homesteads in the American mid-west. Heading south, just past the overgrown remains of a private platform for Knockando House, you come to Tamdhu station with two platforms and a signal box.

With the pure, spring-fed, waters of the Knockando Burn nearby to feed the process at the start, and a steam train to carry away the end result, the site was obviously well chosen. The distillery was completed in 1897, and the first spirit flowed that summer, to be filled into casks for the Glasgow whisky firm, Robertson & Baxter. A year later, Tamdhu was absorbed into the Highland Distilleries Co. to join Glenrothes and Bunnahabhain. The distillery has remained within the group ever since. It shut down for 20 years after 1927, and was extensively modernised in the 1970s when the number of stills was increased to six. Tamdhu malts all its own barley, which makes it fairly unique, though the system employed is a modern one and not the traditional floor maltings which only a handful of distilleries still use.

Having satisfied the requirements of Famous Grouse, where it plays a key role, Tamdhu makes a fragrant, quite sumptuous single malt which trails off in a wisp of smoke.

GLENFARCLAS

Pronunciation: glen**fark**las

Founded: 1836

Founder: Robert Hay as Rechlerich Distillery

Region: Speyside

Production Capacity: 3,000,000 litres

Address: Ballindalloch, Speyside AB37 9BD

Tel: 01807 500 257

website: www.glenfarclas.co.uk

Parent Company: J & G Grant

Visitor Centre: April–September, Mon–Fri, 10am–5pm. June–September, Sat, 10am–5pm. October–March, Mon–Fri, 10am–4pm.

Compared to the relative bustle of Dufftown and Keith, or the sheltered hollows between the woods and the river Spey, Glenfarclas can appear rather bleak and windswept. Sitting in wide open farmland beneath the bare, hump-backed slopes of Ben Rinnes to the north-east, Glenfarclas, like Glenlivet, is just that little bit higher and more exposed than other distilleries in the region. You might almost say it was a lonesome spot for making whisky, though at first it looks more like a farm steading than a distillery.

Both these factors are clues to how Glenfarclas began and evolved into something pretty well unique in an industry dominated by corporate giants. Since 1865 it has remained in the same family's hands as a fully independent distillery now in its sixth generation.

But the story begins some thirty years before when a tenant farmer called Robert Hay first licensed the Rechlerich Distillery, as it was then called, in 1836. Hay is supposed to have used a pair of second-hand stills from the Dandaleith distillery near Craigellachie which had closed some years before. Then, in 1865 he sold out to John Grant, a breeder of champion Aberdeen Angus cattle and owner of several farms in the neighbourhood. It is almost certain Grant was more interested in the land than the distillery which was valued at £511.19s in the deal. The distillery was immediately leased to John Smith, the man who went on to establish Cragganmore. In 1870 the lease expired and John Grant decided to takeover the running of the distillery and set up as J&G Grant with his son George. Gradually the making of whisky began to overshadow the farming side of the business until it became clear that the distillery needed re-building. To raise the necessary funds the Grants went into partnership with the Pattison brothers of Leith to form the Glenfarclas-Glenlivet Distillery Ltd in 1895. The brothers were big-time blenders from Leith, and not the ideal bed-partner for a cash-strapped distillery on Speyside. Only a few years later the Pattisons went bankrupt in spectacular fashion, almost bringing the entire Scotch whisky industry down with them. As they were packed off to jail for fraud, the prospects for Glenfarclas must have looked

Copper Man Hole
In the side of a still it is
only opened to allow
periodic cleaning.

decidedly grim.

The distillery, now in its third generation under John and George Grant, grandsons of the original founder, slipped back into full family ownership to lick its wounds. By 1914 it seemed the worst was over and that the future of Glenfarclas was secure. Perhaps it was the trauma of being caught up in the Pattison crash, which left the Grants vowing never again to lose control and let in outside investors. To this day Glenfarclas proudly proclaims itself as 'the spirit of independence'.

Though whisky was being bottled as 'Pure Old Glenfarclas-Glenlivet malt whisky' and being shipped to the United States as early as 1899, the main business was always that of supplying the big blending houses. Among customers paying 6s 3d a gallon in 1925 were John Dewar of Perth and John Walker of Kilmarnock who took a 100 hogsheads each. In fact one would-be poet laureate, said to have been Tommy Dewar, was so moved by his admiration for Glenfarclas, that he wrote, 'In it is to be found the sunshine and shadow that chased each other over the billowy cornfield, the hum of the bee, and hope of Spring, the breath of May, the carol of the lark, the distant purple of heather in the mountain mist ...'

After the Second World War, George Grant, then in his seventies, held a party in Elgin to celebrate all the events that had happened during the war. There was his silver wedding, the 21st birthdays of his two sons and the centenary of Glenfarclas. It was only

Glenfarclas Warehouse
The locked door to one of
the thirty old dunnage-style
warehouses at Glenfarclas.

**The Fine, Wrought Iron
Entrance to Cragganmore**

later that the earlier roots of the distillery were unearthed.

In 1973 Glenfarclas built a visitor centre and threw open its doors to the public who streamed in through the entrance beneath the old pagoda roof, which used to sit above the kiln when the distillery had its own maltings. It gives the building a curiously oriental feel in this corner of north-east Scotland. Inside guests can enjoy a dram in the reception room done up as a replica of the smoking room aboard the old Empress of Australia. Built in 1913 as a luxury liner she later became a troop-ship until finally being broken up at Rosyth. Years later George Grant, the current chairman, heard on the radio that the original panelling was coming up for auction and promptly put in a bid. The connection between Glenfarclas and the hey-day of ocean liners may not be obvious at first sight, but he evidently got a bargain and it looks great now that the ceiling has been altered to recreate the original from old photographs of the ship.

There are few traces left of the distillery's origins in the farmyard with just the old Mill house dating back to the 1800s and what was once the dairy. Step inside the stillhouse, however, and this is whisky making on a grand scale. The six stills are the biggest on Speyside and are all still direct fired by huge gas-burners — something pretty rare these days. Outside there are thirty old dunnage-style warehouses whose red doors stand out starkly against the black mould-covered walls. The mould is a form of lichen that

seems to love whisky as much as the angels themselves. Here every drop of Glenfarclas destined for single malt is matured in predominantly sherry casks, stacked three high and left in peace for at least eight years. The single malt comes in a whole raft of age statements from 10, 12, 18, 25 and more, as well as the famous 105 cask strength, which at 60 per cent alcohol by volume is one of the strongest whiskies on the market. Perhaps Dewar had been on the 105 when he penned his purple prose?

ALLT'A BHAINNE

Pronunciation: alta**bane**

Founded: 1975

Founder: Seagram Distillers

Region: Speyside

Production Capacity: 4,000,000 litres

Address: Glenrinnes, Dufftown, Banffshire

Tel: 01340 208 37

website: www.pernod-ricard.com

Parent Company: Pernod Ricard

Visitor Centre: Contact distillery for details

CRAGGANMORE

As you approach this modern, flat-roofed building that stands four miles south-east from Dufftown, there is little to suggest that any whisky is made here. It could be a sports centre or perhaps executive flats, but not a distillery. It was built by the Canadian giant Seagram's in 1975 at a cost of £2.7 million.

This was a time of unrivalled confidence in the whisky business when people went out and built distilleries from scratch rather than wait for them to come on the market second-hand. It was the last of a mini building boom that began in the late 1950s, and bears witness to the world-wide success of such Seagram blends as Chivas Regal where a good part of Allt'A Bhainne has always gone.

The name is Gaelic for 'the milk burn' which flows close by and is where local dairy farmers used to wash their equipment after milking, which presumably turned the water cloudy. A couple of new stills were added to the original pair in 1989 to boost the distillery's potential production to an impressive 4 million litres a year. Then, 25 years after the first spirit was produced here, Seagram pulled out of the drinks trade altogether – a business in which they rose to fame during US prohibition bootlegging liquor across the Canadian border.

The whisky is matured on Speyside, though down at Keith, and apart from the occasional independent bottling of this light, floral malt, all of it of is swallowed up in various blends. This may change one day under the new owners Pernod Ricard.

Pronunciation: cragganmore

Founded: 1869

Founder: John Smith

Region: Speyside

Production Capacity: 1,600,000 litres

Address: Ballindalloch, Banffshire AB37 9AB

Tel: 01807 500 202

website: www.diageo.com

Parent Company: Diageo

Visitor Centre: Mon–Fri by appointment only.

Cragganmore is a cracking Speyside malt, a whisky to roll around the tongue and one with a name to match. It lies to the west of the main cluster of Speyside distilleries, a little deeper into the Highlands. With Glenlivet not far to the south towards Tomintoul, this was right in the heart of smuggling country. In fact John Smith, the man who founded Cragganmore in 1869, later discovered it had been the site of an old smuggler's bothy.

Smith had whisky in his blood and was said to be the illegitimate son of George Smith, the founder of Glenlivet. As well as having been the manager at that distillery, John Smith had also managed the Macallan, before taking on a short lease at Glenfarclas. When

that expired he decided the time was right to set up on his own, being one of the most experienced distillers in the country. In 1869 he approached Sir George Macpherson-Grant who lived at Ballindalloch Castle and owned the surrounding estate, to take out a lease on one of his farms and build Scotland's first-ever distillery beside a railway line. It was set on three acres of land facing the Spey, with the wooded slopes of the Craggan More hill behind, connected via its own railway siding to Ballindalloch station, 300 yards down the track. Smith had first tested the water from the spring-fed Craggan burn and found it ideal for distilling. The main burn was also used to power a 14 foot water wheel, while a smaller burn was diverted for cooling purposes. With easy access to good-quality barley and nearby peat, Cragganmore was well conceived from the start.

Apart from whisky, John Smith's great passion in life was the railways and he went everywhere by train. Being somewhat larger than life in the literal sense, his 22-stone girth was too large to squeeze through the carriage doors, so he had to travel in the guard's van. Unfortunately he died in his early fifties a year before the first 'Whisky Special' steamed out of Ballindalloch in 1887 loaded with 16,000 gallons of Scotch on board.

At the time, Cragganmore's annual production of 90,000 gallons of spirit from its two stills was all being sent south to James Watson & Co, a firm of blenders in Dundee who were later swallowed up by the Dewar's empire. Despite the great slump in the whisky trade following the Pattison crash of 1898-99 which brought many to the brink, Cragganmore barely missed a beat. The distillery was never closed for more than a fortnight in all the years from 1870 to the summer of 1901 when John's son Gordon hired the architect Charles Doig. 'The building was too antiquated to do with any further patching up,' he later wrote, 'there was nothing for it but to practically build a new distillery.' Doig was the most famous distillery architect of his day, whose signature was the familiar pagoda-style roofs. In 1923, Cragganmore-Glenlivet became a separate company jointly owned by Sir Peter Mackie's White Horse Distillers co. and the Ballindalloch Estate. Though the Macpherson-Grants sold their shares long ago, they still own casks of Cragganmore at the distillery in case the castle runs dry.

It retains something of the self-sufficient feel of a Highland distillery supporting a small community of houses gathered round the distillery. It had been lit by electric light since 1919 which was powered by a small petrol generator. The rest of the energy needed came from an old water-wheel fed by the Craggan burn. The water-wheel was still running in 1950, the year before the distillery was finally plugged into the national grid.

Cragganmore is famous for its curiously shaped stills. Each of the two spirit stills have the standard swan neck design that bends round to form the lynne arm which connects to copper coils kept in cast-iron worm tubs outside. But the wash stills are something else. Instead of an elegant curve the neck ends abruptly like a sawn-off tree, with the lynne arm jutting out the side like a branch. Most people assume the design was simply in order to squeeze into the stillroom beneath its sloping roof, but Stuart Robinson, the current distillery manager, believes otherwise. He is convinced that John Smith the master distiller, knew exactly what he was doing, and that the shape was the result of many experiments to achieve the result he was looking for. Either way, when the number of stills doubled to four in 1964, no one was going to risk tampering with the design. Whatever it was doing to the wash, it was beautiful. For the parent company, Diageo, this is the jewel of Speyside, and when the 'Classic Malts' were launched in the eighties, no-one was at all surprised it was picked to join the exclusive club.

The use of copper worms also plays its part in making Cragganmore such a complex dram. As with Dalwhinnie, no one would dream of swapping them for condensers even though that would work out a lot cheaper in the long run and certainly be easier to maintain. The only shame is that having produced all that wonderful hot water in the worm tub it is allowed to cool down and flow back into the Spey. If I were distillery manager I would have it piped to my own little outdoor pool. Just imagine wallowing in the steam on a cold winter's day.

TORMORE

Pronunciation: tor**more**

Founded: 1958–60

Founder: Long John Distillers

Region: Speyside

Production capacity: 3,600,000 litres

Address: Advie, Grantown-on-Spey, Moray PH26 3LR

Tel: 01807 510 244

website: www.allieddomecqplc.com

Parent Company: Allied Domecq

Visitor Centre: September–June, Mon–Thurs, 1.30–4pm. All visits by appointment only.

In the days when most Highland whisky was made on the side, away from the prying eyes of the excise man, there were two basic rules regarding a distillery's location. It had to be near a reliable source of cold, crystal-clear water, and it had to be well hidden. When whisky-making moved out of the shadows in the 1820s and 30s, many smugglers' bothies evolved into licensed distilleries. This explains why so many are so remote, tucked down the bottom of some glen.

Remoteness is not something you could accuse Tormore of, built in 1958-60 by the American company Shenley Industries to be the spiritual home

Tormore
Note the stillhouse clock set to chime the tune of 'Highland Laddie' every hour. You can view a scale model of Tormore in the Scotch Whisky Heritage Centre on Edinburgh's Royal Mile.

GLENLIVET

Glenlivet

A thoroughly modern Glenlivet stands out in its remote, desolate setting.

Pronunciation: glen**liv**et

Founded: 1824

Founder: George & James Gordon Smith

Region: Speyside

Production Capacity: 5,500,000 litres

Address: Glenlivet, Ballindalloch, Banffshire AB37 9DB

Tel: 01542 783 220

website: www.theglenlivet.com

Parent Company: Pernod Ricard

Visitor Centre: April–October, Mon–Sat, 10am–4pm. Sun, 12.30–4pm. Group bookings by appointment.

In the whole history of whisky-making in the Highlands few words are so evocative as 'Glenlivet' – a word that seems to capture the very spirit of defiance that set this remote glen in collision with the forces of the law – forces which after the defeat of the Jacobite rebellion of 1745 had robbed the people of their religion, their dress and their language. In 1822, when King George IV arrived on his state visit to Edinburgh and demanded some 'Highland whisky', everyone knew what he meant. And when word reached Elizabeth Grant of Rothiemurchus that the Lord Chamberlain 'was looking everywhere for pure Glenlivet whisky' she wrote later of how she went to empty her 'petbin where the whisky was long in wood, long in uncorked bottles, mild as milk and with the true contraband goût in it.'

The romance of Glenlivet's illicit past almost runs away with itself and cannot possibly live up to the present-day reality of a modern, functional distillery built as a light industrial unit for efficiency rather than looks. On the inside it all feels a million miles from an old smuggler's bothy, but looking out across the wide open bowl and to the hump-backed hill to the south with the braes of Glenlivet beyond, you do begin to get a sense of the past. As one Victorian visitor noted 'there is not a village or town anywhere near the place; the nearest railway station is about seven miles distant. A more lonely spot in winter, or a more delightful one in summer could not be found and, for those who like quietude and rest, truly it is very far from the 'madding crowd'.

The story of the Glenlivet distillery begins with George Smith, who was the first in the glen to take out a licence to operate a distillery at Upper Drummin farm in 1824. The farm had been leased from the Duke of Gordon by George's father some years before. A year later the first whisky trickled from the still, and was soon gushing out at a rate of

of their newly acquired whisky brand – Long John. Nor is it particularly discreet. As the whisky writer, Jim Murray put it. 'After passing the turn to Cragganmore, a vision arrives on your left so unexpected it could land you in the ditch.'

It looms up beside the road like no other distillery in Scotland. It is a huge, white-washed, granite-built affair, with a monster sized stillroom and a towering chimney stack. The architect, Sir Albert Richardson, was a past present of the Royal Academy who clearly believed in making a statement. Some of his plans had to be tamed down, like the idea of building the chimney in the shape of a giant whisky bottle, but others survived. For example, the clock on top of the stillhouse set to chime the tune of 'Highland Laddie' on the hour every hour.

There are now eight stills behind those towering arched windows of the stillroom, producing a malt which at ten years old is a delicate, dry, almost flinty whisky – smooth and faintly smoky in the mouth.

a hundred gallons a week. Yet all was not well, and with two other licensed distillers in the region already bankrupt, Smith went to the Duke's factor in 1827 to confess that he was heavily in debt and could not carry on. In the nick of time a deal was struck, and by selling all his cattle and giving up the lease of a neighbouring farm, he secured a £500 rescue package from the Duke. A year later a company of dragoons arrived in the glen to try and stamp out smuggling once and for all. This helped ease some of the intimidation Smith had been suffering, for by going legal he had upset a lot of people in the neighbourhood, many of whom depended on selling moonshine to pay the rent and get by. As one local farmer recalled, 'there were not three persons in Glenlivet in those days [in the early 1800s] who were not engaged directly or indirectly in the trade.'

By 1834 the battle against the illicit stills was won, and Smith's Glenlivet prospered and spread to Aberdeen, Perth and the Port of Leith by sea. Shipments sometimes shrank en route thanks to the ingenuity of the sailors. A favourite scam was to lift up the top iron hoop on the barrel, drill a hole, siphon off a bit of whisky, then plug up the hole and hammer the hoop back in place. By the mid-nineteenth century Smith was supplying malt whisky to Andrew Usher, the father of blended Scotch, who launched 'Old Vatted Glenlivet' in 1853. Shortly after this the distillery decamped down the glen to its current home of Minmore and was soon pumping out 4000 gallons a week. The whisky was filled into casks and carried by cart to Ballindalloch station on the newly opened Strathspey railway line. When George Smith died in 1871, Glenlivet had become the best-known distillery in Scotland, whose single malt was beginning to penetrate the furthest flung corners of the world. In London alone it was selling over 100 casks a year. The man himself had become something of a legend and the newspapers were curious to learn all about him. Yet how much the fame of Glenlivet was down to Smith or the earlier smugglers is hard to say. When James Hogg's famous Ettrick Shepherd cried 'Gie me the real Glenlivet...', did he have a specific distillery in mind, or was he just looking for something illicit from Speyside? Probably more the latter, since this was written back in 1827.

While distilleries many miles from Glenlivet piggy-backed on the name, creating what was dubbed the longest 'glen' in Scotland, there is no doubt Smith benefited from the romance of the region's illicit past. After a costly two year tussle in the courts, ten distilleries were allowed to keep the word 'Glenlivet' as part of their name in 1882. Many years later the likes of Macallan decided to abandon the practice which says as much for the rise of Macallan as it does for the comparative fall of Glenlivet.

Telford's Bridge
Built at Craigellachie in 1814 and sole survivor of the Great Muckle Spate of 1829 which swept away all the other bridges across the Spey.

This is all relative to the past, for Glenlivet remains one of the top selling single malt whiskies in the world and is especially popular in the United States. The US market was built up by the then owner, Bill Smith Grant, immediately after prohibition when the distillery at last began to bottle its whisky rather than sell everything in cask.

In recent times, Glenlivet teamed up with Glen Grant and then Longmorn until all three distilleries were bought by Seagram in 1977. Then in 2001 Seagram sold its entire whisky business, including its flagship brand, 'Chivas Regal', to the French group, Pernod Ricard. A whole new future awaits Glenlivet.

The main expressions are a sherry-scented 12 year-old that is pale in colour, gentle to the taste and not particularly long on the finish, and a much richer more succulent 18 year-old that has been scooping a fair number of awards.

BRAEVAL

Pronunciation: braeval

Founded: 1972

Founder: Chivas Brothers Ltd

Region: Speyside

Production Capacity: 4,000,000 litres

Address: Dufftown, Keith, Banffshire AB38 9LR

Tel: 01340 871 315

website: www.pernod-ricard.com

Parent Company: Pernod Ricard

Visitor Centre: Contact distillery for details

Who knows how many illicit stills once bubbled away here in the Braes of Glenlivet, especially in the early nineteenth century when smuggling and

The River Avon

One of the major tributaries of the Spey, from Tomintoul.

Speyside were almost synonymous. What is clear is that they had long gone cold by the time Seagram decided to build a new distillery here, five miles from Tomintoul. The first soil was cut by Edgar Bronfman, heir to the mighty Seagram empire, in 1972 and the first spirit flowed a year later.

Its sister distillery at the time was Four Roses in Kentucky, though as if to underline the fact that it was Scotch not Bourbon being distilled here, a decorative pagoda was strapped to the roof. It was originally called Braes of Glenlivet, though once Seagram acquired the real Glenlivet distillery for themselves as part of a £48 million package five years later, the name was changed.

Inside, each of the two large wash stills feeds a pair of spirit stills whose spirit is pumped into giant stainless steel vats, mixed with local spring water and then pumped into waiting tankers for filling into casks at Keith. It may not be romantic but it is efficient and allows one man to control the entire operation on his eight-hour shift. The distillery is hardly the hub of the local community in other words. In fact Braeval stands in glorious isolation at just over a 1000 ft, making it the second-highest distillery in Britain after Dalwhinnie. Some of the whisky seeps out in the form of single malt, bottled by the odd independent, but the vast majority has always gone into the big Seagram blends which, like the distillery itself, now belong to the French group, Pernod Ricard.

TOMINTOUL

Pronunciation: tomin**towl**

Founded: 1964

Founder: Tomintoul Distillery Ltd

Region: Speyside

Production capacity: 2,800,000 litres

Address: Ballindalloch, Banffshire AB3 9AG

Tel: 01807 590 274

website: www.angusdundee.co.uk

Parent Company: Angus Dundee

Visitor Centre: Contact distillery for details

The highest village in the Highlands, Tomintoul grew up as a staging post along the old military road that ran from Corgarff to Fort George. Travellers would stop at the village Inn to refuel. With a dram of whisky costing just a penny in today's money, and with drams being a lot more generous in those days, the Inn built up quite a reputation.

As whisky evolved from the underground to go legal after the Excise Act of 1823, Tomintoul soon got its first licensed distillery, called Delnabo. The first distiller went bust, and the distillery was taken over by George Smith of Glenlivet. It acted as an extension of Glenlivet, until Smith moved his distillery down the glen to its present site in 1858, and that was the last that was heard of Delnabo.

The Tomintoul distillery of today was built five miles from the village, on the road to Glenlivet, in 1964. Though it stands on the banks of the River Avon, the Spey's biggest tributary, it is within the parish of Glenlivet. Thus Tomintoul-Glenlivet had every right to its name.

The distillery is in the same stable as Dalmore and Fettercairn as part of the Whyte & Mackay group, or Kyndal as they now like to call themselves. Compared to other 'Glenlivets' its malt is more delicate and herbal. It forms part of the Whyte & Mackay blend, and is also bottled by its owners as a 12 year-old single malt.

BALMENACH

Pronunciation: balmenakh

Founded: 1824

Founder: James McGregor

Region: Speyside

Production capacity: 1,800,000 litres

Address: Cromdale, Moray PH26 3PF

Tel: 01479 872 569

website: www.balmenachdistillery.com

Parent Company: Inver House

Visitor Centre: Contact distillery for details

James McGregor, a local farmer from Tomintoul took a lease on a farm at Balmenach which lies in a dip in the hills between the Upper Spey and its tributary the Avon, a mile beyond the village of Cromdale. McGregor is said to have made whisky on the side for a few years before going legal and taking out a licence in 1824. The Balmenach distillery was described as among the most primitive in Scotland by Alfred Barnard when he visited in the 1880s, though the fact it was there at all was something of a miracle

On the 28 December 1879, 70 mile-an-hour winds blew down the distillery's chimney stack. It crashed down through the roof of the stillroom and ruptured the stills. The boiling liquid inside spurted out onto the open flames below, but amazingly did not catch fire. Had the distillery burnt down that night, it would have barely made the news the next day, since the papers were totally preoccupied with another victim of the storm — the Tay Rail Bridge. The bridge had been open for less than two years when it collapsed, sending the evening train from Edinburgh to Dundee plunging into the icy estuary, killing 75 of the passengers and crew.

The McGregors were still involved with the distillery when it became a limited company at the end of the century, and one of the grand-children was Compton Mackenzie, author of Whisky Galore. Eventually Balmenach became part of United Distillers who increased the number of stills to six and then mothballed it in 1993. Five years later it was back in production under its new owners Inver House.

SPEYSIDE

Pronunciation: spayside

Founded: 1990

Founder: George Christie

Region: Speyside

Production capacity: 600,000 litres

Address: Kingussie, Invernesshire PH21 1HS

Tel: 01540 661 060

website: www.speysidedistillery.co.uk

Parent Company: Speyside Distillery

Visitor Centre: Contact distillery for details

Otherwise known as Drumguish (pronounced 'drum-ooish'), this is a tiny, totally new Speyside distillery that produced its first dribble of spirit in January 1991. Its construction had been no overnight affair, in fact the foundations were laid almost 30 years earlier. It was in 1963 that Alex Fairlie, a dry-stane dyker by profession, started building on the site at Tronymill. Like William Grant and Glenfiddich a century before, it took the Glasgow blender, George Christie, half a lifetime to realise his dream. Sadly the money ran out four years before completion, and Speyside was sold to a Swiss company. Then in 2000, the distillery was bought by an independent whisky company in the UK, with George's son, Ricky, as one of the directors.

The design belies its youth, because George Christie insisted that it be built using traditional methods. Except for the discreet, modern smoke stack, it could be a century old, though being a squat, low-slung affair, with attic windows in the roof, it looks more like a barn than a distillery. Inside, the two stills stand on stilts to produce 600,000 litres of alcohol a year, making it the second-smallest distillery in Scotland. The plan is to keep some in cask for bottling as a 10 year-old single malt called Drumguish, and sell the rest to blenders.

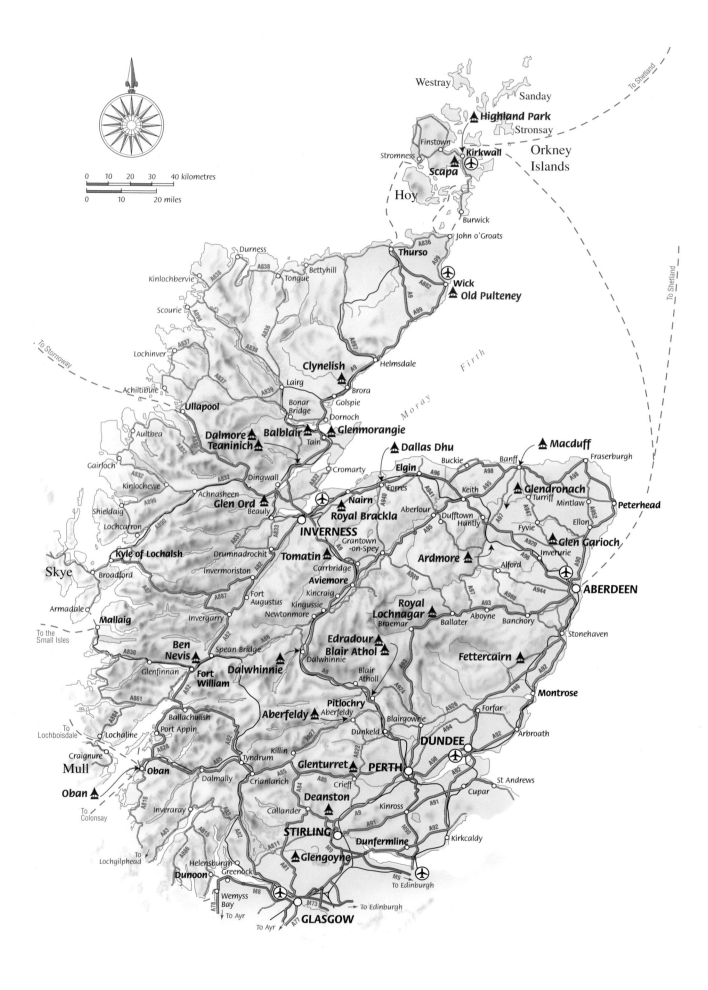

HIGHLAND DISTILLERIES

Two massive geological rifts running southwest to northeast split Scotland from side to side. The furthest north – the Great Glen Fault – runs past Fort William up Loch Ness to the Moray Firth. To the south is the Highland Boundary Fault from the Firth of Clyde to the Tay. Both were the result of a violent collision deep in the earth's crust and both can be seen from space. At the time of their birth the Highlands would have rivalled the Himalayas. Since then, however, 400 million years of Scottish weather has taken its toll.

Yet you only have to drive north along the motorway past Stirling where the mountains suddenly rise up from the plain to see how dramatic the Highland–Lowland divide is. It has always made a natural barrier and been subject to different laws including those concerning whisky. The more enlightened law-makers of the eighteenth century recognised that conditions were tougher in the north where yields of barley were lower on account of the soil and the weather. So to compensate, less duty was charged on the stills. To placate the Lowland distillers who scented unfair competition, the authorities ordered that no Highland whisky should cross the line. It proved impossible to enforce, and illicit whisky began to flood south.

Everything about it was different from Lowland whisky which was mostly being made in big stills worked flat out to produce a rough, raw spirit in large volumes. The typical Highland still was far smaller and allowed to distil at its own pace to produce a much gentler whisky as a result. The fact that most of it had never seen the taxman only added to its charm.

Once the great whisky dynasties like the Haigs and the Steins who dominated the industry for most of the nineteenth century, had converted to continuous patent stills and grain whisky in the 1830s, the north-south split became even more clear cut. From then on, the Highlands became the true home of malt whisky.

It is a vast area and the trouble with relying on the old Boundary Fault is that not many distilleries are excluded. Even Springbank in Campbeltown is technically in the Highlands even though it is actually further south than Berwick upon Tweed. So too is Glengoyne, though only just – the dividing line runs right past its front door. Does Glengoyne have anything in common with Old Pulteney way up on the north-east tip of Scotland? Not much, you would think, at least in terms of location – with one half an hour north of Glasgow and the other buffeted by the North Sea. And so to shed some light on this huge tract of land let's break the Highlands up.

Two whisky regions in the area have separated on their own accord – Campbeltown down in the southwest and Speyside on the other side of the country. What remains are clusters of distilleries in the far north, in Perthshire and in the lone outposts like Oban.

THE FAR NORTH

From Inverness to Kirkwall on Orkney there are a further eight malt distilleries currently working and

The Warehouses at Highland Park on Orkney

A Classic, Slightly Cramped, Victorian Distillery

and turned into a steakhouse which they christened 'The Auld Distillery'. It stands as a poignant reminder of the worst distillery cull in memory, and also demonstrates the downside of being in a town. If your distillery is tucked away in a remote Highland glen and goes silent due to one of the industry's periodic depressions, it can sit peacefully in mothballs for years until demand picks up again. In the meantime not many developers are going to come banging on the door since there is little call for supermarkets and steakhouses in the middle of nowhere.

The coastal distilleries up to Old Pulteney in Wick appear to be thriving, as does Highland Park across the water on Orkney. Of course this is not really the Highlands, but then it's not really 'Island whisky' either, as in Talisker on Skye. Like anything Orcadian it cannot be easily categorised and put in a box. Let's just say it is different, and is all the better for that.

one lone outpost of grain whisky production at Invergordon. All the other grain spirit in Scotland is produced way down south in the Lowlands. The malt whiskies would classify as Highland malts, though the distilleries are all close to if not beside the North Sea whose influence is stronger than the mountains.

Somewhere around Dingwall was Ferintosh, the first ever whisky distillery in Scotland. No-one is sure precisely where Duncan Forbes built the original Ferintosh, but it was certainly operating before 1689 when the local Jacobites razed it to the ground in response to Forbes' support for the new protestant King – William of Orange. In compensation he and his descendents were allowed to produce duty-free whisky for almost a century, earning themselves a fortune and giving Scotland its first-ever brand of Scotch. Afterwards it seems 'Ferintosh' became something of a generic name like 'Glenlivet'. Many distilleries were built close by, including Ben Wyvis which had changed to Ferintosh before being demolished in the 1920s.

Inverness was an important centre of whisky production with three distilleries until the mid 1980s. Throughout the previous decade the whole industry had been distilling away like mad, convinced that the global thirst for Scotch would never be satisfied. Unfortunately forecasts of likely demand proved to be wildly over-optimistic, and the taps had to be turned off fast. Whisky making in the town ceased almost overnight and Glen Mhor and Glen Albyn were soon demolished to make room for a new supermarket. Only Millburn survived, to be gobbled up by the Beefeater restaurant chain a few years later

HIGHLAND PARK

Founded: 1798

Founder: Magnus Eunson

Region: Highlands

Production capacity: 2,500,000 litres

Address: Holm Road, Kirkwall, Orkney KW15 1SU

Tel: 01856 874 619

website: www.highlandpark.co.uk

Parent Company: Edrington Group

Visitor Centre:

April–October, Mon–Fri, 10am–4pm.

June–September, Sat and Sun, 12-4pm.

November–March, Mon–Fri, tour at 2pm.

Group bookings by appointment.

The Kiln at Highland Park

The storms and tidal reaches that swirl round Scotland and the islands make these some of the most treacherous waters on earth. For early geographers this was the 'Ultima Thule' – the northernmost fringe of the inhabited world, or so they thought. Here more than anywhere whisky lit up the long, dark, tunnel of winter before daylight eventually broke through in the spring. Up on Orkney whisky must have felt like the true water of life, long before it became a highly taxed luxury. This certainly helps explain the need for a distillery like Highland Park which began life at the end of the eighteenth century on the outskirts of the island's capital Kirkwall. Today it is the furthest flung distillery in the British Isles having somehow survived long enough to make a virtue of the fact. Sadly this has not been the fate of the island's other distilleries – Stromness, or Man of Hoy, which fell silent in 1928 and today only Highland Park and Scapa are still working.

Until ferries came equipped with stabilisers, the ride through the Pentland Firth, where the Atlantic races round to embrace the colder waters of the North Sea, could be pretty unpleasant. But the compensation of coming in mid summer remains the incredible length of the days, the fact that you can read outdoors all night long, and the warmth of the welcome. At the Castle Hotel in Kirkwall visitors would be greeted with a dram and a slice of ginger cake whatever time they arrived.

The most famous legend about Highland Park is that this was the site where Magnus Eunson carried out his trade as the most notorious smuggler on Orkney. By day he was a Presbyterian minister, but by night he was a distiller of illicit hooch that he used to keep in a cask stashed under his pulpit. Being a minister of the Kirk was not only the perfect cover, it also kept Magnus Eunson in close contact with the community. It was by keeping his ear to the ground that he got wind that the excise officers were finally planning a raid on his Church.

Laying a New Batch of Malt on the Drying Floor

125

The Spirit Safe
Though locked, the stillman can check the strength of the spirit at any moment by diverting a small amount into one of the glass jars containing a hydrometer.

over £100 when it passed to the Revd. James Borwick of Fife. Being a United Presbyterian minister and owning a whisky distillery clearly caused a moral dilemma for James in a way that had never troubled Magnus Eunson, and so the whole place was put on the market for just £450. It was bought by a firm of brokers called Stuart & Mackay who began introducing Highland Park to a wider audience. It was poured for the Russian Emperor and the King of Denmark and was 'pronounced by all to be the finest they had ever tasted'. Most of it however, was being bought by the leading blending houses of the day including Haig, Ballantine's and Dewar's.

The quality of the whisky was put down to the continued reliance on bere – an indigenous, low-yielding strain of barley that distillers on the mainland had all but phased out, and the use of heather which was stored in the distillery's very own 'Heather House'. The heather was cut near to the root when it was in full purple bloom in the summer, and then tied in bundles of a dozen fronds each. One or two of these would be laid on top of the smouldering peat in the kilns to impregnate the malting barley with the scent of honey to offset the bitter aroma from the peat smoke. Visitors were proudly shown the process and invited to inhale the pronounced sweetness that wafted up from the furnace.

In 1895 the distillery was acquired by James Grant of Glenlivet whose descendants sold out to its present owners – Highland Distillers – in 1937 for £185,000. As a single malt it has been appreciated by politicians from Winston Churchill to the Conservative chancellor, Ken Clark. It was apparently a glass of Highland Park that Clark waved to the nation as he read out his budget in 1995. The drink clearly had the right effect for when he came to announcing the rate of excise on whisky, he decided to cut the tax for the first time in living memory, something he repeated the following year. When his successor, Gordon Brown, took over, his glass contained tap water and, sure enough, the level of duty increased.

From the outside, Highland Park appears a neat, slightly cramped Victorian distillery which still malts a fifth of its barley on site. Having its own maltings means using its own peat – cut from the nearby Hobbister Moor as it always has been, and this is why the whisky's floral flavours have lingered on long after the old 'Heather House' was pulled down. The effect of the peat smoke depends on what the peat was formed from – and while that often means sea-weed in the case of Islay, on Orkney it bears the clear imprint of decomposed heather. The result is a moderately peated 12 year-old dram imbued with the scent of orange peel, smoke and heather-honey.

Quickly the barrels were assembled in the aisle and the lid of a coffin placed on top, over which was thrown a white sheet. When the excisemen burst in, the assembled crowd, led by Eunson, let up a great wail for the dead. All that was needed was for one of the congregation to whisper the dread word 'smallpox', the anthrax of its day, and the officer and his men turned and fled.

To make his whisky he used water from a pair of springs that rose in the 'high park' – hence the name. The story goes that the 'minister of moonshine' was finally apprehended in 1813 by John Roberston who promptly took over the High Park estate and its distillery. Robertson was later bought out by his partner, Robert Borwick whose family held on to Highland Park for the next forty years. It remained a very small affair by all accounts and the Borwicks clearly spent very little on it. In the 1860s, the total equipment, including two pot stills, was valued at just

SCAPA

Pronunciation: skapa

Founded: 1885

Founder: Macfarlane & Townsend

Region: Highland

Production capacity: approx 1,000,000

Address: St. Ola, Kirkwall, Orkney KW15 1SE

Tel: 01856 872 071

website: www.allieddomecqplc.com

Parent Company: Allied Domecq

Visitor Centre: All year, Mon–Thurs,
8am–12noon and 1–5pm. Friday, 8am–1pm.

To a certain extent Scapa suffers from the same syndrome as Glen Scotia right the other side of Scotland in Campbeltown — that of having a much more famous distillery for a neighbour. In the case of the latter, it is Springbank, in the former it is Highland Park which takes all the kudos. Curiously enough Scapa and Glen Scotia shared the same owner for a while. Whisky books wax lyrical and in

considerable length about the Orcadian delight that is Highland Park, then make a perfunctory nod towards 'poor Scapa', before crossing back to the mainland to continue their trawl down the east coast. Well, it is true that Scapa has been mothballed rather a lot recently, but rumours of its demise have been a little exaggerated. In 2001, it distilled whisky for a three month period and hopes to continue on that basis in the future.

The distillery was opened by John Townsend, a whisky maker from Speyside in 1885. Some 33 years later, it had a ringside seat from its position on the north shore of Scapa Flow when the German High Seas Fleet decided to scuttle itself at the end of the First World War. Long afterwards the masts of great battle cruisers could be seen poking above the waves at low tide.

Before its recent troubles, Scapa managed a whole century of almost unbroken production, apart from a couple of years in the mid 1930s. It was rebuilt in 1958 and upgraded in 1978, by then part of Hiram Walker which later merged to form Allied Distillers. It no longer malts its own barley, and relies on the brackish water of the Lingro Burn for any peatiness in the whisky. With just two stills and such a short distilling season, this heathery, salt-flecked, soft-centred malt, is rare indeed.

Marking the Barrels with a Stencil

With their huge inventories of maturing whisky, the larger companies now use bar-codes to keep track of their stocks.

**The Sturdy,
Hard-Working Stills
at Highland Park**

OLD PULTENEY

Pronunciation: old **pult**ney

Founded: 1826

Founder: James Henderson

Region: Highlands

Production capacity: 1,000,000 litres

Address: Huddart Street, Wick,
Caithness KW1 5BA

Tel: 01955 602 371

website: www.oldpulteney.com

Parent Company: Inver House

Visitor Centre:
April–September, Mon–Fri, 10.30am–12.30pm and
1.30-3.30pm.
October–March, restricted hours.

Huddled beside the North Sea, half battered to death by fierce winds, the small town of Wick, just eighteen miles south of John O'Groats, can feel pretty bleak at times. Inland the flat, featureless scenery is pretty much devoid of trees to shelter from the fierce and near constant onshore breeze, while along the coast the sandstone cliffs and towering stacks of rock have been sculpted by the sea. Apart from Dounreay, a few local services and some inshore fishing there is not much in the way of work to keep hold of the young, and like other Highland outposts, Wick's population is shrinking slowly. It is hard to believe therefore that this was once the boom town of the north whose size was doubling every ten years in the latter half of the nineteenth century. The reason for such dramatic growth was the herring for which Wick became Europe's biggest fishing port, far larger than Hull or Grimsby, with a fleet of up to a thousand boats at its peak. When the fleet was in, the boats were packed so tight you could walk across the decks from one side of the harbour to the other. The sight of all those masts was probably as close as this wind-swept stretch of coast has ever got in the way of a forest.

Every summer a huge itinerant workforce assembled by the harbour wall to gut the herring and pack them into salt barrels ready for export across the North Sea. Hauling nets and gutting fish all day could lead to a serious thirst, which is where James Henderson comes in. After thirty years of making moonshine inland, Henderson decided to move to the coast and set up a licensed distillery here in 1826.

The distillery was named after Sir William Johnstone Pulteney, a herring baron who had helped establish the town twenty-five years earlier for the British Fisheries Society. It had lofts to store the barley which came from nearby Moray and Ross-shire and two malting floors. Since only peat was used to fire the kilns the whisky would have been pretty pungent especially if it was not allowed time to mellow. Even the water, which came from the Loch of Hempriggs, three miles away, was prized for its peaty character. But with daily life impregnated with the constant smell of the sea and the reek of pickled herring from the barrels lined up along the harbour front, a good, tarry spirit was probably just what the locals wanted.

As well as satisfying this burgeoning demand on his doorstep, Henderson had little to fear from illicit competition, since the town's customs officers were ever on the prowl for any unlicensed activity. There was easy access by sea to other markets along the east coast and above all to Russia, Germany and the Baltic States where most of the herring was shipped. In fact from Henderson's point of view, the place was just about perfect. Sadly it was not to last.

The outbreak of the First World War hastened

the demise of the fishing fleet which was already losing out to the larger Scandinavian drift netters. Meanwhile the 10,000 strong seasonal workforce was being blamed for all manner of drunken depravity and for not respecting the Sabbath, although Iain Sutherland, a local historian, denies that it was ever quite the Wild West. Yet 1922 was the high water mark of the temperance movement, the year when Neddy Scrymegeour, Britain's one and only prohibitionist MP, finally defeated Winston Churchill in Dundee. In that year, along with 56 other towns in Scotland, Wick voted to go dry and remained so right up until after the Second World War.

There was little appeal in being the only distillery in a dry town having to compete with others who were a lot closer to the main markets of the south. By then all the other distilleries of Caithness such as Murkle and Brabster had long since folded. So Henderson decided to sell out to the Distillers Company in a deal worth over £2 million that also included the distilleries of Ord and Parkmore. DCL promptly closed Pulteney down in 1930 and kept it in mothballs for the next twenty years. It was then bought by a lawyer in Banff who also owned Balblair and was then sold to Hiram Walker who completely re-built it in 1959. This explains its pared down functional design as a back-street distillery with just a modern chimney stack and no pagoda roofs to advertise its presence.

Feeling not a little unloved by this stage, Pulteney was next adopted by Allied Distillers who decided its main purpose in life was to be one of the fifty or so malts that went to make up Ballantines. The odd bottle of young spirit occasionally appeared in town, but its raw, throat-stripping qualities were seldom appreciated.

Not being a Speyside or an island whisky, Pulteney was neither fish nor foul, and doubtless suffered a sense of neglect as a remote asset in Allied's global portfolio. And yet Wick's isolation helped protect it from real estate predators during the periodic bouts of inactivity as had been the fate of Inverness's three distilleries in the early 1980s.

Today Pulteney belongs to Inver House Distillers, who decided in 1997 to launch Old Pulteney as a 12-year-old single malt. The company has drawn heavily on the whisky's maritime heritage, the way the barley and barrels were transported by boat and how the distillery workers were often fishermen as well. A fishing boat is etched on the bottle – indeed there does seem a trace of salt and sea spray on the nose together with something sweeter like walnut cake. While in the mouth this amber malt with a reddish tinge is decidedly dry particularly on the finish.

Inver House recently restored an old herring drifter, the *Isabella Fortuna*, to tour the coast spreading

The Boil-Ball Wash Still at Pulteney
The spherical chamber, or boil-ball, above the main body of the still encourages the heavier vapours to condense back into the pot to create a cleaner spirit.

the word of Pulteney's new-found identity as the northernmost distillery on the British mainland. With its solitary pair of stills it is a small, traditional operation which you can now visit. Inside is a weird looking wash-still whose neck appears to have been lopped off whilst being installed. In fact both stills have seriously kinky lyne arms that curve round to join their respective condensers. Perhaps this helps account for the fresh, whistle clean freshness of the spirit produced.

Checking the Level of Maturing Casks of Old Pulteney

CLYNELISH

Pronunciation: clyne**leesh**

Founded: 1967

Founder: United Distillers

Region: Highlands

Production capacity: 3,400,000 litres

Address: Brora, Sutherland KW9 6LR

Tel: 01408 623 000

website: www.malts.com

Parent Company: Diageo

Visitor Centre: January–Easter,

by appointment only.

Easter–September, Mon–Fri, 10am–5pm.

October, Mon–Fri, 11am–4pm.

November–December, by appointment only.

The New Clynelish
Built in 1969, this functional, box-like distillery offers its staff great views and a warm, well-lit space compared to the original Victorian Clynelish.

Just past the pretty coastal town of Brora on the last stretch of the A9 heading north, you finally reach Clynelish. Built in 1967, it is as functional a distillery as you are likely to find. The views looking out from the glass-plated stillroom can be beautiful, especially at dawn with the sun rising up out of the sea. But the views looking in are distinctly less so. Aesthetics were not part of the architect's brief, which at first seems a shame when you consider the original Clynelish.

In 1819 the Marquess of Stafford, later the first Duke of Sutherland, decided to erect a distillery here on the north side of the river Brora where it flows into the sea. It was the latest in a string of ventures to encourage his tenants to move off the land. There had already been a salt works and a brick factory. The 'land' was the Sutherland estates which at one stage covered over half a million acres, while the tenants were mainly crofters living in widely scattered communities. It was only a few miles north from the Duke's fortress of Dunrobin Castle with its thirteenth-century keep and Disneyesque turrets and garden, supposedly based on Versailles. It was also close to some recently opened mines that would hopefully provide fuel for the new distillery. Unfortunately the coal was very poor quality, so the manager was soon relying on additional peat cut from a nearby bog.

Another reason for spending £750 on setting up a licensed distillery, was to wean people off supplying their grain to the makers of illicit Scotch. This had nursed the people 'in every species of deceit, vice, idleness and dissipation,' thundered James Loch, Stafford's Land Commissioner, in 1820.

When it came to persuading his tenants to abandon the land, the Marquess adopted what you might call a carrot and stick approach. This was the height of the Highland Clearances, when a total of 15,000 people were evicted from the estate and replaced with sheep. In the same year as Clynelish was built, 250 of their crofts were burnt down.

Though fully integrated into a pig farm, Clynelish was one of the earlier purpose-built distilleries that was not just an adjunct to the farming year. It was first let to James Harper from Midlothian who produced 10,015 gallons in 1820/21. By 1846 the distillery had passed to George Lawson, the brother of a local bank agent which probably explains why he had the means to expand the business. He extended the buildings, brought in a new kiln, replaced the stills and, by the end of the century, had doubled the capacity. Much of the production was reserved for private customers, some of whom would have no doubt picked up their whisky at the distillery gate while up in Sutherland on their annual fishing holiday. The salmon running up the Brora into Loch Brora, two miles to the west, was the town's main attraction.

In its present form the original Clynelish dates from 1896 when the distillery was bought by a Glasgow firm of blenders who completely rebuilt it. It has all the feel of a classic late-Victorian distillery with its tight-knit buildings arranged around a courtyard dominated by a pair of pagoda roofs. With its horizontal steam engine and screw and band

The Original Clynelish
The last spirit flowed from this classic, late nineteenth-century distillery in 1983, and though its stills remain it would take more than a miracle to bring it back to life.

'There's Gold in Them There Hills'

You can still obtain a permit to pan for gold in the Clynemilton burn behind the distillery.

conveyors to move the raw materials about, it was at the cutting edge of distillery design with manual labour cut to a minimum. After this initial burst it appeared to lag behind the white heat of technological change and was only connected up to mains electricity in the early 1960s. Soon afterwards the last delivery of coal was made to the distillery as it converted fully to internal steam coils to heat the stills and oil to fire the boiler. The water source remained unchanged, being piped from a weir on the Clynemilton burn. It is said to run over rock containing gold. In 1860 news that there was gold 'in them there hills', known as the Strath of Kildonan, sparked a mini gold-rush if not of Klondike-like proportions. Today you can still obtain a local permit to pan for gold, and if you are lucky you might find enough for a ring.

The new distillery had six stills which tripled the amount of spirit produced, though by modelling the stills on the original ones and by keeping to the same water source the essential character of Clynelish was not lost. A couple of years later in 1969 the old distillery was started up again as Clynelish B. Its name was quickly changed to the Brora Distillery, because the whisky it produced was unlike anything made there before. For fourteen years Brora was the most powerful, full-flavoured single malt on the Scottish mainland, packed with enough peat smoke to rival all but the Ardbegs and Laphroaigs of this

world. But that was just the idea since the parent company had run short of Islay-style malts for its blends.

Then in 1983, the old distillery died seemingly forever. Though you can just make out the old stills through a grimy window, it would take more than a miracle to bring it back to life this time. Besides no-one working in the modern Clynelish would swap their warm, well-lit space for something cold and Victorian and if you came here on a damp, dreich day, not unknown in this part of the world, you would hardly blame them.

BALBLAIR

Pronunciation: bal**blair**

Founded: 1790

Founder: James McKeddy

Region: Highlands

Production capacity: 1,330,000 litres

Address: Edderton, Tain, Ross-shire IV19 1LB

Tel: 01862 821 273

website: www.inverhouse.com

Parent Company: Inver House

Visitor Centre: Contact distillery for details

The first Balblair distillery was built near the village of Edderton in Ross & Cromarty in around 1790 by James McKeddy. There are records of whisky being made here 50 years before which would have been in the glory days of Ferintosh down on the Black Isle.

This was the oldest distillery in Scotland which began making whisky way back as the 1670s. Ferintosh had long gone by the time Andrew Ross, whose family had been involved with Balblair from its earliest days, decided to build a new distillery in 1872. He chose a site half a mile from the original, that was on higher ground and right beside the railway line.

It was taken over and rebuilt by Alexander Cowan in 1894 and, apart from a few tweaks here and there it has changed little. Viewed from the train as it chugs past on its final leg of the East Coast line to Wick, Balblair remains a classic late Victorian distillery, small and attractive.

Balblair closed during the First World War and its solitary pair of stills went cold for the next thirty years. It was then bought and fired up again by a lawyer from Banff, who later rebuilt Pulteney. It was then sold at the end of the 1960s for around £200,000 and became part of Allied Distillers who used its malt in Ballantine's Finest and other blends. After a short spell standing idle it was bought and brought back to life by its present owners – Inver House.

GLENMORANGIE

Pronunciation: glen**mor**anjee

Founded: 1843

Founder: William Mathieson

Region: Highlands

Production capacity: 2,900,000 litres

Address: Tain, Ross-shire IV19 1PZ

Tel: 01862 892 477

website: www.glenmorangie.com

Parent Company: Glenmorangie

Visitor Centre:

All year, Mon–Fri, 9am–5pm.

June–August, Sat, 10am–4pm.

Sun, 12–4pm.

Things are fairly hectic these days in the glen of tranquillity where they make Scotland's favourite single malt whisky. Such is the demand that all but a fraction of what is produced is bottled as Glenmorangie. Just 5 per cent disappears into blends, and to prevent any independent bottler riding on the distillery's success and bringing out their own version, a spoonful of the Glen Moray, Glenmorangie's sister distillery in Speyside, is added to every cask to be swapped or traded.

Balblair Distillery – A Victorian Gem

The original distillery was uprooted and moved half a mile to be beside the newly constructed Wick-Inverness railway line in the 1870's.

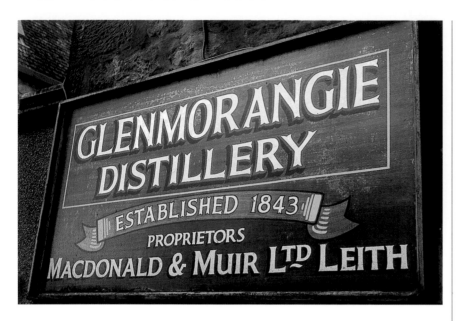

Scotland's Most Popular Malt

The New Stillhouse at Glenmorangie

Note the 17ft stills in the background – the tallest in the industry.

The roots of Glenmorangie date back to the early 1840s when William Matheson took over the lease on the Morangie farm on the southern shores of the Dornoch Firth. With the farm came an old brewery that had been brewing beer since the early eighteenth century, and Matheson took out a license to convert it into a distillery in 1843. Initially he seems to have been more preoccupied with the farm, as the first record of any spirit being produced was not until six years later. For the next forty years Matheson carried on in a rudimentary, ad-hoc fashion, somehow managing to produce 20,000 gallons a year by the time Alfred Barnard, the Victorian Whisky writer paid a visit in the 1880s. He described the distillery as 'the most ancient and primitive we have seen.' Soon

afterwards, the sudden boom in whisky sales allowed Matheson to attract outside investors in the Glenmorangie Distillery Co. which he formed in 1887. At last he could undertake the complete renovation of the distillery, before it collapsed altogether. Barnard had described it as 'almost in ruins'.

The whisky was being sold in England and Scotland, and a few casks were even shipped as far afield as San Francisco. On seeing some destined for Rome the local paper wondered whether the Pope himself had requested 'the Mountain Dew of Easter Ross' as they charmingly dubbed Glenmorangie.

The new distillery was the first to have stills fitted with internal steam coils to prevent scorching. With a life-span of just 15 years on average, these stills have been faithfully copied many times to retain the unique shape. Small and spherical at the base, they bulge out in a boil ball like a large Adam's apple before rising straight upwards in an elegant neck to form the highest stills in the industry at just under 17 foot. The first are said to have come second-hand from a gin distillery – certainly one of the largest investors in the original company was a distiller from London's Chelsea where he may well have been making gin. Production doubled, and the distillery survived the boom-bust years at the start of the twentieth century and limped through the First World War when recruits from the Argyll & Sutherland Highlanders were billeted in its malt barns. But by the end of the war Glenmorangie was up for sale. In April 1918 Macdonald & Muir, a prominent firm of blenders from Leith, paid £74,100 cash for the distillery and its stock.

Roll Out The Barrel
New-filled casks
queue up for a place in
Glenmorangie's warehouse.

With a new owner prepared to spend money on the buildings and equipment and one with a number of important blends to supply like 'Highland Queen' Glenmorangie was in good hands. Production was cranked up by a third to 110,000 gallons a year, and the business proved highly profitable at first. Most of the barley was bought locally and delivered to the malt barns that used to sit by the entrance at the top of the hill. From there the process of making the whisky flowed via the floor maltings, to the mash tuns and eventually the stillroom at the bottom as if by gravity. Peat was used exclusively up until the late 1940s. At first this had been cut from the Tarlogie hills behind the distillery, but by the 1920s was being shipped in from the Orkneys.

The worldwide slump sparked off by the Wall Street Crash of 1929 led to the distillery shutting down in March 1931 for five years. In the meantime the ending of US prohibition signalled a light at the end of the tunnel for firms like Macdonald & Muir. By the outbreak of the Second World War, almost 80 per cent of all the whisky produced by the company was being shipped to the United States. Much of the US success was down to M&M's brand; 'Martin's VVO'. So long as Glenmorangie had a role in supplying malt whisky to such popular blends, its future would be secure.

At least that is how it probably seemed during the 1960s when American consumption of Scotch, all of it blended, tripled to reach 36 million cases by

1971. The subsequent collapse of sales there, the large stocks of maturing whisky and the early success of fellow independent, William Grant, in promoting Glenfiddich, led Glenmorangie to dip its toe in the

**Close-up of
Glenmorangie's
Unique Stills**
The man hole cover is
tightly closed before the
stills are fired up.

135

Across the Cromarty Firth to Dalmore Distillery

world of single malts. These had made an occasional guest appearance on price lists in the past, but only on a very local level. As word of this high quality, ten year-old malt spread, it soon became clear that the distillery had to be enlarged. In the late 1970s it was decided to cease malting and convert the building into the new stillroom, adding more stills and boosting production by a half. Within ten years, Glenmorangie was catching up fast with its great rival Glenfiddich in the UK. Today, by expanding its presence on the supermarket shelf by an ever more exotic range of 'finishes', it plans to become the most popular malt whisky in Britain and not just Scotland. This idea of sending the maturing whisky to 'finishing school' and putting it in a barrel that previously contained anything from Port to red Burgundy for its final months before bottling, has become quite an obsession. Whether it is passing fad, or something more permanent, remains to be seen, but with the possible exception of the 'Madeira' finish, I find the original is best. And if you pick up that delicate alluring scent of orange peel amidst other spices and a whiff of smoke, it can at least help you get one thing right – the pronunciation. The emphasis is on the second syllable– as in Glen-MOR-angie.

DALMORE

Pronunciation: dal**more**

Founded: 1839

Founder: Alexander Matheson

Region: Highlands

Production capacity: 3,200,000 litres

Address: Alness, Ross-shire IV17 0UT

Tel: 01349 882 362

website: www.kyndal.co.uk

Parent Company: Kyndal International Ltd

Visitor Centre: Contact distillery for details

This is the whisky at the heart of the Whyte & Mackay blend, as well as being the flagship single malt of the new parent company, Kyndal. The company was created after a management buy-out in 2001, when the former US owners finally lost their taste for Scotch after an unhappy few years. The significance of Kyndal is that it brought almost a century of North American involvement in the whisky business, which was at one time massively important, to a virtual close. The connection between Whyte & Mackay and Dalmore, however, goes back well over a century.

The distillery was originally established in 1839 on the banks of the Cromarty Firth by Alexander Matheson. With exclusive rights to draw water from the River Alness, plentiful supplies of fuel and some of the best barley grown in the north-east on its doorstep, its location was hard to fault. Yet for some reason, Matheson barely lasted a decade and it passed to Mrs Margaret Sutherland, described as 'sometime distiller', before it was taken over by a well-known local family, the Mackenzies, in 1878. Having known James Whyte and Charles Mackay since they set up in partnership four years later, the family firm, Mackenzie Bros., finally merged into Whyte & Mackay in 1960.

Dalmore's capacity was doubled in 1966 to eight stills, but the overall feel of the distillery is as solidly Victorian as the stones used to build it. The shape of the stills is eccentric to say the least, with necks swaddled in giant copper cooling jackets to speed up early condensation. It seems to work, because Dalmore 12 year old has a spicy richness to it, part plum pudding, part candied fruit.

TEANINICH

Pronunciation: **teen**ineekh

Founded: 1817

Founder: Hugh Munro

Region: Highlands

Production capacity: 2,700,000 litres

Address: Alness, Ross-shire IV17 0XB

Tel: 01349 885 001

website: www.diageo.com

Parent Company: Diageo

Visitor Centre: Contact distillery for details

This distillery up beside the Cromarty Firth, in Easter Ross, was established by Captain Hugh Munro in 1817. It was named, not after a game of Scrabble when stuck with too many 'n's, but after the Captain's estate beside the River Alness a short distance upstream from Dalmore.

Whether it was originally just for personal consumption by the laird's family, Teaninich was only leased out in 1852. Thirty years later it had become quite a modern operation making up to 80,000 gallons of 'pure Highland Malt' a year. It was the first distillery north of Inverness to have electric light and even boasted a telephone linking it to the owner's

house and that of the excise officer. At the time Alness was a small country village a mile away across fields of barley and grazing cattle, while the distillery itself was surrounded by a broad belt of fir trees. Today Alness has expanded outwards such that Teaninich now sits in the middle of an industrial estate which is not quite how it began life under Captain Munro. Then again, extensive modernisation in the 1970s stripped Teaninich of any remaining old-world charm.

Expansion has also meant that there are now more-or-less two distilleries on site, whose spirit is vatted together as at Linkwood on Speyside before being filled into cask. As a 10 year-old in Diageo's Distillery Malt range, this is a lively, gently peat-smoked, citrus flavoured single malt.

The Cooling Jacket on Dalmore's Spirit Still

This ancient copper sleeve was made in 1874 and helps speed up the process of condensing the hot vapours into spirit.

**The Pagoda Roofs
of Glen Ord**

A traditional image of
whisky making – note the
blackened gables in front.

GLEN ORD

> **Pronunciation:** glen**ord**
>
> **Founded:** 1837
>
> **Founder:** D. MacLennan
>
> **Region:** Highlands
>
> **Production capacity:** 3,400,000 litres
>
> **Address:** Muir of Ord, Ross-shire IV6 7UJ
>
> **Tel:** 01463 872 004
>
> **website:** www.glenord.com
>
> **Parent Company:** Diageo
>
> **Visitor Centre:** March–June, Mon–Fri,
> 10am–5pm.
>
> July–September, Sat, 10am–5pm. Sunday,
> 12.30–4pm.
>
> November–February, 11.30am–3pm.

There were good historical omens for building a distillery in the village of Muir of Ord, between Beauly and Dingwall, in 1837. For a start this was within a few miles of the mighty Ferintosh, which by the end of its 100 year reign had become known throughout Scotland. Its demise prompted Robert Burns to write in 1784 'Thee, Ferintosh! O sadly lost! - Scotland lament frae coast to coast! ' in his poem 'Scotch Drink'.

Unfortunately Glen Ord began life leasing its site from a mill owner who had first crack at the water supply. After two bankruptcies, the widow of the second would-be distiller married a local banker who at least had the funds to maintain the operation. In the 1880s it was bought by James Watson & Co, a substantial blending operation in Dundee. When the company went bust in 1923, it was swallowed up by the joint forces of Dewar and Johnnie Walker. Glen Ord found itself part of a £2 million-plus package that included Pulteney and Parkmore distilleries and what was later described as 'one of the most important stocks of old whisky in the country.' That was no exaggeration considering the stocks amounted to a staggering eight million gallons!

After spending the Second World War in mothballs, Glen Ord was spruced up and connected to the National Grid, and then expanded in the 1960s when the number of stills tripled to three. Meanwhile a big modern malting plant was built alongside to supply UDV's seven northernmost distilleries, which meant that all Glen Ord's barley is malted on site, if not in the old-fashioned romantic way beneath its now-redundant pagoda. Having had all sorts of names from 'Muir of Ord' to 'Glenordie', the single malt has decided to settle for Glen Ord – a finely tuned 12 year-old that starts with a caramelised sweetness and seems to dry in the mouth.

TOMATIN

Pronunciation: to**mat**in

Founded: 1897

Founder: Tomatin-Spey District Distillery Co. Ltd

Region: Highlands

Production capacity: 7,000,000 litres

Address: Tomatin, Inverness-shire IV13 7YT

Tel: 01808 511 444

website: www.tomatin.com

Parent Company: Tomatin Distillery

Visitor Centre: All year, Mon–Fri, 9am–5pm, last tour 3.30pm.

May–September, Sat, 9am–1pm, last tour 12pm.

Closed Sundays.

The village of Tomatin is just off the A9 after the great north road has swung away from the Spey for its final run into Inverness. Far from the crowd on Speyside, the distillery looks isolated in the treeless, windswept site, almost 1000 feet up and surrounded by menacing peaks. Yet Tomatin hardly cowers beneath their presence, for it is a giant of a place, with no less than 23 stills, making it the largest malt whisky distillery in Scotland. Something about the scale is reminiscent of an old-style Soviet farm co-operative, the sort that processed grapes into vast quantities of bulk wine whether there was demand for it or not.

The Tomatin-Spey District Distillery Co. was established in 1897 and went bust eight years later. Soon it was back on its feet, eventually becoming a public limited company before going bankrupt for good in the mid-1980s, when the distillery became Japan's first venture into Scotch whisky.

The move into the big time league happened relatively recently. Up until 1956 it had existed on just one pair of stills. Thereafter Tomatin grew in leaps and bounds, doubling, and re-doubling its capacity every few years. Whether the distillery has ever been run flat out is another matter, and certainly the new owners are happy to have half the stills sitting idle which is something of a relief. After all, if they did go for broke and pump out 7 million litres of alcohol a year, Tomatin could create a whisky loch all on its own, which is not something the whisky business needs right now.

As well as supplying whisky for the 'Big T' blend, the distillery makes a nicely toffee-scented, quite peppery single malt in various ages from 10 years and up.

DALWHINNIE

Pronunciation: dal**hwin**ee

Founded: 1897

Founders: John Grant, Alex Mackenzie and George Sillar

Region: Highlands

Production capacity: 1,300,000 litres

Address: Dalwhinnie, Inverness-shire PH19 1AB

Tel: 01540 672 219

website: www.malts.com

Parent Company: Diageo

Visitor Centre: Easter–June, Mon–Fri, 9.30am–5pm. July–Sept, Mon–Sat, 9.30am–5pm. July-August, Sun, 12-4pm. October, Mon–Sat, 11am-4pm. November–Easter, Mon–Fri, 1–4pm.

Photographs of Dalwhinnie often show the distillery caked in snow above a caption declaring it to be 'the height of perfection', reinforcing the fact that this is the highest place in Britain making whisky – as far as the authorities know. It stands at just over 1000 feet above sea level in the heart of the Central Highlands. Anyone visiting Dalwhinnie is likely to hear tales of huge dumps of snow, of the time distillery workers had to come to work via the first-floor windows of their cottages, and of their children using the tops of telegraph poles for goal posts. In fact 20 ft drifts are not unheard off in this huge windswept bowl that lies between Loch Ericht and Glen Truim. According to the Met. Office the mean

The Modern Face of Glen Ord

Like many distilleries, Glen Ord underwent dramatic expansion in the 1960's in response to surging world-wide demand for Scotch.

139

annual temperature is just 6° C, making this the coldest inhabited place in Scotland and presumably Britain as well. So why did John Grant, Alex Mackenzie and George Sillar, three local men from Kingussie and Grantown-on-Spey, decide in 1897 to build what was then the Strathspey distillery in such sub-Siberian desolation?

Well, the romantic answer would be access to the cold, pure spring water that collects in the Lochan an Doire-uaine 2000 feet up in the Drumochter hills before flowing underground to emerge as the Allt an t-Sluic, or distillery burn. Though the water is crucial and may add to the surprising softness of the whisky made here, being right beside the railway was probably just as important. Far from being cut off, Dalwhinnie, whose name is Gaelic for meeting place, was strategically placed at a cross-roads. It was where the old droving routes that ran the length and breadth of the Highlands met; a place to rest and gather up the herd before continuing south over the Drumochter pass to market. Later it became an important junction in the eighteenth century road-building schemes of General Wade which linked up Fort William and Inverness.

The first spirit flowed from Strathspey in the spring of 1898 at the height of the speculative boom when the amount of whisky being produced in Scotland bore absolutely no relation to the amount being drunk. When the inevitable crash came, the

Strathspey distillery came tumbling after. By the autumn of 1898 it had been bought by the boss of a whisky firm in Leith for his son. The new owner re-christened it Dalwhinnie and hired the celebrated distillery architect, Charles Doig, to make 'considerable improvements' before selling out to Cooke & Bernheimer, the biggest distillers in America for £1250 in 1905. This was the first direct American involvement in whisky, beyond just drinking the stuff, and some in the industry feared it might be the start of a U.S. take-over. As if to compound such fears, Cooke & Berheimer immediately hoisted the Stars and Stripes above their massive warehouse in Leith where Scotch whiskies were blended 'to suit the American palate.'

But as things turned out US prohibition intervened in 1919 and Dalwhinnie slipped back into Scottish hands and the well-known blenders Macdonald Greenlees of Leith, who were in turn swallowed up by the Distillers Co. in 1926. Twelve years later it was licensed to James Buchanan & Co. as a key filling in their 'Black & White' blend with its famous Scottie dogs logo. The distillery's dark slate roofs and gleaming, whitewashed walls, are an obvious visual pun on the name.

Before the new A9 effectively by-passed the distillery in the 1970s, back when the 'Great North Road' ran past its door, the distillery must have felt less isolated than it does now. There would also have been many more people employed and hence a larger community of workers and their families clustered round the distillery. There was plenty of manual work since Dalwhinnie was never exactly state-of-the-art. When it suffered a bad fire in 1934, it was still being powered by steam engines as there was no electricity here or in the village. Without telephones or modern snow ploughs it would have to have been a pretty self-sufficient operation especially in the depths of winter.

According to the current manager this spirit of self sufficiency is alive and well, such that the day-to-day running of Dalwhinnie is largely left to the distillery workers themselves. In the old days, provided there was sufficient stocks of grain and fuel to fire the stills and heat the kilns, whisky could be made here whatever the weather even when the place was completely cut off by snow. The barley was malted on site right up until 1968.

Because it was built facing the railway line to which it was connected with its own siding, Dalwhinnie now appears rather back-to-front. As a result the first thing you notice today, are a pair of raised up, wooden worm tubs steaming away in the outside air. The fact they now enjoy pride of place is just as it should be, since using an old-fashioned copper worm as opposed to a modern condenser helps capture the essence of Dalwhininie. The heavy, almost sulphurous spirit is achieved by having two large, broad-necked stills which allow the vapours to rise up easily with little reflux and then condensing them back into liquid as quickly as possible. The aim is to keep the contact with copper to a minimum — too much and you would get a much lighter spirit. You might make a nice whisky, but it wouldn't be Dalwhinnie.

Even now the rate at which the stills can be run is partly determined by the temperature of the water to cool the worm. In a mild year when the snow disappears early off the surrounding hills, the water in the burn can start to warm up by the summer, forcing the stillman to slow down the stills. Any drop in quantity is clearly going to have an impact on the costs of production. So perhaps the reason for building a distillery here within reach of some of the coldest, clearest water in the Highlands wasn't so romantic after all.

THE EASTERN HIGHLANDS

Angus and Aberdeenshire had plenty going for it as a whisky region in the nineteenth century. Its distillers had some of the best barley grown in Scotland on their doorstep and a ready market keen to drink the proceeds from Aberdeen to Dundee and all the coastal towns in between. No fewer than 76 distilleries were built here, but barely a handful have survived into the present. In fact now that Montrose has lost Glenesk and Glencadam has been mothballed in Brechin, there is only one distillery left south of Aberdeen. The city itself has seen a dozen distilleries come and go, the last being Strathdee which survived for over hundred years before being closed for good in 1938.

Though the region started out with many more licensed stills than Speyside, it was effectively passed over in the great building spree of the 1880s and 90s when so many wannabe-Glenlivets were built further north. Perhaps the whole whisky boom on Speyside simply pushed the eastern Highlands into the shade, and they never really recovered.

Due west of Aberdeen is Royal Lochnagar in the heart of Royal Deeside beside Balmoral. By today's standards this would classify as a boutique distillery making less than half a million litres each year, but by the end of the nineteenth century it was producing enough to fill eight warehouses in Aberdeen. It was also a key filling in Vat 69.

The city's most famous whisky was the predominantly Speyside blend, Chivas Regal. It was the flagship of Chivas Brothers on King Street — a grocery store to rival Fortnum & Mason in London. At its height it supplied everyone from Queen Victoria to the Emperor of Austria with anything from tinned ox tongues to 'curious brandies' to wax and sperm candles. Whisky was bottled in the shop's basement, and included some of the earliest aged blends which later became known as 'deluxe whiskies'. Chivas Regal remains a huge international brand with sales of around 3 million cases a year. The shop has long gone and is now a Chinese restaurant at 13 King Street.

North of Aberdeen by Oldmeldrum, the long-established Glen Garioch was brought back into production in 1997 after a period in mothballs. Meanwhile Glendronach has been idle since the mid 1990s, leaving its stable mate Ardmore, close by at Kennethmont, to carry the Teachers blend. A couple more are up on the north coast of Aberdeenshire on the edge of Speyside around Banff. MacDuff produces whisky for the William Lawson blend and its own single malt — Glen Deveron, while Glenglassaugh has been shut down, seemingly for good.

Tomatin Distillery Beside the Alt Fritte Burn

With its 23 stills and the capacity to produce no less than 7 million litres of alcohol a year, it is hard to believe this was just a modest distillery with a single pair of stills as recently as 1956.

Dalwhinnie – Scotland's Highest Distillery

At just over 1000 ft. the average annual temperature is a cool 6 deg.C.

ROYAL BRACKLA

> **Pronunciation: brack**la
>
> **Founded:** 1812
>
> **Founder:** William Fraser
>
> **Region:** Highlands
>
> **Production capacity:** 2,400,000 litres
>
> **Address:** Cawdor, Nairn, Morayshire IV12 5QY
>
> **Tel:** 01667 402 002
>
> **website:** www.dewars.com
>
> **Parent Company:** Bacardi
>
> **Visitor Centre:** Contact distillery for details

The Brackla distillery was not born into the Royal Family, but it took just 23 years for its owner, Captain William Fraser, to secure a Warrant from the king in 1835. The early years as a licensed distillery competing with the flood of moonshine flowing out of Glen Livet cannot have been easy, but once the Excise Act came in and he had William IV's blessing, Fraser was on a roll. Soon early advertisements were calling it 'The King's Own Whisky' and urging Londoners to seek out a bottle from Graham & Co. 'opposite the Marylebone workhouse.' Fined for

misconduct five times from 1827 onwards, Fraser may have risked losing his royal status, but when Queen Victoria arrived on the throne the Warrant was duly extended. A few years later Fraser decided to play by the rules, having paid out one final fine of £600.

The distillery was rebuilt in 1890 and then passed through a series of blenders and brokers in Aberdeen before belatedly joining the great whale of the whisky trade, DCL, midway through the Second World War.

When the time came to modernise Royal Brackla and add an extra pair of stills in 1970, the refurbishment was somewhat stark. The glass-fronted shed with corrugated steel-roof – is not exactly in the Prince Charles school of architecture, but then Deeside is some distance away. If United Distillers had put Royal Lochnagar through the same sort of re-fit, His Highness might well have had something to say, what with Lochnagar being on Balmoral's doorstep. The distillery now belongs to Bacardi.

DALLAS DHU

> **Pronunciation:** dallas **doo**
>
> **Founded:** 1899
>
> **Founder:** Wright & Greig
>
> **Region:** Highlands
>
> **Address:** Mannachie Road, Forres, Morayshire IV36 2RR
>
> **Tel:** 01309 676 548
>
> **website:** www.historic-scotland.net
>
> **Parent Company:**
> In the care of Historic Scotland
>
> **Visitor Centre:** Contact distillery for details

Prettier than its Forres neighbour, Balmenach, but no longer in production, Dallas Dhu is now a whisky museum, like Bladnoch way down in Galloway.

Unlike Bladnoch, however, which does still produce a little whisky, a trip round Dallas Dhu will not satisfy all the senses because distilling stopped here in 1983. As a result the stillroom lacks the warmth and those beautiful spirity fumes given off by a working still. For all that, the museum's curators, Historic Scotland, do their best to create the atmosphere of a fully functioning, traditional malt distillery with models of distillery workers who deliver their pre-recorded spiel at the press of a button.

Having peeked into the stills, crawled over the mash tun and played with the spirit safe you can sample 'Roderick Dhu', a blend that contains a little of Dallas Dhu.

The distillery was built in 1899 by Alexander Edward, only to be sold a year later. Then, in common with about half the distilleries on Speyside, it was swallowed up by DCL. After closing for most of the 1930s it re-opened, only to suffer a serious fire in 1939. If it had been a remote rural distillery it would have burnt to the ground, as it was, the local Forres fire brigade took four hours to bring the blaze under control.

There were never any complaints with the whisky which was sumptuously smooth and sweet, and well regarded by blenders, but its water supply from the Scourie burn could be erratic. Also, Dallas Dhu never quite embraced the twentieth century, still relying on a waterwheel for some of its power as late as 1971. This is part of its charm, but perhaps one reason why it is now a museum.

MACDUFF

Founded: 1962

Founder: Consortium including George Crawford, Morty Dykes and Brodie Hepburn

Region: Highlands

Production capacity: 2,500,000 litres

Address: Banff, Banffshire AB4 3JT

Tel: 01261 812 612

website: www.dewars.com

Parent Company: Bacardi

Visitor Centre: By appointment only, contact distillery for details

In the 1960s something of the same air of excitement was blowing down the Spey that had last blown this way 70 years before. The depression and the war-time restrictions that followed were well in the past, and Scotch whisky was enjoying a golden period. Demand was expanding on all fronts, new markets were opening up all the time, and every stillroom on Speyside was feeling the heat. Against this background, a consortium of various business interests began building a two-still distillery they called MacDuff, in 1962.

It sits beside the river Deveron facing the coastal town of Banff, and soon acquired another pair of stills. Being on the right bank, looking towards the sea, theoretically makes Macduff an 'Eastern Highland' malt, but as a 12 year old, sold as 'Glen Deveron', it is every inch a Speyside, in its gentle, lingering, sweet-natured way. The distillery was bought in 1972 by William Lawson, the Liverpool whisky blenders who had recently moved back to Scotland. Ever since, Macduff has provided the heart and soul of the company's eponymous blend. Today it is all part of the Bacardi empire which means 'William Lawson's' gets to share a stable with the infinitely more famous Dewar's 'White Label'.

ARDMORE

Pronunciation: ardmore

Founded: 1898

Founder: Adam Teacher

Region: Highlands

Production capacity: 3,530,000 litres

Address: Kennethmont, Aberdeenshire AB54 4NH

Tel: 01464 831 213

website: www.allieddomecqplc.com

Parent Company: Allied Domecq

Visitor Centre: Contact distillery for details

Crossing the river Deveron at Huntly heading east, the whisky towns of the Spey with their skylines of pagoda roofs and chimney stacks have long slipped into the distance. There is plenty of good barley grown here, but not much distillation going on, on the road to Kennethmont. But just beyond this small village, stuck out on the hillside, is one last bastion of whisky-making in the north-east in the shape of Ardmore. The name actually comes from the west coast of Scotland near the ancestral home of the Teacher family.

The rags to riches rise of William Teacher is a classic tale of 'can do Victorian spirit'. Born in 1811, he joined his mother at a cotton spinning mill at the age of seven, having had just six months' education at the local village school. His first break was becoming apprenticed to a Glasgow tailor whose wife taught him from books as he stitched in the workroom, and his second was marrying Agnes McDonald in 1834.

Agnes inherited a grocery store from her mother in Anderston, just west of the city, which William helped run. First he obtained a licence to sell drink, and then, some time later, opened a shop of his own at No. 50 Cheapside Street, down by the Glasgow docks. By the 1850s Teacher had decided to move from selling bottled whisky to selling glasses of his own vattings over the counter. At first these would have been malts, but with the change in the law in the 1860s he moved on to selling blends.

No other blender was as directly involved as William Teacher with the end consumer. Teacher's dram shops became a famous institution in and around Glasgow that lasted until 1960.

There were already eighteen in the chain by 1876, the year William died, to be succeeded by his youngest son, Adam, four years later. The company's most popular blend became the 'Highland Cream' brand. With demand growing at home and abroad — the first shipment arrived in New Zealand in 1878 — there was an increasing need to control production to ensure supply.

Adam Teacher was actively looking for a site to build a distillery when he went to stay at Leith Hall, the fine eighteenth-century manor house on the edge of Kennethmont that now belongs to the National Trust for Scotland. While there he discovered an excellent source of spring water on the nearby hill of Knockandy. In 1895 a suitable plot of land was found and three years later, construction of Ardmore began.

Just before completion and the first run of spirit in the summer of 1899, Adam Teacher died. Ardmore was built on a grand scale, and as with John Dewar and Aberfeldy, the proximity of the railway was crucial. An early advertisement for 'Teacher's Old Scotch Whiskies' shows Ardmore as an industrial, large-scale distillery right beside the tracks on the main Aberdeen to Inverness line. It was ambitious in scale but left the business saddled with punitive interest charges for years at a time when whisky was deep in the doldrums.

The distillery was powered by a giant steam engine until the late 1950s, by which point a second pair of stills had been added. Further expansion in the seventies gave Ardmore the capacity to produce 3.5 million litres of alcohol a year by doubling the number of stills to eight, all of them exact copies of the original design of Adam Teacher in 1899. Soon after, in 1976, the old family firm was bought out by Allied Breweries.

To this day, most of the malt goes to make Teacher's Highland Cream such a fine blend. Some is bottled as a luscious, quite oily single malt whose initial sweetness fades on the tongue to a dry, smoky finish.

GLENDRONACH

Pronunciation: glen**dron**ach

Founded: 1826

Founder: James Allardyce

Region: Highlands

Address: Forgue, By Huntly, Aberdeenshire
AB54 6DB

Tel: 01466 730 202

website: www.allieddomecqplc.com

Parent Company: Allied Domecq

Visitor Centre:
All year, Mon–Fri, 10am–2pm.

Just a short drive north, past Huntly on the other side of the main Aberdeen – Inverness road, lies Glendronach, the spiritual sister to Ardmore and fellow contributor to the Teacher's blend. The family connection goes back a lot further than 1960, when Wm. Teacher & Sons bought the distillery. Whether the distillery's malt was already a component part of 'Highland Cream' when Ardmore was built is another matter, but if so it may explain why Adam Teacher was looking in that part of the world.

Glendronach sits in a dip amidst the rolling hills of the Valley of Forgue [or 'brambles'] beside the Dronach burn. It was established by the Glendronach Distillery Co, a partnership of local farmers and traders, headed by James Allardyce, in 1826. The company was still going strong when Alfred Barnard, visited in the 1880s, while compiling 'The Whisky Distilleries of the United Kingdom'. Barnard described it as 'quaint and picturesque, and puts the production at 'pure Highland Malt' at 50,000 gallons a year. He also mentions a rookery in the trees surrounding 'the charming House of Glendronach'. The presence of rooks was meant to bestow good luck on the distillery – a custom dating from the days of illicit stills when the birds would act as an early warning system if anyone approached.

The Gledronach Distillery Company was bought out by a whisky firm in Leith just before the Pattison crash in 1899, and was 'acquired by the Crown' during the First World War. In 1920 the distillery was bought by Captain Charles Grant, younger son of William Grant of Glenfiddich, in whose family it remained for the next forty years.

Apart from adding a second pair of stills in 1966, the new owners have done little to alter the old-world charm of Glendronach. The warehouses have retained their traditional earth floor and the stills are still fired

by direct flame, or rather they would be if Glendronach was actually operating. The distillery was mothballed by Allied Distillers in the late 1990s and not a drop of whisky has been produced since. At least it is genuinely 'mothballed', and kept in readiness for the day when demand for Scotch, and especially 'Teacher's', picks up. Sometimes the term 'mothballed' can be a euphemism for permanent closure, but so far that does not seem the case at Glendronach. Tour groups are still taken round, and despite the quiet and the depressingly cold stills, there is much to see. For a start Glendronach, along with a tiny handful of distilleries, has retained its own floor maltings, which last malted barley, some grown in the adjacent fields, in 1997. The single malt is a golden, medium dry 12 year-old, quite spicy and with good length.

GLEN GARIOCH

Pronunciation: glen**geer**ee

Founded: 1798

Founder: Thomas Simpson

Region: Highlands

Production capacity: 1,000,000 litres

Address: Old Meldrum, Aberdeenshire AB5 0ES

Tel: 01651 873 450

website: www.morrisonbowmore.co.uk

Parent Company: Suntory

Visitor Centre: Contact distillery for details

This attractive, traditional stone-built distillery, stands in the old market town of Old Meldrum, 18 miles north of Aberdeen on the road to Banff. Built by Thomas Simpson in 1798, and still with some of its original buildings intact, one wonders how many distilleries it has seen come and go in the last 200 years. Today it stands as something of a lone outpost, a sole survivor among the whisky-making fraternity in this lush pocket of Aberdeenshire farmland.

It was surrounded by some of the best barley in the country, but unfortunately ran into occasional problems with its water supply from the nearby Percock hill. By the 1880s Glen Garioch was producing around 50,000 gallons a year from its two stills and belonged to J.F. Thomson, a firm of blenders in Leith.

At some point the quality of this hefty, peat-packed malt caught the eye of William Sanderson, who had just started bottling Vat 69. How much Glen Garioch went into the famous blend is unclear, but Sanderson liked the distillery enough to buy it in 1908. Some sixty years later it was bought by Morrison Bowmore whose whisky empire is widespread if not vast. Always keen on conservation, the new owners diverted waste heat from the kilns into greenhouses to grow tomatoes on a commercial scale. Later the same idea was applied to Bowmore on Islay where the excess heat was used to heat the town pool.

As a single malt, the peat content has been reduced to release Glen Garioch's underlying flavours of heather-blossom, and a faint prickle of spice.

Royal Lochnagar on Deeside

Discreetly hidden from the main road, this boutique distillery is barely a stone's throw from Balmoral.

ROYAL LOCHNAGAR

Pronunciation: lokhna**gar**

Founded: 1845

Founder: John Begg

Region: Highland

Production capacity: 400,000 litres

Address: Crathie, Ballater, Aberdeenshire AB35 5TB

Tel: 01339 742 700

website: www.malts.com

Parent Company: Diageo

Visitor Centre: May–September, Mon–Sat, 10am– 5pm. Sun, 12–4pm.

October–April, Mon–Fri, 11am–4pm.

This small, wonderfully discreet distillery is tucked away off the main road which follows the north side of the river Dee all the way to the sea. Coming from the west you drive past rows of Scots pines – the remnants of the great Caledonian forest – before turning south at Crathie as if visiting Balmoral. With the Queen just a mile away, Royal Lochnagar is at the epicentre of 'Royal Deeside' – a concept that the tourist board chiefs and estate agents have extended right down the valley as far as the suburbs of Aberdeen.

The first Lochnagar distillery was set up in 1825 on the north bank of the river by James Robertson of Crathie, a one-time smuggler who had decided to go straight. Unfortunately it was burnt down some years later, in an arson attack by another smuggler who had evidently decided not to go straight. What remained was washed away by a great spate the following year.

The next incarnation was on the southside of the river, set up by the firm of Begg & Buyers in 1845 as the New Lochnagar distillery. The name comes from the 3800 ft peak of the same name that the poet Byron described as the 'most sublime and picturesque amongst our Caledonian Alps.' Byron had stayed here as a boy when recovering from scarlet fever.

It was an ideal setting for a distillery. There was no shortage of water for cooling worms and mixing with the mash. This flowed from a mountain spring down a series of burns to collect behind the Cragnagall dam where it formed a reservoir. There were peats to be had from nearby moors and good quality barley from the distillery's own farm. And to consume the spent grains there were a hundred head of cattle.

Three years after it was built Queen Victoria and Prince Albert moved into Balmoral next door and after an invitation from John Begg, decided to call on the distillery with their children that September. 'We have come to see through your works, Mr Begg,' Prince Albert declared, and with that the royals were led on possibly the world's first distillery tour. Afterwards Begg recorded every detail of the trip in his diary.

[At the end of the tour] 'I called for a bottle and glasses and, presenting one glass to Her Majesty, she tasted it. So also did his Royal Highness the Prince. I then presented a glass to the Princess Royal and to the Prince of Wales and Prince Alfred, all of whom tasted the spirit.' ... as they progressed to the still house, Prince Alfred, noting the spirit safe said 'I see you have got your locks there'. On my replying 'These are the Queen's locks', Her Majesty took a very hearty laugh.' What beggars belief when you consider the

hoops of protocol you would have to go through now, Begg's invitation was only delivered to Balmoral at 9pm the evening before!

In 1851 John Begg became sole proprietor and once the first orders began rolling in from Balmoral, Lochnagar quickly changed its prefix from 'New' to 'Royal'. Apart from the prestige, they were good, regular customers – there were all those decanters to fill in the various royal residences and there was John Brown's hip flask. Once Prince Albert died, the Queen spent increasing amounts of time in the Highlands with her loyal man-servant, prompting much gossip at Court. One story doing the rounds was that on one occasion Brown was so 'drink taken' that he stumbled and fell flat on his face, at which point the Queen instantly announced that she too had felt the earth move.

Much of the whisky's early role was in Vat 69, blended by Begg's friend, William Sanderson. Begg himself was involved in blending and as the business grew, he established an office in Aberdeen with eight bonded warehouses along the water-front. The distillery was rebuilt in 1906, and then bought out by Dewars ten years later. With its grey granite walls, solitary pair of rather dumpy stills and three-storey

Maintenance work in the mash tun at Lochnagar

warehouse, it remains little changed. In terms of production it is the smallest owned by its parent company, Diageo – pumping out just 430,000 litres of spirit per annum. For all its size, Royal Lochnagar is clearly a cherished jewel in the company's portfolio. With the woodwork picked out in matt blue paint after a £2 million refurbishment it has become a showcase for all the malt whiskies produced by Diageo. It also plays host to the various malt advocates' courses which teach whisky salesmen round the world all about single malts. They get a total immersion in whisky for four or five days. In the warehouse are casks from a wide range of the company's distilleries so that those who have come here to learn can taste and compare different whiskies at different stages in their up-bringing drawn straight from the barrel.

As for Royal Lochnagar it is used in premium expressions of Johnnie Walker, for the blue and the gold labels. Nowadays the royal connection is played down. There are occasional visits from Balmoral, though arranged with more warning than Queen Victoria's, and Prince Charles did come here on an official visit to mark the distillery's 150th birthday in 1995. There is a photo of the Prince clutching a bottle of Royal Lochnagar's 'Selected Reserve', wearing that worried, hang-dog expression of his. Lips slightly parted, he seems to saying 'How much, did you say it was worth !?' The answer is the best part of £200 a bottle. For something slightly more affordable, is the standard 12 year-old – an amber, sweet-scented malt with a curiously rich, buttery flavour.

FETTERCAIRN

Pronunciation: fetter**cairn**

Founded: 1824

Founder: Jas. Stewart

Region: Highlands

Production capacity: 1,600,000 litres

Address: Distillery Road, Fettercairn, Laurencekirk, Kincardineshire AB30 1XY

Tel: 01561 340 205

website: www.kyndal.co.uk

Parent Company: Kyndal International Ltd

Visitor Centre: May–September, Mon–Sat, 10am–4pm.

Situated in the prime barley-growing country of the Mearns in Kincardineshire, this is one of the few distilleries on the east coast south of Aberdeen to have survived into the twenty-first century. The area had all the raw ingredients, but never the safety in numbers nor the prestige of neighbouring Speyside.

The original distillery was two miles from the village of Fettercairn and sat higher up the slopes of the Cairn o'Mount, the hill which guards one of the prettiest routes over the Grampians and down into Deeside. In the 1860s Queen Victoria herself made the trip, declaring that Fettercairn was 'a small, quiet town'. The whole place erupted at such heartfelt

praise and immediately set about building a commemorative arch in celebration.

The distillery was a grain mill which was converted into a licensed distillery as soon as the 1823 Excise Act was passed. Various private individuals tried and failed to make a go of it, until the Fettercairn Distillery Co. was formed in 1887 with Sir John Gladstone as chairman. This no doubt inspired his son William, the famous Liberal Prime Minister, to enshrine the concept of the 'Angel's Share' in law. As a result distilleries were no longer taxed on the estimated two per cent that evaporates from a cask each year. Today that is a saving to the whisky business, or a loss to the Treasury – depending on your point of view – of, very roughly, £14 million a year, if my maths is correct.

Fettercairn was bought for the Americans by the Scottish-born whisky magnate, Joseph Hobbs, on the eve of World War Two, and then passed to Whyte & Mackay in the 1970s, in whose eponymous blend much of the malt disappears.

CENTRAL HIGHLANDS

Moving in a sweep round from Loch Lomond to Perth taking in the Campsie Fells and the Ochils, there are currently five malt distilleries in operation. If you follow the Tay upstream along the A9 to the Drumochter Pass and Loch Ericht and then loop back to Loch Lomond you can add another four distilleries. This total of nine is all that survives out

of almost 130 licensed distilleries that were known to have been producing whisky at some point in the region. Add in all the illicit stills and this area was probably producing more malt whisky than anywhere else in Scotland. The smugglers had a good passing trade along the old drove routes that snaked across

Scotland, connecting upland grazing with the giant Lowland cattle markets like Falkirk. In the little pocket of land around Glengoyne there were as many as twenty unlicensed stills operating at one stage. The burgeoning Lowland towns provided a ready market.

On the other hand these were probably the first to be stamped out as the campaign to crack-down on illicit whisky-making moved northwards into the Highlands. Then at the other end of the eighteenth century there was a demand for 'Perthshire malts' to add their characteristic sweet, floral body and dry finish to the newly created blends. Perth was long-established in the drinks trade, principally wine, and was also an important hub of the railways. It was perfectly placed to become a major centre of the whisky business and was soon home to the big blending houses like Arthur Bell & Sons and Matthew 'Famous Grouse' Gloag. It was entirely due to the demand for their 'White Label' brand, that the Perth-based firm of Dewars built Aberfeldy in 1896.

EDRADOUR

Pronunciation: eedra**dowr**
Founded: 1825
Founder: John McGlashan
Region: Highlands
Production capacity: 90,000 litres
Address: Pitlochry, Perthshire PH16 5JP
Tel: 01796 472 095
website: www.edradour.com
Parent Company: Signatory Vintage Scotch Whisky Ltd.
Visitor Centre: March–October, Mon–Sat, 9.30am–5pm. Sun, 12–5pm. November–Mid-December, Mon–Sat, 10am–4pm.

When the big bosses of the booze trade periodically worry that too much whisky is being made, the last place they look is Edradour in the hills beyond the Perthshire town of Pitlochry. This dolls'-house distillery is the smallest in Scotland, and its annual production of 90,000 gallons, is what a self-respecting Speyside distillery pumps out in a week.

This last survivor of the many Perthshire farm distilleries went legal soon after the Excise Act of 1823. It was a cottage industry then and remains so today, and the methods used are as traditional as you will find. There is the 1930s refrigerator to cool the wort (the mix of grist and hot water) at one end of the

processes to the use of a copper worm at the other. If the quality of smuggled Highland whisky owed something to the tiny size of the pot stills used, then it can only help Edradour, whose stills are just above the legal minimum.

Edradour was used in premium aged blends like House of Lords, which was slipped into the US market in the 1930s inside steel torpedoes fired at night to land on the beach. Later it went into the King's Ransom, a super-deluxe blend created by William Whiteley who bought the distillery in 1933. It was the world's most expensive whisky when 200,000 bottles went down aboard the *SS Politician* wrecked off Eriskay in the Outer Hebrides in 1941 bound for America. This was the inspiration behind Compton Mackenzie's *Whisky Galore*.

Edradour – A Classic Farm Distillery
Before blended Scotch became a global spirit, virtually all whisky made in the Highlands would have been on this scale.

Loading the Draff
This by-product of the mashing process is mixed with pot-ale, the residue from the wash, to make a protein-rich cattle cake, known as dark grains.

BLAIR ATHOL

Pronunciation: blair**ath**ol

Founded: 1798

Founder: John Stewart and Robert Robertson

Region: Highlands

Production capacity: 2,000,000 litres

Address: Pitlochry, Perthshire PH16 5LY

Tel: 01796 482 003

website: www.diageo.com

Parent Company: Diageo

Visitor Centre: November–Easter, Mon–Fri, 1–4pm.

Easter–September, Mon–Sat, 9.30am–5pm.

June–September, also Sunday, 2–5pm.

October, Mon–Fri, 10am–4pm.

The village of Blair Atholl and its famous castle are actually two or three miles down the road from the distillery, which sits just off the A9 on the southern edge of Pitlochry. While Ben Nevis distillery has every right to the name of Britain's highest mountain given how it sits in its shadow, Blair Athol is stretching a point. This tourist boom-town and 'gateway to the Highlands' is largely the creation of the Victorian era when all things of a heathery or tartan disposition were deeply cherished.

Back in 1798, when Pitlochry was just a village, John Stewart and Robert Robertson began a distillery here. There are some doubts over its precise name; it may have been Aldour - 'the burn of the otter' – or the Pitlochry distillery, no one is quite sure. Either way it soon floundered. There was nothing wrong with the location – there was good access to water from the Kinnaird Burn fed by the run-off from Ben Vrackie and there were plentiful supplies of local barley. But there was also a thriving underground trade to compete with, and given the way taxation on spirits was then levied it was extremely hard for anyone to run a viable business out of making whisky as opposed to moonshine. Unless you were into serious volumes that is, which was clearly not the case at this little, farmyard operation. Still at least it meant Blair Athol could celebrate its two hundredth anniversary recently.

In the 1820's, the distillery was resuscitated by Alexander Connacher and began to flourish under the more enlightened tax regime ushered in by the Excise Act of 1823. Meanwhile down the road in Perth, a young boy had recently moved up from London with his family. The boy was Arthur Bell who, at the age of fifteen, was to join Sandeman & Roy, a local firm of wine & spirit merchants. He was later to achieve fame with his top-selling blend – a blend which almost from the start had Blair Athol at its heart. He began as a traveller, taking orders and collecting money from a variety of inns, hotels and private customers. At some point he started buying whisky for the firm which made him a partner in 1851. This whisky,

The Ivy-Clad Walls
of Blair Athol Distillery

Blair Athol in Bond

Filling the spirit into casks to begin the slow process of maturation is all done 'in bond' – under lock and key. Only when it is released from bond prior to bottling does excise duty become payable.

The Stillroom at Blair Athol

A sense of calm has returned to Blair Athol, after the mad dash for growth that took Bells to the top of the charts as Britain's best-selling blend in the 1970's.

bought from grain distilleries like Cameronbridge in Fife and malt distilleries like the nearby Edradour, was clearly being used to make blends. When asked for the recipe by a customer in 1867, he replied "I do not usually give the mixture of my whiskies, but may mention that the best is made in Banffshire's Glenlivet district and the others are Pitlochry and Stirlingshire whiskies.' The Pitlochry whisky was almost certainly Blair Athol.

The first known connection between what was now Arthur Bell & Sons and Connacher came in 1873 when Bell took on the agency to sell Connacher's malt in Glasgow. It proved as unsuccessful a venture as the company's earlier attempts to enter the London market for blended whisky. Arthur Bell then found himself caught up with the law after Connacher was caught trying to fiddle his Excise receipts. For Arthur Bell, a slightly nervous fellow at the best of times with an almost pathological fear of debt and impropriety, it was a terrible blow. The feeling of being wronged never left him.

By looks and inclination Arthur Bell had more than a touch of Captain Mainwaring about him – as in the bumbling, provincial bank-manager of 'Dad's Army'. He was a most unlikely whisky baron – there was nothing flash about him like Tommy Dewar; in fact he refused to allow any advertising or even for his name to appear on his blends which, in any case, he preferred to sell in bulk.

In 1882, Connacher sold out to Peter McKenzie, a wine and spirits broker from Liverpool, who extended and improved the lay-out of the distillery, upping production to 60,000 gallons a year from the single pair of stills. It was fitted out with all the latest distilling equipment and according to one contemporary report used 'none but the finest quality of barley' and had its 'peat brought from Orkney' which must have been quite a trek in those days.

Having relied on the whisky for its main blend for

**The Distillery Burn –
Blair Athol**

The spring-fed water from
Ben Vrackie is diverted past
the distillery to mix in the
mash tuns, cool the
condensers and reduce
the new-make spirit to
its filling strength. What
remains flows back into
the River Tummel.

so long, Arthur Bell & Sons finally bought Blair Athol in 1933. It was their first venture into distilling, but curiously the recently mothballed distillery was not brought back into production until 1949. By the 1970s, when Blair Athol gained another pair of stills, it was clear that the mother company was on a roll.

As Bell's cranked up the stills to increase production by 300 per cent in an all-out campaign to increase volume and steam ahead of their rivals, some of the quality considerations may have gone astray. If you work the stills too hard eventually unpleasant compounds like fusel oils manage to stray up the neck of the still, through the condensers and into the final cut. Some of the distilling equipment was showing its age and complaints began to surface that not only was Blair Athol not what it used to be, but that its role as the heart and soul of Bell's was doing the blend no favours.

Now in the hands of Diageo after one of the most bitterly contested take-over battles in the industry's history, Bell's has changed radically, becoming an 8 year-old with over a third of the blend now composed of malt whisky. Not for nothing is it still Britain's most popular blended whisky. If Bells ever crashed, perhaps plucked to death by that Famous Grouse, the distillery would go down with it. With half the bottles going through the distillery shop, there is not much chance that sales of its 12 year-old malt will somehow sustain Blair Athol the distillery.

ABERFELDY

Pronunciation: aber**fel**dee

Founded: 1898

Founder: John Dewar & Sons

Region: Highlands

Production capacity: 1,800,000 litres

Address: Aberfeldy, Perthshire PH15 2EB

Tel: 01887 822 010

website: www.dewarsworldofwhisky.com

Parent Company: Bacardi

Visitor Centre: April–October, Mon–Sat, 10am–6pm. Sun, 12–4pm. November–March, Mon–Fri, 10am–4pm. Last tour one hour before closing. Groups by appointment.

The verdant, undulating uplands of the Tay valley beyond Perth were for many years a hotbed of illicit distillation. Home-grown whisky evolved organically out of the myriad of little farms in the district, its supply spreading outwards from just friends and family to passing trade to the larger towns. As you turn off what is now the A9 at Ballinluig and cross over the River Tummel to follow the Tay westwards to Aberfeldy you enter what was

broken up and a few casks were confiscated. The four tending the still that night escaped and fled to America, only to return ten years later as respectable members of society.

The Grandtully distillery itself had been producing whisky, albeit on a tiny scale of just 5000 gallons a year, for over seventy years when Dewar's, the famous firm of blenders from Perth, decided to set up a distillery of their own. Their main brand, White Label, had become one of the best-selling Scotch whiskies of its day, and they needed to be sure of a supply of good-quality Perthshire malt for their blend. At the time, speculators were buying up stock and sitting on it, forcing up the price of whiskies required by the blending houses.

The decision to move a little further west of Grandtully to the edge of the gentle, Perthshire town of Aberfeldy was partly family attachment and partly sound commercial logic. The site had a fine source of water and was near to the main railway line so that it could be linked directly to Dewar's new headquarters in Perth. It was also just a few miles from the croft where the original John Dewar was born. According to family folklore he had walked all the way to Perth where he founded the firm of John Dewar & Sons in 1846. It was a growing business engaged in wines and spirits, but its success was purely local. It took his two sons, John and Tommy Dewar, to transform the family name into a big brand, sold throughout the world.

Aberfeldy had grown up around the last of the many bridges built by General Wade as part of his campaign to tame the Highlands after Bonnie Prince Charlie and the revolt of 1745. It was also where the Black Watch standard was first raised. The town had already seen the demise of the Pitillie distillery in 1867, and waited to see what Dewar's could do on the 12 acres they leased from the Marquis of Breadalbane.

The first spirit flowed from Aberfeldy's two stills in 1898 and was put in casks which were dispatched via a siding onto the railway for warehousing in Perth where it would go for blending. Sales of the blends were growing, but the rivalry with other whiskies, notably Buchanan's Black & White, was becoming increasingly intense. 'Competition is the breath of business, but the death of profits,' declared Tommy Dewar, and with that John Dewar & Sons decided to merge with their age-old rivals, James Buchanan & Co, in 1915.

Ten years later the joint company decided to come under the fold of the Distillers' Company, and brought with them a fistful of other distilleries to add to Aberfeldy.

The distillery was closed during the Second World War, and then reopened in much its original

Aberfeldy and the Dewar's Pipe Major

The bronze statue was a gift from the Schenley Corporation, Dewar's American importers, to mark the brand's centenary in 1986. The Pipe Major stares over to the site of the croft where the original John Dewar was born.

once true bandit country in the war against smuggling.

Among the many bothies that housed illicit stills, was a lone farmhouse on top of a hill near Grandtully, half way between Aberfeldy and the main road north. According to legend, a trapdoor in the kitchen floor led beneath the farmhouse to a wide underground cave through which water was channelled for making whisky. The still was hidden in the cave's depths, while the smoke from the fire was carried seventy yards by a flue up through the trapdoor and out through the farmhouse chimney. It was a brilliant disguise and for years the gaugers were none the wiser until one of the locals grassed. There was a midnight raid and the still, tubs and worm were form until the early 1970s when the stillhouse was rebuilt to house an additional pair of stills. From the outside the extension sits a little uneasily next to the weathered stone of the original late-Victorian distillery. But from the inside looking out, with the shutters pulled right up as they are for much of the year, the view is superb. It is great to feel the cool fresh air mingling with the heat from the four pairs of copper stills. Needless to say the shutters come down at week-ends and in winter, otherwise snow would blow in.

Below stands the sculpture of the famous Pipe Major facing up the glen to the croft. His image has adorned every bottle of the White Label brand beneath a necklace of medals garnered in the last decade of the nineteenth century. Today the distillery has become something of a shrine to the blend, after the £2 million 'Dewar's World of Whisky' opened in 2000.

Visitors wander at their own pace after spending time sitting in a plush red armchair watching a short video about the life and times of Tommy Dewar. Displays trace how the brand's advertising has evolved to the Pipe Major's latest bare-chested incarnation carrying a surf-board in the 'just add water' campaign. There is a faithful reconstruction of the blending room in Dewar House in Perth as it would have been in 1929, as well as Tommy Dewar's London office. You can even try your hand at a spot of blending with the help of the interactive master blender. Unlike every other distillery tour which is keen to promote the individual fruit of their stills, the Aberfeldy experience is entirely focussed on blends, and at the end you get offered a dram of White Label. This is however, one of the few places you can obtain a drop of Aberfeldy as a single malt with its scent of vanilla and boiled sweets and its luscious, oily flavours.

'Dewar's World of Whisky'
One of the few places in Britain you can enjoy a drop of Dewar's White Label.

The Stillroom at Aberfeldy
The small console in the foreground is used to control the steam to heat the stills.

pounce, one mouse short of 28,900, a total which propelled her into the *Guinness Book of Records*.

Illicit whisky from five separate smuggling bothies was said to have been made here for over 50 years when Glenturret was founded in 1775. For the first hundred years it was known as the Hosh distillery and changed hands regularly. Then as Glenturret, it struggled on until 1923, when it shut down. It seems no one was interested in a cute little distillery tucked down one of the prettiest glens in Perthshire, and so it slipped back into the farm it had once been. Some 30 years later it was miraculously brought back to life by James Fairlie, and is now part of Highland Distillers who produce a range of malts including a honeyed, rich, oaky 12 year-old. In the summer of 2002, the distillery's visitor centre reopened as the official 'Home of the Famous Grouse'. It is packed with interactive razzmatazz to rival 'Dewar's World of Whisky' at Aberfeldy.

The Stills at Aberfeldy
The new stillroom was built in 1972 when the number of stills was doubled to four.

GLENTURRET

Pronunciation: glen**turr**et

Founded: 1775

Founder: began as Hosh distillery

Region: Highlands

Production capacity: 340,000 litres

Address: The Hosh, Crieff, Perthshire PH7 4HA

Tel: 01764 656 565

website: www.glenturret.com

Parent Company: Edrington Group

Visitor Centre: The Famous Grouse Experience is open all year, Mon–Sat, 9am–6pm.

This classic pocket-sized distillery beside the river Turret, a mile from Crieff, has a number of claims to fame. For a start it is the oldest distillery of Scotch whisky in the Highlands, if not the world. The title is disputed by Littlemill in the Lowlands which is said to have been established three years earlier in 1772. What is undeniable is that nobody gets as many visitors as Glenturret, which receives anything up to 200,000 people each year, each one of whom is told about Towser, the distillery cat. Unlike the cartoon cat in Tom & Jerry, this cat knew what was what. Having averaged five and a half mice a day for 14 years, Towser died mid

DEANSTON

Pronunciation: deanston

Founded: 1966

Founder: Deanston Distillery Co. Ltd

Region: Highlands

Production capacity: 3,000,000 litres

Address: Doune, Perthshire FK16 6AR

Tel: 01786 841 422

website: www.burnstewartdistillers.com

Parent Company: Burn Stewart

Visitor Centre: Contact distillery for details

If this Perthshire distillery near Doune on the River Teith does not look like a distillery, that's because until the 1960s it never made a drop of whisky in its

GLENGOYNE

life. This listed building, founded by James Arkwright in 1784, was one of the original cotton mills which kicked off the Industrial Revolution in Scotland. Step inside this cavernous space beneath its huge vaulted ceiling supported by strategically placed columns and one wonders what it was like to weave cotton here. Apparently they once grew grass above to preserve the right level of humidity for the textiles, while today the great water driven turbines provide so much power the current owners can sell the excess back to the National Grid.

It is an undeniably glorious place to mature whisky however, and the casks are stacked no more than three deep and left to slumber in the dark in what resembles a cathedral for its sense of calm.

The original company that converted Deanston into a distillery sold out after a decade to Invergordon who closed it down in 1982, and finally sold it to its present owners, Burn Stewart, in 1990. Burn Stewart also own Tobermory on Mull, from where the spirit is shipped ashore almost as soon as the casks are filled.

At first it seems a shame to deny them the chance to breathe in some Hebridean air, but if an island malt has to be matured on the mainland there can be no better place than here. Deanston's own malt is bottled in various age-statements, but the smooth-as-honey, unpeated 12 year-old is hard to beat.

Pronunciation: glen**goyn**

Founded: 1833

Founder: George Connell

Region: Highlands

Production capacity: 1,200,000 litres

Address: Dumgoyne, Killearn, Stirlingshire G63 9LB

Tel: 01360 550 254

website: www.glengoyne.com

Parent Company: Edrington Group

Visitor Centre: All year, Mon–Sat, 10am–4pm. Sun, 12–4pm.

Joining the tourists heading out of Glasgow in mid-summer on the road north to Aberfoyle and the Trossachs, it is hard to imagine this area was once bandit country – a land of robber barons and illicit distillation. As you continue along the A81, near the village of Killearn the view becomes dominated by Dumgoyne hill. This 1400 ft high volcanic plug is the first outcrop of the Campsie Fells. Running down its steep, south-facing flank is a burn which plunges the last 50 ft into a pool creating its own secret glen. In the

Glengoyne – The First Highland Distillery
Built on the edge of the Campsie Fells just north of the Highland Line, this was once bandit country, immortalised by Sir Walter Scott in his novel *Rob Roy.*

eighteenth century the only link between here and the outside world would have been a rough track that picks its way round the contours of the hill. It may well have been the sound of cascading water that attracted the first smugglers to come here and set up their stills. Just as important as water was the seclusion – the fact that the dense canopy of trees and shrubs made this little glen all but invisible. There was also a good passing trade with this part of the Campsies being criss-crossed with drove roads along which the herds of sheep and cattle would be driven to the 'trysts' or cattle-markets. All in all it was a near-perfect spot for making moonshine, and at one point there were over twenty stills in this small pocket of Stirlingshire.

In fact, smuggling was rife across the whole floor of Strathblane, as was cattle rustling. Rob Roy, the celebrated rustler and romanticised hero of Sir Walter Scott, once managed to escape his pursuers by hiding in a tree whose stump still stands just 300 yds from the present day distillery.

Glengoyne began life as the Burnfoot distillery, when George Connell took out a license in 1833. Now that it was making whisky legally, the distillery could emerge into the open, 50 yds from the burn's little waterfall. Though brief, this journey downstream had almost taken the distillery into the Lowlands, since the geological fault that splits Scotland in two – the Highland Line – runs literally right past the entrance to Glengoyne. One benefit of being on the edge of the central belt, was the early arrival of the railway in the late 1840s which gave Connell a head start over distilleries further north. There was also the bonus of having easy access to Perth which had become an important centre for the wine trade bottling large quantities of wine imported by barrel. Once emptied they represented a good, cheap source of second-hand casks for all the local distillers.

If Connell had been a bean-counter by nature he could have sent his casks to Glasgow from Dumgoyne station in the afternoon full of the spirit made that morning. It would have ensured a quick return, if not the greatest whisky. But it seemed Connell understood from the very start that decent Scotch needs time to mellow and lose its hard edges, for the old warehouse, which still stands, was one of the first buildings he put up.

Undoubtedly the whisky was sold in Glasgow and at some point it must have come to the attention of Hugh Lang and his sons who ran a pub in the Broomielaw district, right in the heart of the city's port area. From selling malt whisky in five gallon stone jars straight from the cask, the Langs progressed to blending. Having established Lang Brothers Ltd. in 1861, the three sons built up a flourishing business for their main blend. With the growth in exports shipped down the Clyde from the

firm's front door, the Lang's decided they needed to indulge in a little 'vertical integration'. So in 1876 they bought the distillery.

By the mid 1880s Glen Guin, as it was then called, was producing a modest 45,000 gallons from its pair of old pot stills and had a staff of nine. Meanwhile the Lang brothers had just moved their operation into the basement of the Argyll Free church in Glasgow's Oswald Street. It seems the congregation, who continued to worship there, gave their blessing, much to the amusement of the local press. As one paper put it:

'The Spirits below were the spirits of Wine
And the spirits above were the spirits of Divine.'

Langs were always fiercely independent and managed to survive intact as a family business until 1965 when they were taken over by Robertson & Baxter, a large firm of blenders and brokers. At least the new owners were fellow Glaswegians and had nothing to do with the giant Distillers' Co., who seemed to own just about everything else in the industry. Today the distillery is ultimately owned by the Robertson Trust – an umbrella organisation which also controls The Macallan, Highland Park and Famous Grouse. Despite such famous siblings, Glengoyne is still a cherished jewel for the company.

The distillery was rebuilt in the late 1960s, when the number of stills was increased to three, and the boiler was converted from coke to gas. The tall chimney erected by George Connell was knocked down and smoke no longer billows from the pagoda roof. Other than that the distillery has changed little. It has always fitted snugly into its tight-sided glen and further expansion is not an option. Due to lack of space the eight warehouses where some two million litres of Glengoyne matures in casks are across the road from the distillery.

The whisky is aged in American oak which is shipped over to Spain and seasoned outdoors before being assembled into casks in Jerez and filled with sherry. Two or three years later they are inspected and if pronounced OK, they are shipped over to Scotland. How much easier things must have been in the days when Perth had a ready supply of hand-me-down wine barrels.

Whether this had any bearing on a recent decision to invest in Scottish oak casks – something unique to Glengoyne – is hard to say. It is a radical move none-the-less, but one with a nice ring to it compared to some of the weird wood finishes doing the rounds. So far only 15 casks have been made, so the standard expressions of Glengoyne are unaffected. The 10 and 17 year-old Glengoyne are both quite flowery, unpeated whiskies with the sweet smack of American oak. The older version has a bit more spice and structure.

The Stillroom at Glengoyne
Note the different shapes between the smaller spirit still in the foreground and the big wash still in the background.

Oban Harbour Showing the Distillery Chimney

Note McCaig's tower in the background – Oban's answer to the Coliseum in Rome.

WEST HIGHLANDS

If you unravelled the shoreline of Argyll and stretched it out flat it would be longer than the coast of France. That little boast from the local tourist office may well include all the islands within the county, but it demonstrates how jagged this whole coastline is. If you want to take the scenic route north from Oban make sure you have all the time in the world. The road is like an endless ribbon of single-track tarmac that dips and curves its way past lumps of exposed rock over coastal moorland and peat-bogs, until it finally spools into Ullapool. As a wilderness to hide out in beyond the long reach of the law it appears ideal even now, and in the days of rough tracks and horse-drawn carts, the law-makers can scarcely have bothered. Imagine being an excise officer in these parts – you would hardly know where to begin.

At one stage almost every isolated farm steading must have had a still which would be put to work if there was grain to spare after the harvest. Early travellers to the region spoke of whisky flowing freely

in the west coast glens. There were caves and bothies to stash the odd cask if need arose, though chances were that if ever a gauger did appear in the district, the whole community would have heard of his coming well in advance.

But if widespread, it seems no one was making whisky on a large scale, which would have meant the hassle of having to source barley from the east coast. Most were content to provide for their own needs and perhaps the occasional passing trade, and few saw the need to go legal when home distillation was banned. There have been less than thirty licensed distilleries in the whole history of whisky making in the region, and today there are just two – Oban, and Ben Nevis in Fort William.

This does seem strange when you consider Islay has three times as many. It is perfectly true there were severe obstacles to overcome. The barley had to be brought in from outside since the ground was too wet and infertile to ensure a reliable crop. The main centres of population were a long way off and local trade was in decline as the community was thinned out by the Clearances. Yet these were all problems shared by the island distillers. The fact that communications on the west coast have always lagged behind those on the east, must have been a critical factor in why only two west coast distilleries are still going. In the case of Ben Nevis, Fort William was a well-established garrison town at an important military cross-roads, while Oban was the 'Gateway to the Isles', as it was dubbed by the early tourist industry. Both later benefited from the arrival of the railway, though Ben Nevis happily continued shipping its considerable production down Loche Linnhe in its own fleet of steamers.

OBAN

Pronunciation: oaban

Founded: 1794

Founder: Hugh Stevenson

Region: Highlands

Production capacity: 700,000 litres

Address: Stafford Street, Oban, Argyll PA34 5NH

Tel: 01631 572 004

website: www.malts.com

Parent Company: Diageo

Visitor Centre: Easter–June, Mon–Sat, 9.30am–5pm. July–September, Mon–Friday, 9.30am–7.30pm. Sat, 9.30am–5pm and Sun, 12–5pm. October, Mon–Sat, 9.30am–5pm. March and November, Mon–Fri, 10am–5pm. December–February, 12.30–4pm.

Approaching Oban from the south, speeding along the A816, you would hardly be aware of this part of Argyll's supernatural past, or the legend of Sarah of the Bog – the whisky witch. Sarah hung out in the woods around Knapdale where she indulged in black magic and smuggling moonshine. The superstitious locals, clearly believing in her powers, reckoned it was best to keep on the right side of her and ensure that she was well supplied with peats, potatoes, grains and whatever else she needed. But as Sarah grew old her love of the hard stuff was to be her undoing. One night having drained the contents of her whisky keg she stumbled blind drunk into the fire. By the time her body was discovered her blackened head was said to be 'burned to a cinder'.

To find a distillery like Oban bang in the middle of a town is actually quite rare when so many of them evolved out of the farm. This was obvious given the need for barley, and a reliable source of water as well as providing a ready use for all the draff produced as a by-product. Moreover a remote rural location

ensured a healthy distance from the forces of law and order.

However in this instance one could almost say that the distillery in Oban predates the place itself. It did exist, but only as a tiny fishing village when the three Stevenson brothers began making whisky here in 1794. In fact it was the same family who effectively put Oban on the map. Having built themselves a pretty Georgian town-house complete with a peep-hole from the sitting room to check up on the distillery next door, they appear to have become distracted by their other ventures. As with John Sinclair on Mull whose Tobermory distillery had to fit in with his main business of supplying the soap and glass industry with kelp, so it was with the Stevensons and their distillery. Whisky making was a sideline to their real interests which lay in property, ship-building and quarrying slate.

Apparently the distillery used to be by the water's edge, but for some reason the sea has retreated, and today it sits tucked down an alleyway off the main street well back from the harbour. Now that its pagoda roof has been lopped off, it appears to have almost disappeared amongst the town that has grown up around it. That said the distillery is easy enough to find because it sits directly below one of Oban's most prominent Victorian landmarks, McCaig's

**The View Across
Oban Bay**

But for its towering chimney
stack, the distillery would
have all but disappeared
behind the town that grew
up around it.

Tower. Commissioned by a local philanthropist, apparently solely to give work to the town's unemployed stone masons, it is not a tower at all, but a model of the Coliseum in Rome.

In its present form the distillery dates from 1883 when a man called Walter Higgin bought it and spent four years rebuilding it. As future owners have all discovered, Oban is seriously compromised by its position hemmed in by a 40 ft cliff immediately behind. When Higgin attempted to blast into the rock-face and extend the warehouse in the summer of 1890 he found he had burrowed into a secret cave that contained the remains of some of the earliest inhabitants known to have lived in these parts. These were the Scoti, a tribe of ancient cave-dwellers from around 5000 BC whose bones and tools are now kept in the National Antiquities Museum in Edinburgh. Sadly no evidence of a prehistoric still was discovered and the caves were subsequently blocked up. With water coming from two lochs in Ardconnel, a mile behind the distillery, and a shed containing two years' supply of peat, Oban was a self-contained operation under Higgin, producing a

modest 35,000 gallons each year.

It was then merged into a joint operation with Glenlivet and Aultmore, before all three distilleries were sold off to John Dewar & Son and as a result passed to DCL in 1925. Apart from six years in the 1930s and a brief spell in the early 1960s when the distillery was closed to allow for the rebuilding of the stillroom, Oban has been in continuous production since the end of the eighteenth century. Along the way it has done precious little to add to the perennial curse of the industry, that of overproduction, for the simple fact that this remains one of the smallest distilleries in the Highlands with just a solitary pair of stills. The quality of the spirit which is fairly lightly peated, quite smoky and with a faint prickle of spice, has long been recognised in the trade. In 1990 it was elevated to the status of a 'Classic Malt' and today rubs shoulders with the mighty Talisker and Lagavulin in Diageo's exclusive club of that name. As something of a boutique distillery this suits Oban perfectly, since there was never enough of the stuff to go round for it to become a major component in any of the mainstream blends.

BEN NEVIS

Pronunciation: bennevis

Founded: 1825

Founder: 'Long John' Macdonald

Region: Highlands

Production capacity: 2,000,000 litres

Address: Lochy Bridge, Fort William PH33 6TJ

Tel: 01397 700 200

website: www.bennevis.co.uk

Parent Company: Nikka

Visitor Centre: All year, Mon–Fri, 9am–5pm.
Late June–September, Sat, 10am–4pm.
July–August, Mon–Fri, 9am–7.30pm. Sun, 12–4pm.

With no legal distilleries within 50 miles, 'Long John' Macdonald built Ben Nevis beneath the black, brooding bulk of Britain's tallest mountain in 1825. The family were part of the Keppoch branch of the Macdonalds whose ancestors had sent over 2000 men to fight for Bonnie Prince Charlie and whose clan chief was killed at Culloden in 1745. Years later

his name reappeared as a popular brand of blended whisky with which Long John International sought to rival the dominant blends of Bell's and Teacher's. Since 1989 it has belonged to the Japanese distillery giant, Nikka.

Fort William stood at a strategic military crossroads and changed its name from the Garrison of Inverlochy, the nearby castle, during William III's campaign to stamp out revolt in the Highlands, and bring the Jacobites to heel. The distillery was always on the big side and by 1884 was pumping out over 150,000 gallons of whisky a year from just four stills. Most of the whisky was shipped down Loch Linnhe in Macdonald's own fleet of steamers loaded from the distillery's own pier. It must have been a real hive of activity, with its on-site smithy, joinery, engineer's shop and saw-mill which together with the distillery and the attached farm employed a workforce of thirty. The farm was largely arable, but also had 200 head of cattle all fed from the spent grains from the distillery.

On the birth of Edward, later Prince of Wales, John Macdonald presented Queen Victoria with a cask of 'Long John's Dew of Ben Nevis'. By 1878 such was the demand for the whisky that another distillery had to be built alongside the original one. The new venture was known as the Nevis distillery

Ben Nevis

Built in the shadow of Britain's highest peak in 1825, there cannot have been much doubt over what to call this famous west coast distillery.

**The Stillroom
at Ben Nevis**
One of the few distilleries
left where you can still buy
your own personal cask
of whisky and have it
warehoused until ready
to drink.

**The Allt a' Mhuilhin
burn flowing past
empty casks of
Ben Nevis** (opposite)
The casks lie waiting to
be filled and matured
on site in the distillery's
six warehouses.

and operated completely separately until being absorbed into the old Ben Nevis in 1908. It had seven stills arranged in a line, two to hold the wash and five to carry the spirit, which were housed in a stillhouse that was said at the time to be as 'modern in style and construction as any in Scotland'. It boosted the firm's overall production to over 400,000 gallons a year and increased the total workforce to 230, all housed in what were described as 'most picturesque dwellings' built by the Macdonalds. Although this included those employed on the farm it does seem an incredible number when compared to Ben Nevis today where just fifteen men produce 500,000 litres of pure alcohol (lpas) a year.

Despite the scale of the operation nearly all the energy required came from the River Nevis which powered the giant water wheel which was only supplemented by steam turbines when necessary. Not that anyone was boasting of its environmentally friendly credentials at the time, since the idea of being 'green' and doing one's bit to save the planet would have made little sense in late Victorian Britain. And yet any visitor would have to have been impressed by the way the whole thing was so

brilliantly integrated with the distillery at the hub of an almost self-sufficient nucleus of industries with one feeding off the other. The barley grown to supply the distillery became the cattle cake for the cows and horses. At one stage there were as many as twenty horse-drawn carts ferrying a constant stream of casks down to the pier for loading on to the waiting steamers.

The Macdonalds took care to keep to the same supply of water from Buchan's Well and the Allt a' Mhuilinn (the Mill Burn) which starts above the snow line on the mountain itself for making their 'dew of Ben Nevis'. They claimed it was the highest and if not the purest source of water in the whole of Britain.

The water remains unchanged, but the Nevis distillery now lies buried beneath a housing estate built in the 1980s. Meanwhile Ben Nevis, which had stayed in the family fold until the 1950s was bought by Joseph Hobbs, an ex-pat Scot who had made his fortune in Canada. Hobbs had been buying up distilleries since the late 1930s including Glenesk and Bruichladdich, and decided for some strange reason that what Ben Nevis lacked was grain whisky and so

promptly installed a Coffey still. The decision may have been inspired by his belief that to make the best blended whisky, the component parts —the grain and the malt — had to be 'married' in a cask for as long as possible before bottling. He also bequeathed to Ben Nevis an ugly pair of concrete washbacks which were later ripped out and replaced with stainless steel when he sold out in 1981. The new owners were Long John International who had at last got their hands on the distillery which had been supplying them with malt whisky for their blend for so long. The sale also finally completed the circle which had begun with 'Long John' Macdonald over 150 years before.

When Glenlochy, the only other distillery in Fort William, shut down for good in 1983, Ben Nevis became the most northerly distillery on Scotland's west coast. Apart from Oban, at the far end of Loch Linnhe, you have to travel all the way down to Campbeltown where today only two distilleries remain. The vast majority of malt produced here disappears into blends including the famous 'Dew of Ben Nevis'. A trickle is allowed to mature and be bottled as single malt. Some years ago an ancient cask of 63 year-old Ben Nevis was unearthed and found to contain enough for just 90 bottles which were sold for up to £2000 each. Another solution is to call in and buy your own cask — definitely not something you can do at your average distillery. In fact this

might make Ben Nevis pretty well unique. The cask will be kept on site under bond as it matures in return for warehouse charges, then when it's ready and you have paid the tax, you can walk away with your very own 'hoggie'. It may not be as cheap as buying wine in bulk direct from the vineyards of continental Europe, but for £400 for a hoggshead of West Highland malt, it sounds tempting.

Crest of the Clan MacDonald on the front gate at Ben Nevis

(below) The crest, showing the red hand of MacDonald, relates back to the distillery's founder — 'Long John' Macdonald.

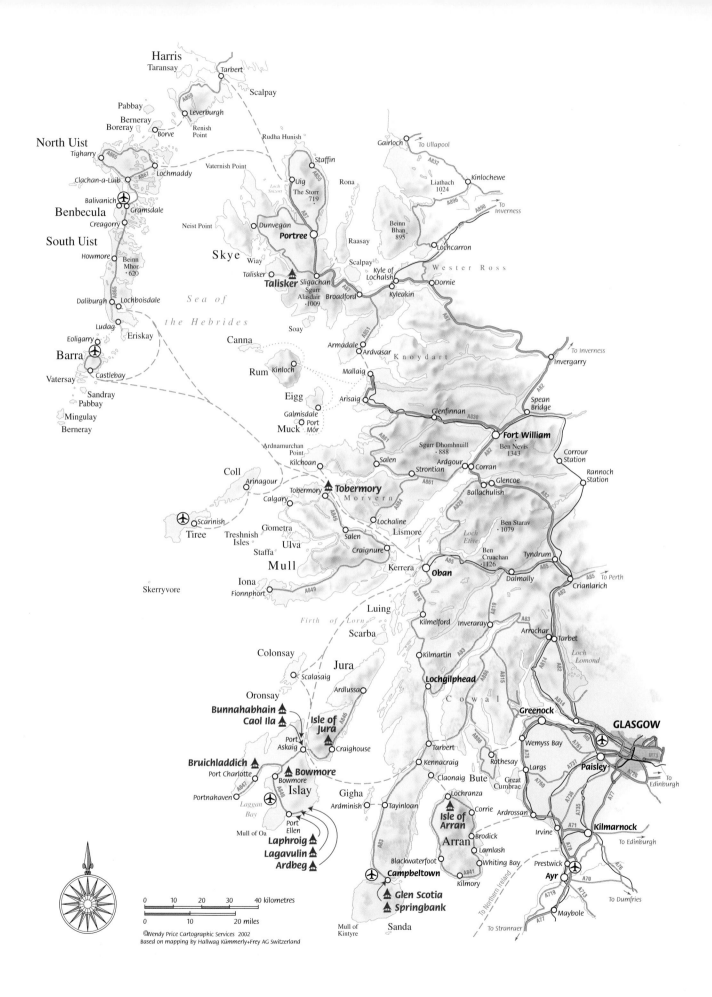

Harris
Taransay
Tarbert
Scalpay
Pabbay
Leverburgh
Berneray
Renish
Boreray
Point
Borve
North Uist
Tigharry
Rudha Hunish
Clachan-a-Luib
Lochmaddy
Vaternish Point
Balivanich
Benbecula
Gramsdale
Creagorry
South Uist
Howmore
Beinn
Mhor
·620
Daliburgh
Lochboisdale
Ludag
Eoligarry
Barra
Vatersay
Castlebay
Sandray
Pabbay
Mingulay
Berneray

Sea of
the Hebrides

Canna
Rum
Kinloch
Eigg
Galmisdale
Muck
Port
Mór

Gairloch
To Ullapool
A832
Liathach
1024
Kinlochewe
A896
A890
To
Inverness
Beinn
Bhan
895
Lochcarron
Wester Ross
Uig
Staffin
Rona
The Storr
719
Raasay
Dunvegan
Portree
Scalpay
Wiay
Kyle of
Lochalsh
Talisker
Dornie
Talisker
Sligachan
Sgurr
Alasdair
·1009
Broadford
Kyleakin
Skye
Neist Point
Soay
Armadale
Ardvasar
Knoydart
To Inverness
Invergarry
Mallaig
Spean
Bridge
Arisaig
Glenfinnan
A830
A82
Fort William
Ardnamurchan
Point
Kilchoan
Salen
Sgurr Dhomhnuill
· 888
Ardgour
Ben Nevis
1343
Corrour
Station
Strontian
Corran
Rannoch
Station
Coll
A861
Glencoe
Arinagour
Tobermory
Ballachulish
A828
A82
Scarinish
Tobermory
Morvern
Calgary
Tiree
Lochaline
Ben Starav
· 1079
Treshnish
Gometra
Isles
Salen
Lismore
Loch
Etive
Ben
Cruachan
·1126
Tyndrum
Staffa
Ulva
Craignure
Mull
Kerrera
A85
Oban
Dalmally
A85
To Perth
Iona
Crianlarich
Fionnphort
A849
A816
A82
Firth of Lorn
Luing
Kilmelford
Scarba
Kilmartin
Inveraray
Arrochar
Colonsay
A83
Tarbet
Loch
Lomond
Jura
Scalasaig
Kilmartin
Ardlussa
A819
A82
Oronsay
Cowal
A83
A815
Greenock
GLASGOW
Bunnahabhain
Isle of
Jura
Lochgilphead
Caol Ila
A846
Wemyss Bay
A761
Paisley
Port
Askaig
Craighouse
Tarbert
Rothesay
Largs
A737
A78
Bruichladdich
Kennacraig
A886
Claonaig
Bute
Great
Cumbrae
A760
Kilmarnock
Port Charlotte
Bowmore
Islay
Gigha
Lochranza
To
Edinburgh
Portnahaven
Bowmore
Ardminish
Tayinloan
Corrie
Ardrossan
Laggan
Bay
Isle of
Arran
Irvine
To Edinburgh
Port
Ellen
Brodick
Mull of Oa
Laphroig
Lamlash
Prestwick
Lagavulin
Arran
Ayr
Ardbeg
Blackwaterfoot
Whiting Bay
A841
Campbeltown
Kilmory
Maybole
Glen Scotia
A70
Springbank
To Dumfries
Mull of
Kintyre
Sanda
To Northern Ireland
To Stranraer

0 10 20 30 40 kilometres
0   10   20 miles

©Wendy Price Cartographic Services 2002
Based on mapping by Hallwag Kümmerly+Frey AG Switzerland

ISLAND DISTILLERIES

There has been whisky-making on the necklace of islands round Scotland's coast for centuries. It was only a year before the first recorded mention of Scotch whisky being made in 1494, that the King of Scotland forced the head of Clan MacDonald to surrender his title 'Lord of the Isles'. Not that the island chiefs became loyal subjects overnight, and sporadic inter-clan warfare continued for over a century. An attempt to impose some sort of order on this Hebridean anarchy was made with the Statutes of Icolmkill of 1609, but how much notice was ever paid to it is unclear. The Statutes laid much of the blame on 'the extraordinary drinking of strong wines and aquavitae'. It was claimed that these were being brought in by 'merchants of the mainland' and 'traffickers dwelling amongst [the isles]'. The solution was to ban all imported liquor. Five years later Sir John Campbell of Cawdor, a close ally of the King, finally brought the MacDonalds to heel by taking over their power base on Islay.

Some sort of harmony began to descend on the isles, and the whisky-fuelled blood-baths of the past slowly faded into history. Household drink allowances for the clan chiefs were reduced, but not excessively. MacLean of Duart on Mull was still allowed up to four tuns of wine a year, equivalent to about 18 bottles a day. The amount of alcohol around caused amazement to some early visitors. Martin Martin, in his book 'A Description of the Western Isles' (c 1695) wrote of Lewis:

'There was plenty of Corn was such, as disposed to the Natives to brew several sorts of Liquors, as common 'Usquebaugh', another call'd 'Trestarig' ...three times distill'd, which is strong and hot; a third sort is four times distill'd, and this by the Natives is call'd 'Usquebaugh-baul', which at first taste affects all the Members of the Body: two spoonfuls of this Last Liquor is a sufficient Dose; and if any Man exceed this, it would presently stop his Breath, and endanger his Life. The 'Trestarig' and 'Usquebaugh-baul' are both made of oats'.

His description is reminiscent of those nineteenth-century explorers who penetrated deep into the jungle to witness tribes getting completely stoned on some hallucinogenic plant. Later the scholar Samuel Moorewood was to describe in his book 'Inebriating Liquors' (1838) the ancient customs on the Isles. He wrote of how the clan would sit in a circle for anything up to two days at a time. A goblet or shell of whisky would be passed round again and again until there was no more, or until everyone had collapsed and been carried off in a wheelbarrow.

With the exception of Islay and Tiree, the poor quality soil of the Western Isles hardly encouraged the growing of crops, which could easily be ruined after a rain-soaked harvest, though maybe it was watching the wet grain start to ferment of its own accord that first set the islanders on the path to *Usquebaugh*. Such natural fermentation would have produced a rough, coarse beer which could only benefit from being boiled up and purified into a spirit. There were plenty willing to have a go as John Knox [no relation to Edinburgh's fire and brimstone preacher of the 16th century] wrote of Mull on his Hebridean Tour of the 1780s:

'Of grain, this coast cannot raise, with the greatest exertions, a sufficiency for the use of the inhabitants; and of every year's production of Barley, a third or fourth part is distilled into a spirit called whisky, of which the natives are immoderately fond.'

In all the Hebrides, excluding Islay there were only 13 distilleries ever licensed, of which seven were on Skye. The two distilleries on Tiree may have had enough barley, but the locals were well supplied with moonshine and the mainland was simply too far away. Once illicit Scotch died out in the nineteenth century, and the main market became the blenders, any island distiller would have felt isolated. If Tobermory spent much of the twentieth century asleep, what hope was there for distilleries further out. Today of course being able to call yourself 'the only distillery on the island', as is the case with Tobermory, Talisker, Jura and Arran, is a big plus. It gives your single malt a unique cachet that Speysiders can only dream of.

Talisker

Beside Loch Harport with the Cuillins behind.

TALISKER

> **Pronunciation: tal**isker
>
> **Founded:** 1830
>
> **Founder:** Hugh and Kenneth MacAskill
>
> **Region:** Islands
>
> **Production capacity:** 1,900,000 litres
>
> **Address:** Carbost, Isle of Skye IV47 8SE
>
> **Tel:** 01478 640 314
>
> **website:** www.malts.com
>
> **Parent Company:** Diageo
>
> **Visitor Centre:**
>
> Easter–October, Mon–Sat, 9.30am–5pm.
>
> November–Easter, Mon–Fri, 2–5pm.
>
> Last tour 4.30pm.
>
> Group bookings by appointment.

The Isle of Skye's only distillery pumps out the equivalent of 1.5 million litres of pure alcohol a year from its five stills. Around 50,000 cases of this are eventually bottled as a single malt. The rest disappears into blends, especially Johnnie Walker – the world's best-selling Scotch whisky, without which Talisker may have closed down long ago.

Skye is the largest of the Inner Hebrides with its 672 square miles and a population of around 9000 that swells in the midsummer months until every spare bed is taken. Tucked up close to the mainland it was always the most accessible of the Western Isles even before the controversial bridge was built in 1995, which some say has debased its character as a true island. All this begs the question – why just the one distillery?

The Scotch Whisky Industry Record of 1823 records seven licensed distilleries on Skye, none of which has survived. There were inevitably a good number of illicit stills supplying local needs on an irregular basis depending on the availability of grain, but for anyone distilling on a larger scale conditions were far from easy. The mainland may have been just a few hundred yards away across the straights of Kyleakin, where the bridge now stands, but it was still a huge distance from good quality east coast barley, the soil on Skye being much less fertile than on Islay, which at the time had three times the number of legal distilleries.

The story of Skye's sole surviving distillery began soon after, when a couple of farmers from Eigg, Hugh and Kenneth MacAskill, arrived on Skye to take on the lease of Talisker House on the west side of the island. Here in the parish of Bracadale, round the back of the Cuillin Hills, facing the Atlantic, the locals scraped a living harvesting seaweed which was turned into kelp and from that into soap and glass. By then the trade in kelp was already in decline, prompting the start of mass migration from Skye to North America. The MacAskills, in true nineteenth century Highland tradition, helped speed them on their way by replacing them with Cheviot sheep. In 1830, after a failed attempt to site a distillery five miles north at Fiskavaig, they settled on a plot of land beside Loch Harport and spent £3000 building Talisker. The name came from the Gaelic 'Talamh Sgeir', or 'Echo Rock' which stood on the shore.

The local minister, the Rev Macleod, was passionately opposed to liquor and, speaking of his parish, called 'the erection and establishment of a whisky distillery… one of the greatest curses which, in the ordinary course of Providence, could befall it'. In 1854, his prayers were answered and Talisker was put on the market for a third of the price it had cost to build. There were various attempts to make a go of the distillery until it passed into the capable hands of Roderick Kemp, an entrepreneur from Aberdeen. Business began to take off as visitors noted from the regular sight of 'puffers', or small steamers, calling at Talisker to deposit grain and load up with whisky.

Unfortunately, the lack of a pier meant the casks had to be set afloat and towed three or four hundred yards out into the Loch to be winched aboard. Despite increasingly desperate letters to the laird, Macleod of Dunvegan, the pier was only built in 1900. By then Kemp had long since given up on Skye, selling out to his partner before buying the Macallan.

Talisker, meanwhile, had merged with Dailuaine, on Speyside, then the biggest distillery in the Highlands, as a limited company which was taken over in 1915 by the Distillers company in one of their first ventures into malt whisky.

Today little of the old Talisker remains, thanks to the distillery's recent £2 million re-fit and a fire in 1960, when low wines trickled out of a still through an open manhole onto the coal fire below. The stillhouse was gutted along with the stills which were replaced exactly as was, apart from having steam coils inside to avoid risking another fire. One relic from the past, and part of what makes the flavour of Talisker with its beguiling mix of smoke and pepper so unique, stands on the outside. The lyne arms pass from the neck of the two spirit stills straight through the wall of the distillery into the open air, then kink upwards to form a giant U-bend before plunging into a pair of wooden worm tubs. These are kept brimful of cool water diverted from the Carbost burn.

Very few distilleries have worm tubs any more, and none have such weird-shaped lyne arms. One theory has it that the coppersmith was experimenting to create a style similar to the original Talisker, that

Stillroom at Talisker
The lyne arms of the two spirit stills pass straight through the wall of the stillhouse into the outside air where they loop round in a giant U-bend before plunging into a pair of wooden worm tubs.

The Picturesque Harbour Front of Tobermory on Mull

Viewed from the distillery.

until 1928 was triple distilled like an Irish whiskey. Possibly too many off flavours were finding their way into the final cut – and with no other distillery close by to seek advice the only solution was to improvise. Either way, it seems to work, and no one now among its current owners would dare change a thing.

But the island's connection with whisky does not quite end with Talisker.

The Pràban na Linne whisky company was set up on the south-east corner of Skye overlooking the Sound of Sleat by the financier and entrepreneur, Sir Iain Noble in 1974. This is Gaelic whisky where the word *pràban* meant a place where moonshine was sold and sometimes made.

The whisky is not actually made on Skye, though Sir Iain says 'he can neither confirm nor deny', but the head-quarters of the company are undeniably here, which is not something Talisker can lay claim to. On offer are Té Bheag [pronounced 'chey vek' and not tea-bag] an excellent blend in its own right, and Poit Dhubh [pronounced potch ghoo] – a 12 year-old vatted malt. Perhaps one day the island might yet have a second distillery. A site has already been found and the water has been analysed and pronounced good, all that's needed is for sales of Té Bheag to really take off.

TOBERMORY

Pronunciation: tober**moar**ee

Founded: 1797

Founder: John Sinclair

Region: Islands

Production capacity: 1,000,000 litres

Address: Main Street, Tobermory, Isle of Mull PA75 6NR

Tel: 01688 302 645

website: www.burnstewartdistillers.com

Parent Company: Burn Stewart

Visitor Centre:

Easter–October, Mon–Fri, 10am–5pm.

October–Easter, by appointment only.

Whatever the past problems of Tobermory, Mull's one and only distillery, a lack of water was never one of them. Watching the weather roll in off the Atlantic, it is little wonder the clouds are so content to spill their load after 3000 miles of nothing but sea between here and the coast of Canada. Like Islay, it shares that warm, damp feel of

Ireland — a connection reinforced by a geological bond beneath the sea.

Sixty million years ago there was intense volcanic activity in these parts as the Atlantic Ocean was taking shape. As the landmass that was to form Greenland and North America began to break off and drift westwards, the outpouring of lava was like a departing fanfare. As the lava cooled it turned to black basalt, at its most spectacular in the Giant's Causeway of Northern Ireland and Fingal's cave just off the west coast of Mull. Today the water that feeds the Bushmills distillery in County Antrim flows over the same basalt rock as the water which nourishes Tobermory.

Long after these volcanic ructions, St Columba landed his coracle on the shores of Iona off the south-west tip of Mull in 563. If he was carrying the secret of the water of life along with the Christian faith, then perhaps the Mullachs were distilling before the Ileachs had even dreamt of it. Not that anyone knows of course.

What is true is that Tobermory was built as a model village in the late eighteenth century by the British Society for Promoting the Fisheries. Part of its aim was to wean the locals onto fishing and off the burgeoning cottage industry of making moonshine. So when in 1797, a local merchant called John Sinclair tried to surreptitiously build a distillery there, having failed to mention the dreaded 'd' word in his submission, the Society promptly sussed him out. They suggested he might try a brewery instead.

Some time between then and its 'official' start date of 1823, Tobermory began producing whisky.

Sinclair only dabbled in whisky making, his main business was with kelp which he exported off the island in his own fleet of ships to the soap and glass factories of Glasgow and Liverpool. When he died in 1837, the distillery died with him and remained quiet for the next 50 years. There would have been enough island peat and barley to supply the raw materials and a population approaching its peak of 10,600 to drink the results, but it was not cranked back into life until 1878. After a string of what the current distillery manager calls 'enthusiastic amateurs', it passed to the Distillers' company in 1916. After the war, Tobermory became one of the many casualties of the 1930s recession and shut down, seemingly for good. Then in 1972, in one of the most extraordinary acts of resuscitation ever witnessed by the whisky industry, Tobermory was brought back to life. It had been a 40 year siesta when a consortium backed by some well-known figures in the trade took it on. They replaced the stills and the wash backs that had been ripped out years earlier, and began distilling again. Whether they momentarily lost their heads in the distillery's dreamy setting beside the blues, pinks and yellow of Tobermory's houses reflected in the bay, who knows. Possibly the size of the cheque from the development agency had something to do with it. Either way it was not the best moment to be going back into production on the eve of a recession and

The Unique Stills at Tobermory

As with many distilleries the original owner probably played around with the stills and the angle of the lyne arm until he achieved what he was looking for, and now no-one would change a thing.

THE SCOTCH WHISKY BOOK

Port Ellen Maltings, Islay

Port Ellen distillery was one of the casualties of the whisky loch, when DCL closed a large number of distilleries in the early 1980's to bring production into line with consumption. Since then Port Ellen's role in life is to supply malted barley to the island's other distilleries.

with the whisky loch filling up nicely.

Once again, the venture failed, but when Tobermory was bought by Burn Stewart in 1993, the previous owners had done enough to make the distillery viable again. With the success of single malts from Islay, there was a real cachet in being the only malt whisky from Mull — a cachet that had never existed before. And perhaps Tobermory had survived because it was so remote. It is hard to imagine a dormant distillery on the mainland holding out against the developers' diggers for that length of time.

The first priority of the new owners was to clear out all trace of Isle of Mull cheddar that had been maturing in part of the distillery. With wild spores buzzing about there was a hygiene disaster waiting to happen. On the other hand there was nothing wrong with the equipment that the new owners inherited, not least the stills themselves.

As Burn Stewart's managing director, Billy Walker, later recalled, 'their unique shape was compelling.' The spirit stills, which can hold an impressive 18,000 litres apiece, appear to dominate the cramped still room with their necks craning right up to the ceiling. Then instead of coming off at right angles, the lyne arms display a dramatic kink, almost as though they were bent to fit the space. The effect is a very heavy reflux of low wines and foreshots back into the spirit still, and a final cut that is extremely clean with none of that oily character you can find in Islay malts.

The two wash stills are slightly bigger and can be connected to their own spirit still in such a way to produce two completely different styles side by side. Traditionally there has been Ladaig, named after the burn that flows right beside the distillery, which shares the same level of peatiness as a heavier Islay like Caol Ila, if not Laphroaig. And then there is Tobermory itself — a much lighter restorative style than Ladaig, more akin to Bunnahabhain or old-style Bruichladdich, but less oily. There is an attractive trace of smoke and a faint wisp of peat as well from the water that collects in a peat bog in the hills behind the distillery. From here it flows for a few

Isle of Jura Distillery From the Sound of Jura

With a population of less than 200, Red deer outnumber islanders by 30:1

Pyramids of Peat
Peat is traditionally cut in the springtime and left to season in the open air.

miles, picking up trace minerals from the basalt until collecting behind a dam from where it is piped directly to the distillery. Its colour varies from pale brown, tinged with red, to being as dark and brackish as builder's tea. The level of peat is said to remain pretty constant however.

The brief distillery tour, on the southern side of the bay looking across to possibly Scotland's most photographed waterfronts, ends abruptly with distillation. Unlike tours round Bowmore and Macallan, where you will be shown the slumbering barrels and hear about the Angel's share, at Tobermory the whisky is unromantically dispatched off the island by tanker. In truth few distilleries age more than a token amount of their whisky on site nowadays. In the case of Tobermory, the spirit is pumped back into casks at its sister distillery of

Deanston in Perthshire. Here it is laid to rest in the most perfect vaulted cellars this side of Burgundy. The building was one of those dark satanic mills, built by Richard Arkwright in 1785, and with walls a metre thick and from summer through to winter, the temperature hardly varies.

ISLE OF JURA

Pronunciation: joora
Founded: 1810
Founder: James Ferguson
Region: Islands
Production capacity: 2,500,000 litres
Address: Craighouse, Isle of Jura,
Argyll PA60 7XT
Tel: 01496 820 240
website: www.isleofjura.com
Parent Company: Fortune Brands
Visitor Centre:
All year, Mon–Thurs, 9am–4pm.
Fri, 9am–1pm.
All visits by appointment.

Sometimes looking at whisky labels can be instructive. That of Jura, shows the island all alone surrounded by water as if its big, brash,

Cutting Peat
Hand-cut peat is a rarity, most is cut by machine nowadays.

Empty barrels at Bunnahabhain

Five years later Isle of Jura was up and running with twice the capacity and looking nothing like the 'castle' of the 1880s; not even after lying under the still for a week could you say that. But perhaps if its huge stills could be tamed to produce something really special and if Islay could somehow be towed off to the other end of the Hebrides, Jura might stand a chance.

ISLE OF ARRAN

Pronunciation: aran

Founded: 1995

Founder: Harold Currie

Region: Islands

Production capacity: 750,000 litres

Address: Lochranza, Isle of Arran KA27 8HJ

Tel: 01770 830 264

website: www.arranwhisky.com

Parent Company: Isle of Arran Distillers

Visitor Centre:

Mid-March–October, daily, 10am–6pm.

November–December,

contact distillery for details.

limelight-hogging neighbour did not exist. We are talking of Islay, a place of pilgrimage for those who take their malt whiskies seriously (perhaps too seriously). Unfortunately as every fan of Manchester City football club knows, it is no good just going to bed at night wishing one's glamorous neighbour would simply drop dead and disappear, for by morning they will be back as smug as before and more famous than ever.

When Alfred Barnard visited the island on his great distillery tour of the 1880s, he declared that Jura 'is one of the handsomest we have seen, and from the bay looks more like a castle than a distillery.' By then it had been going for around 75 years as a licensed distillery, and no doubt as a smugglers' bothy for a lot longer than that.

It was abandoned during the First World War and left to decay. Then in 1958, two local landowners approached the brewer, Scottish & Newcastle, to see if the distillery could be rebuilt, which would, if nothing else, create much-needed jobs on the island.

When Harold Currie, the former managing director of Chivas Brothers, decided to build a distillery on Arran in the early 1990s he knew what had happened to the last attempt. Despite producing the best whisky in Scotland, so it was claimed, the Lagg distillery on the south of the island folded in 1837, after just thirteen years. Apart from the difficulty of shipping the casks up the Firth of Clyde to the drinkers of Glasgow, those behind Lagg were fighting a losing battle against the island's illicit distillers, who were still making whisky until 1860.

The smugglers may have gone and the shipping service to Arran has improved, but in some ways the new distillery faces even worse odds – that of trying to survive as a one-off in an age of corporate giants. The distillery is in Lochranza on the north of the island which faces across the Kilbrannan sound to Kintyre. Production began in 1995, and two years later the Queen, who was touring the Western Isles on the Royal Yacht *Britannia*, came and opened the visitor centre.

In 1998, after three years in a sherry cask, Isle of Arran was now officially whisky. At present Isle of Arran appears surprisingly mature for its youth, with a rich malty aroma and a fresh, almost pepperminty sweetness on the tongue.

Ardbeg at Sunrise
Appropriately for a distillery so close to the shore, the whisky of Ardbeg is impregnated with the salty, tarred rope aromas of the harbour.

ISLAY

Looking at a map, Islay, the southernmost island in the Hebrides, appears to have been pushed out to sea by the isle of Jura. It is two hours from the mainland by ferry, while heading due west, there is nothing but open sea for 2500 miles until you hit the shores of Canada's Newfoundland. Meanwhile the coast of Northern Ireland is less than twenty miles south. Such close proximity is clear the moment you step off the ferry. In summer the lush, almost phosphorescent green of the pasture, the dank farm buildings and moss-covered walls, the names of forgotten hamlets like Ballygrant and Kilmeny… all sounds too Irish for words.

If our Celtic cousins invented the pot still and the knowledge of distillation was carried across the water by Irish monks, then it would seem only natural for the first Scotch whisky to have been distilled on the west coast. If true then it was surely here on Islay or else Campbeltown on the southern end of the Argyll peninsular. Not that any of this can be proven, of course, for no firm evidence has been discovered, but maybe one day a fragment of some ancient still will be unearthed from one of the island's many peat bogs.

The abundance of peat to fuel the fire to boil the contents of the still, is one good reason why the knowledge of making whisky never left once it had blown in from outside. Nor was there ever likely to be

a shortage of that other vital ingredient — water. Although the island is pretty low lying with even its highest hills less than 1500 feet, it is still high enough to scrape the bottom of passing rain clouds. These regularly roll in off the Atlantic to keep the burns, rivers and bogs well topped up. If the sound of trickling water is what drew the first distillers to a particular spot, those on Islay would have been spoilt for choice.

With few trees and no outlying island to act as a windbreak, Islay takes the full brunt of the onshore breeze, though the word 'breeze' is a bit tame for what is often closer to a gale ripping in off the sea, shaking the roof-tops and flattening the vegetation. Even modern, short-stemmed varieties of barley are no match for winds that can reach up to 130mph. It is also too wet for a reliable crop, and today what little barley is grown is fed to the cattle. All six distilleries currently making whisky buy their grain from the east coast barley belt that runs from the Moray Firth to the flatlands of East Anglia.

Arable farming on Islay may not make economic sense nowadays, but it is the most fertile of all the Hebrides, and originally grew enough cereal to get the island's whisky makers off to a good start. How much of it was actually barley is hard to tell — not that the early distillers were too bothered about that. It was probably just as often oats, wheat and whatever else was at hand. They would have doubtless added wild mint, thyme, bog myrtle or anything to produce

Bowmore Beside Loch Indaal

The oldest surviving distillery on Islay produces a complex, less heavily peated whisky than the likes of Lagavulin and Laphroaig.

something vaguely palatable from the stew bubbling inside the still.

The name Islay is possibly derived from 'Ella' – the daughter of a Viking ruler. It took until the twelfth century for the Western Isles to shake off their Norwegian overlords, and start developing into an independent state under the Lords of the Isles. At its peak in the following century, this island empire stretched from the Orkneys via Northern Ireland to the Isle of Man. It had its own parliament, held court, negotiated treaties with foreign powers, and was a constant thorn in the side of monarchs like James IV in his bid to create a united Scotland. The Lord of the Isles evolved into the great house of Macdonald whose main power-base on Islay was Dunyveg castle, now in ruins and sharing the same bay as Lagavulin distillery. The Macdonalds used to slip out in their flat-bottomed boats beneath the stone sea-gate of Dunyveg to try and bring their island kingdom to heel. With powerful clans like the MacLeans of Duart on Mull and the MacLeods on Lewis and Skye, this was something they never quite achieved. Finally in 1614, the Macdonalds were driven out of their power-base on Islay by the Campbells of Cawdor, who were among the King's closest allies.

After the Act of Union in 1707, the Scottish Board of Excise was set up to raise revenue from drink to pay for the country's administration. On Islay and Jura, all whisky tax remained 'in farm' to the laird – a happy state of affairs that existed for most of the eighteenth century. In 1725, a prominent Glasgow MP, Daniel Campbell, had his mansion in Shawfield burnt to the ground by the mob because he voted to increase the Malt Tax. With the compensation paid out by the city fathers, Campbell bought the entire island from his namesake, John Campbell, for £9000. This sounds rather a bargain considering the amount would be something under £1.2 million in today's money.

Daniel and his descendants helped modernise farming on the island, and introduced the two-rowed strain of barley which increased yields. The amount of whisky distilled on the farms depended on the harvest. In good years there was no conflict with the grain needed for food, but in poor years it could result in famine. In the 1770s the parish report for Kildalton, the southern strip that includes the distilleries of Laphroaig, Lagavulin and Ardbeg, knew exactly who to blame.

'We have not an excise officer in the whole island. The quantity therefore of whisky made here is very great; and the evil that follows drinking to excess of this liquor, is very visible on this island.'

The laird was not overly impressed with this argument and realised that distilling on a commercial scale could provide much needed employment on the island whose population was already over 7000. At the time of the Kildalton report, Bowmore had just been built as the new capital and soon boasted the island's first official distillery, established by David Simpson in 1779.

There was always a certain amount of smuggling taking place especially in the south-east tip around the Mull of Oa, but the lack of local grain was such that it would have been for domestic consumption only. There appear to be no records of moonshine being spirited off the island to feed demand on the mainland, which was certainly growing due to tough new measures which were hitting whisky makers on either side of the law. The first excise man landed on Islay in 1797 and within three years there was a call for armed militia from the mainland to give support, though it never came. David Simpson of Bowmore and Donald McEachern who had begun distilling nearby at Bridgend, both signed a petition denouncing the illegal distillers who were denying them their share of the barley.

Imported grain did not arrive until the end of the Napoleonic Wars in 1815. From this point on various legal distilleries started up like Daill in 1814, Scarabuss in 1817 and Newton a year later, though none of these survived more than a couple of decades. Under the benign stewardship of William Frederick Campbell, the last of the family to own Islay, the island's whisky industry was given much encouragement to help it through its adolescence. In all there were 21 licensed distilleries operating here at some point during the nineteenth century. Among the early survivors were the famous Kildalton distilleries of Ardbeg, Lagavulin and Laphroaig which had absorbed first Ardenistiel and then Kildalton.

Word of Islay whisky and its growing reputation had reached the Royal Household, who requested Campbell to send 'a cask of your best Islay Mountain Dew' in 1841, an order repeated two years later. Meanwhile the island's population, which had peaked at 15,000, was being thinned out by the Highland Clearances. Though the forced eviction of crofters was brutal, it proved a blessing in disguise. Ignorance and overcrowding had led to horror-stories of degenerative diseases, in-breeding and of mentally handicapped children being chained to their bedsteads.

In the 1880s, Islay gained two more distilleries that have survived into the present – Bruichladdich and Bunnahabhain which face each other across Loch Indaal. It hardly rivalled the incredible distillery boom happening on Speyside, but it does show that Islay malts were in demand from the blenders who already formed the biggest customers for malt whisky. In time Ardbeg's main role was to add flavour to Ballantine's while Lagavulin was doing the same for White Horse and to a lesser extent Johnnie Walker. Laphroaig was added to Long John and Caol Ila to Bells. There was also a following for unblended Islay whisky, thanks to the salesmanship of Peter Mackie who never lost his taste for Islay whiskies, having begun his career at Lagavulin. Mackie finally bought the distillery as part of his 'White Horse' empire.

Leaving aside Laphroaig's little coup of being allowed into the United States as a 'medicinal spirit' during prohibition, the vast majority of Islay whisky went into blends. Like highly flavoured oil in a

Early Morning at Lagavulin

Note the jagged rocks in the bay. Sailors from Viking times to the present day have often come to grief here by misjudging the tide.

**Bunnahabhain –
with the Paps of Jura
in the Distance**

dressing, it was always esteemed by those who used it in their blends, but it was used sparingly. More than 3 or 4 per cent in a predominantly Speyside blend could make it unbalanced. One option was to go for a lighter style like Bunnahabhain, which could slip into the mix in greater quantity before it became too apparent. The trouble with that approach is that you could lose your identity. If you were not heavily peated you were not really an Islay – in which case some blenders might think, 'Why bother?' There was probably a malt closer to hand on the mainland offering a similar style.

The Islay peat-reek has come to define the island's malts. The peat is certainly all from the island and is laid on top of coke in the vast kilns at the Port Ellen maltings. This is just down the road from Laphroaig and is run almost like a co-operative to supply all the distilleries. Laphroaig and Bowmore have retained their floor maltings which gives them about a third of the malt they need. The fact that the peat is all home-grown is one of the reasons Islay malt whisky is special. Mainland distilleries, as far away as Brora right at the other end of the Highland fault beside the North Sea, have tried to make an 'Islay style' of whisky, but it just wasn't the same.

Locked in every brick of Islay peat is a compacted

sample of ancient vegetation, of heather, gorse and sphagnum moss. It is, if you like, a little fragment of the island's DNA and the imprint it gives on the malting barley transfers directly into a dram of Islay malt even after a decade or two in cask. The local peat has a relatively high moss content which is said to soak up some of the brine and salt blown in off the sea and may account for some of those medicinal aromas that waft out of a glass of Laphroaig. Whether it makes it a better dram who knows, some find that slightly antiseptic smell hard to enjoy, but it certainly makes it different. The peat is also rich in bog myrtle which adds a sweet resinous aroma to the smoke.

The whiskies also derive some of their smoky character from the dark peaty water of the island, though the effect is pretty subtle to be honest. In most cases this is the last influence the island exerts on its whiskies. There is much purple prose about casks of whisky slumbering beside the sea breathing in the smoky, peaty, seaweedy, briny atmosphere. All very evocative, except that practically every barrel of Islay is shipped over to the mainland and aged in some vast Lowland warehouse a long way from any seaweed or brine. The exception is Bruichladdich which is now matured on site, and it will be interesting to see what effect this has on its malts in years to come.

Per capita the island contributes something like £250,000 to the Scottish economy and is rewarded with expensive fuel bills and an inadequate ferry service, though it is not about to declare UDI. With a population of 3,500 it does face the old dilemma of any island community – how to hang on to its young who have seen the life and opportunities offered on the mainland. Whisky is of vital importance to Islay and does provide year round jobs in a way tourism does not. After some hard times in the 1970s and 1980s, Islay whisky is booming right now. Let's hope its popularity continues.

BUNNAHABHAIN

Pronunciation: boonahavan

Founded: 1881

Founder: Greenlees family

Region: Islands

Production capacity: 2,500,000 litres

Address: Port Askaig, Isle of Islay,
Argyll PA46 7RP

Tel: 01496 840 646

website: www.edringtongroup.com

Parent Company: Edrington Group

Visitor Centre:
March–October,
Mon–Fri, 10am–4pm.

Above the words 'Westering Home', the label of this Islay malt shows an old sea-dog, one hand clasped to the wheel of his ship, the other shielding his eyes from the sun. There is no empty bottle of Scotch poking from his pocket and he looks in control. This was evidently not the case with the Captain and first mate of the ocean-going trawler which ran aground in 1974, missing Bunnahabhain's pier by inches. The wreck still lies rusting in the shallows between the distillery and the Paps of Jura. With its shingle beach and sheltered bay it is a fairly idyllic spot to build a distillery, but not the most practical, as the Greenlees brothers, a pair of local farmers, discovered in 1881.

Up on the north-west corner of the island, beyond Port Askaig, there was nothing, and the contractors had to build a row of cottages for the workers, a schoolroom, and a pier, as well as the distillery itself. Yet despite the £30,000 spent, the Islay Distillery Co. was making a profit of nearly £10,000 by year two. The directors were so impressed with their manager, Mr Smith, that they told him to name his terms. In addition to his £350 salary, free lodging and keep for a cow, he demanded 'not less than £30 be spent on furniture' which is precisely what he got.

Five years later Bunnahabhain became one of the founding distilleries of Highland Distillers who still own it to this day, and use its malt as a key filling for Famous Grouse. Its malt is famous for being virtually unpeated, which is not what you would expect on Islay, though it does share that fresh salty tang of the sea.

The Pier at Bunnahabhain Distillery
In 1974 the Captain of a large trawler missed the peer by inches only to run aground. Its wreck lies rusting in the shallows to this day.

Caol Ila Distillery and its Glass-fronted Stillhouse

For years Caol Ila has been highly popular among blenders, now at last more is to be bottled as single malt.

CAOL ILA

Pronunciation: koel**eel**a

Founded: 1846

Founder: Hector Henderson

Region: Islands

Production capacity: 3,600,000 litres

Address: Port Askaig, Isle of Islay, Argyll PA46 7RL

Tel: 01496 840207

website: www.malts.com

Parent Company: Diageo

Visitor Centre: March–October, Mon–Thurs, all visits by appointment only.

Islay's other west coast distillery is nothing like as picturesque thanks to its seventies refurbishment which imposed the same off-the-peg design found in half a dozen distillery re-fits carried out at the time.

But if the views looking in at the shed-like still-room are nothing to write home about, those looking out are stunning. No stillman at Caol Ila could ever tire of peering out across the Sound of Islay though giant plate glass windows above the shimmering copper sides of his stills.

It was built by a Glasgow distiller called Hector Henderson in 1846, and like Bunnahabhainn developed its own little community and relied on its own pier. By the 1880's David MacBrayne's company, the forerunner of Caledonian MacBrayne, was sending two steamers twice a week to deliver grain and collect the whisky. The distillery then belonged to the mighty Bulloch Lade, once a serious rival to DCL until going bankrupt in 1920. Ever since Caol Ila has been part of DCL, or United Distillers as the became.

As a big busted, strongly peated, pungent heather-smoked Islay malt it adds weight to such blends as Bells 8 year-old and Johnnie Walker Red Label. On its own as a fifteen year-old, it is almost a meal in itself.

ARDBEG

Pronunciation: ard**beg**

Founded: 1815

Founder: Alexander McDougall

Region: Islands

Production capacity: 1,000,000 litres

Address: Port Ellen, Islay PA42 7EA

Tel: 01496 302 244

website: www.ardbeg.com

Parent Company: Glenmorangie

Visitor Centre: All year,
Mon–Fri, 10am–5pm. June–August,
Sun–Sat, 10am–5pm.

The last of the Kildalton distilleries shares much with Laphroaig and Lagavulin – the same predilection for peat for a start – but its history, certainly in recent years, has been a lot more precarious. The distillery only produced whisky for two years during the whole of the 1980s, and while it was cranked back into life in 1990 it was back in mothballs five years later. Curiously the man who shut it down that time, Allied Distillers' Alistair Cunningham, reportedly called it 'heaven's own nectar' adding that 'if you knew exactly the amount to take each day you could live forever.' The trouble was that from a blender's point of view its heavyweight, peat-packed flavours were not sufficiently different from those of Laphroaig, its sister distillery next door. Like a family where praise is disproportionately heaped on the first born, poor Ardbeg inevitably suffered from neglect. And yet when it was put on the market, bids flooded in from all sides. In an eight-horse race, Glenmorangie eventually stomped home, paying around £7 million in 1997 before beginning the slow process of restoring it to its rightful position. For anyone who saw it in its moment of despair and has returned to see it now, the transformation has been awesome. What it is to be loved.

The story of Ardbeg begins with the MacDougalls, a family of tenant farmers who were known to have signed a lease with the laird of Islay, Walter Campbell, to continue farming here in 1798. There is some record of a previous whisky-making on

The Gleaming Stills of Caol Ila

On a clear day, the stillman at Caol Ila enjoys one of the finest views in the industry, across the Sound of Islay to Jura.

Ardbeg Distillery at Dusk

this spot and of the excise men seizing a large quantity of illicit whisky and destroying a still. Old Duncan MacDougall was probably making a bit on the side, before his son Alexander first licensed the Ardbeg distillery some time around 1815. 'Distillery' is probably too strong a word for what was barely one step on from a cottage industry that operated for a brief period after the harvest, producing a few hundred gallons of whisky each year. It was said that Alexander, who died in 1853, had been well-known in the spirit trade in Glasgow, and that he was intensely clannish. When he discovered an unknown namesake in court, he demanded to pay the fine declaring that it was impossible that a MacDougall could do anything wrong.

By the time of his death, Ardbeg was supporting a 200-strong community which soon had its own school. Ownership of the distillery passed to Alexander's sisters, Margaret and Flora, who were entered in a lease at the time as 'co-partners' carrying on business at Ardbeg as Distillers under the firm of Alexander MacDougall & Co. Whether they really were 'Scotland's first lady distillers' is hard to know, for the old laird's former coachman was also down as managing the distillery. This was Colin Hay who became owner of Ardbeg on the demise of the MacDougall sisters, and continued to send the whisky to Buchanan's — a firm of whisky merchants in Glasgow who later became partners in the distillery.

When Alfred Barnard visited in the 1880s he spoke of the distillery's lonely position on the very verge of the sea and how 'the isolation tends to heighten the romantic sense of its position.' From its pair of spirit stills it was then producing 250,000 gallons of pure Islay malt which Buchanan's sold on to the big wine and spirit merchants in Glasgow, Liverpool and London. In the space of fifty years, it had grown into a relatively big fully-fledged distillery with a staff of 60 from a small farmyard operation pumping out just 500 gallons a week.

The firm of Alexander MacDougall &Co. carried on until the 1950s the distillery having been bought outright from the laird of Kildalton in the 1920s for £19,000. Then Ardbeg was consumed by the Canadian giant, Hiram Walker, which in turn was subsumed into Allied Distillers. As well as playing second fiddle to Laphroaig in Allied's portfolio of distilleries, it was claimed that Ardbeg's personality was being tweaked to suit the blenders. Perhaps the still-run was cut back slightly to reduce the proportion of heaver oils making it into the final cut – who knows. But it does seem true that when Glenmorangie took it over in 1997, it took some time to work out exactly what Ardbeg should be. Its past form could be second to none, or strangely disappointing. Once the distillery stopped malting its own barley the phenolic content of the malt tended to vary at first, but has since become much more uniform. One reason why Ardbeg can cope with such highly peated malt is the curious piece of copper tubing attached to the wash still which helps purify the wash before sending it through to the spirit still. It is said that if you put Ardbeg's wash through a

standard spirit still, the result would be undrinkable.

Another problem stemmed from the serious gaps in past production. Where whisky making has been carried on uninterrupted year after year, the distillery owners are completely free to decide at what age to bottle – in the case of Ardbeg, that simply had not been possible for many years. Finally, as the millennium drew to a close, sufficient stocks were found to launch a ten year-old – a smooth, contemplative dram where the smells of the harbour, of wet rope and smoked fish come wafting out of the glass. And beneath those layers of dense peat smoke lies something tart and tangy – TCP perhaps?

Checking the Spirit Safe at Ardbeg
Note the wooden spirit receiver below the spirit safe.

Rolling the Barrels at Ardbeg (opposite)
The 250 litre 'hoggies' are rolled off their racks onto foam landing mats, to be re-racked or tankered off the island and re-filled into casks on the mainland.

Maturing Casks in the Warehouse at Ardbeg
With the exception of Bruichladdich, most of the whisky made on Islay is matured on the mainland where the big whisky groups have their central warehouses.

LAGAVULIN

Lagavulin in the Early Morning Light

Each cask of Lagavulin destined to be a single malt is laid down for sixteen years, which makes the task of predicting future demand well nigh impossible. If its popularity keeps growing, Lagavulin may soon have to be rationed.

> **Pronunciation:** laka**vool**in
>
> **Founded:** 1817
>
> **Founder:** John Johnston
>
> **Region:** Islands
>
> **Production capacity:** 1,700,000 litres
>
> **Address:** Port Ellen, Isle of Islay PA42 7DZ
>
> **Tel:** 01496 302 730
>
> **website:** www.malts.com
>
> **Parent Company:** Diageo
>
> **Visitor Centre:**
>
> Contact distillery for details

From the very start it was inevitable that the history of this great island distillery should be intertwined with its close neighbour – Laphroaig. There have been times of shared ownership, and times of bitter dispute and rivalry, but today such feelings have long since softened into mutual respect. The truth is they are different – each producing their own very personalised style of malt whisky which belies the fact that they live so close together.

It is hard not to be swept up in the deep sense of history that pervades Lagavulin Bay and has done for so long. It was here that Robert the Bruce fled after his defeat by the Earl of Pembroke in the early fourteenth century. It was here that the Lords of the Isles had their stronghold at Dunyveg Castle whose tattered ruins still guard the entrance to the bay. And it was here in the mid eighteenth century that moonshine whisky was being produced by up to a dozen bothies which had banded together to form some sort of smugglers' co-operative. These bothies were gathered around a communal mill which supplied the necessary malt – in fact the name Lagavulin comes from the Scots Gaelic – 'laggan mhouillin' meaning the mill in the hollow.

The name Dunyveg is a similar corruption of Gaelic for the 'fort of little ships' – a reference to the way the Lord of the Isles could send forth a fleet of flat-bottomed boats through the castle's sea-gate. If attacked by someone without an intimate knowledge of the waters round here, the Ileachs [Islaymen] could watch with glee as their enemy's ships caught on the vicious rocks that lurk just below the surface. It may be beautiful, but this is no natural harbour; indeed

for many years the barrels of whisky made at the distillery had to be floated out across the bay to boats waiting beyond the rocks.

The smuggling bothies had merged into what became a recognisable distillery by 1817. In fact, for the first 20 years there were two distilleries operating side by side, until one was wound up and Lagavulin carried on alone. The first man to distil here was John Johnston of Tallant, father of Donald who we met at Laphroaig. It appears that Johnston had fallen into debt with Alexander Graham who was an Ileach by marriage and a whisky merchant by day - running the 'Islay Cellar' in Glasgow in partnership with John Logan Mackie. So when he died in 1836, Graham took over the lease. This was periodically renewed, but seldom without rows about who should pay for necessary repairs and extensions. These clearly happened as Laphroaig became one of the biggest distilleries on the island with three malthouses and two kilns and with an annual production of 75,000 gallons by the 1880s. By this stage John Mackie had taken over the Glasgow business, and was training up his nephew for succession. Peter Mackie had done his apprenticeship in whisky making at Lagavulin and was busy developing the blended side of the business

– which eventually gave birth to White Horse. The success of the brand with Lagavulin at its heart, secured the future of the distillery and made Mackie a personal fortune. Yet the quality of the spirit produced here was not just appreciated by blenders, for long before the creation of White Horse, this was

Looking West to the Hills Behind Lagavulin

The View Across Lagavulin Bay

one of the most prominent single malts around. In fact, by the time Glenfiddich decided to re-invent the world of single malt whisky in the 1960s, people had been drinking Lagavulin for the best part of a century. One hopes for their sake that these early drinkers were getting a reasonably matured dram. The thought of Lagavulin, now sold as a 16 year-old, being drunk under-age almost fresh from the still is hard to swallow.

Having lost his connection with Laphroaig as sole agents in a bitter court case in 1907, Peter Mackie decided he could build a replica distillery of his own within the grounds of Lagavulin. Thus was born the Malt Mill Distillery in a hopeless bid to reinvent Laphroaig, copying the stills and even hiring the old distiller who used to work there. The Malt Mill was a small, highly traditional distillery with floor maltings and a peat kiln, but its whisky was not Laphroaig. For a start it drew its water from the same source as Lagavulin, the Surnaig burn, while Laphroaig had always been supplied by a bog – something Mackie must have known. Those who tried a drop of malt from the Malt Mill – one of the peatiest malts ever produced – were unlikely to confuse it with the whisky made down the road. The distillery was demolished in the 1960s and for a brief period its two pear-shaped pot-stills joined those of Lagavulin while its old maltings were transformed into a visitor centre. Apart from that, all that remains today is a pair of mill stones painted with a white horse beside the gate.

Finally in 1921 Sir Peter Mackie, as he then was, managed to negotiate the outright purchase of his beloved Lagavulin for £16,000 from Iain Ramsay, the laird of Kildalton. Three years later Mackie died, and his company changed its name to White Horse Distillers Ltd which came under the yoke of the Distillers Company in the late 1920s. Supplies of grain would arrive from the *Pibroch*, a coal-fired puffer which would land at the distillery's own pier and leave with newly filled casks of malt. In 1937 the *Pibroch* famously rescued 22 trawler men whose two vessels had struck rocks in the treacherous waters round Islay's southern coast, while during the war it had a narrow escape from a German U-boat. Had the commandant known the puffer was packed full of Islay malt – it could have added a whole new twist to Compton Mackenzie's classic yarn, *Whisky Galore*.

With the advent of a modern ferry the puffers disappeared in the mid 1970s when the distillery abandoned its own maltings in favour of the Port Ellen maltings nearby. For Lagavulin, each kiln-load of barley is left to soak up the aroma of locally cut peat for no less than 22 hours. At the other end of the process the spirit run off the two spirit stills is slowed to a trickle to increase the contact with the copper. The result is a dram like no other, filling the mouth with deeply scented smoke where the initial fruit-cake sweetness gives way to a long, dry, slightly bitter finish.

Laphroaig Contemplates its Reflection

The home of what is said to be Prince Charles' favourite malt, has hardly changed in a hundred years.

LAPHROAIG

Pronunciation: la**froa**eeg

Founded: 1815

Founder: Donald Johnston

Region: Islands

Production capacity: 2,400,000 litres

Address: Port Ellen, Argyll PA42 7DU

Tel: 01496 302 418

website: www.laphroaig.com

Parent Company: Allied Domecq

Visitor Centre:

Contact distillery for details

Famed for its raw, uncompromisingly pungent taste as one of the most heavily peated single malts around, Laphroaig the distillery is in a very beautiful spot for sure, in its sheltered bay with the low hills of Kildalton behind and the gently shelving sea in front. Marketed as a whisky of no half measures that you will either love or hate, I somehow pictured the distillery perched on a cliff jutting out into the Atlantic, pounded by breakers and enveloped in a permanent cloud of spray.

Yet if one lets the whisky speak for itself, Laphroaig is somehow like a conch shell found on the beach – pretty to look at, but if you hold it to your ear or, in this case, your lips, you can feel the power of the sea. There is an inescapable aroma of sea weed and iodine in Laphroaig, which was apparently the reason it could be legally sold in the States as a medicinal spirit during prohibition. But one should not get carried away trying to trace the source of why a whisky tastes and smells the way it does. When Alfred Barnard visited the distillery in the 1880s, he was told that the sea air had absolutely no effect whatsoever on the whisky and that its unique taste was all down to peat.

The people behind Laphroaig for most of its history were the Johnstons – a local family of tenant farmers and distillers from Tallant a few miles east along the southern coast of Islay, near the famous Kildalton Cross on Ardmore Point. With his father, John, already involved with Lagavulin down the road, Donald Johnston established Laphroaig, which is

The Sheltered Cove at Laphroaig

The dreamy setting belies the raw intensity and peat-smoked brilliance of the whisky – as fulsome and uncompromising a dram as you could wish for.

Gaelic for 'hollow by the bay', in the 1820s. With Port Ellen nearby for access to supplies by sea and for shipping whisky out, and with plentiful cold water and peat, it was a well-chosen site. Others thought so too, and within ten years, Johnston was joined by the Ardenistiel distillery next door. At first this was run by James and Andrew Stein from the famous dynasty of Lowland distillers, but they soon pulled out. By then Donald Johnston had died, apparently from falling into a vat of his own burnt ale in 1847. The distilleries limped on side by side until the two were amalgamated into Laphroaig in the 1860s. There was much family feuding with contested wills and disputed water rights, until Donald's niece, Catherine, took over in 1907.

The distillery was making a loss by then and it was felt that the Glasgow firm of Mackie & Co., who had been Laphroaig's agents for as long as anyone could remember, were not giving the Johnstons a fair deal. To terminate the contract, they took Peter Mackie to court. The great whisky baron, the man behind White Horse who also represented Lagavulin, was furious. If this was the reward for all those years of hard work promoting Laphroaig and giving Glaswegians a taste for Islay malts, he would teach the Johnstons a lesson they wouldn't forget. In a fit of pique he ordered stones to be ripped up from the lade to stop water flowing to the distillery, but this merely ended in another trial which again he lost.

The role of Catherine Johnston as the first lady distiller of Laphroaig was eclipsed by Bessie Williamson, who arrived as a temporary short-hand typist in the early 1930s. By this stage the distillery was owned and run by Ian Hunter, Catherine's nephew, who had invested all his time and money on modernising Laphroaig, doubling the number of stills to four in the early 1920s. An early photo shows Hunter in the middle astride a barrel, surrounded by his staff, with Bessie very much on the edge of the group. However she soon became a pivotal figure at Laphroaig. When Hunter was struck down by a mild stroke in the Caribbean where he was trying to drum up post-prohibition sales to the States, he sent for Bessie to continue the tour. Gradually as his health drained away, his former secretary took on more and more of the running of the distillery, for which she became company secretary. When Ian Hunter died in 1954 without an heir, he left his entire estate, including the distillery to Bessie Williamson. Not a bad legacy for a girl from Glasgow who had come for a holiday job some twenty years earlier and decided to stay. In the early 1960s she sold out to Long John Distillers Ltd who added another pair of stills and kept Bessie on as MD until 1972.

Three years later Long John was purchased by Whitbread who later sold out to its current owners, Allied Distillers in 1990. Laphroaig is very much Allied's flagship single malt, whose best known consumer is probably Prince Charles. The Prince once dropped in by private plane to pick up a case or two, only to overshoot and land nose-down at the end of the runway on Islay's pocket-sized airport.

The secret of Laphroaig is in the peat and being able to exploit it to maximum effect because the distillery has its own maltings. This may only account for a third of the barley used and have more than a little to do with PR, but those who work here believe that somehow it gives them the edge. By allowing the damp barley 18 hours to soak up the warm, hazy blue smoke from the peat, before turning up the heat to dry the grains, you can achieve a unrivalled degree of control. Buying malt in you can specify the degree of peat, the so-called phenolic content, but you cannot insist on a process like that.

The Towering Pagoda of Bowmore

For all but a handful of distilleries, the pagoda chimney is purely decorative, but at Bowmore with its own floor maltings, it helps draw the smoke up from the kiln to dry the malt and infuse it with the scent of peat.

Feeding the Kiln at Bowmore

At Bowmore the malted barley is smoked with a precise quantity of Islay peat and then dried by blowing air from radiators filled with waste water from the distilling process.

BOWMORE

Pronunciation: boamore

Founded: 1779

Founder: David Simson

Region: Islands

Production capacity: 2,000,000 litres

Address: Bowmore, Isle of Islay, Argyll PA43 7JS

Tel: 01496 810 671

website: www.morrisonbowmore.com

Parent Company: Suntory

Visitor Centre: Open all year.

Tour times: Summer, Mon–Fri, 10.30am, 11.30am, 2pm and 3pm. Sat, 10.30am. Rest of year, Mon–Fri, 10.30am and 2pm only. Free guiding and tasting.

All the distilleries on Islay are to be found beside the sea, but none quite as close as Bowmore which was literally built into the harbour wall of the island's capital. Its whitewashed walls are regularly bathed in the salty ozone-rich spray blowing in off Loch Indaal, while the damp air penetrates deep into the underground cellars. Here a few thousand select casks, including one laid down to mark the Queen's Golden Jubilee in 2002, slumber in peace, though most of the whisky produced is matured on the mainland. This is common practice among island distilleries who simply do not have room to give their malts the long years needed to come round and mellow into well balanced whiskies. In the case of Bowmore there is even less space now than there used to be, as the ghost of an old warehouseman would discover if he drifted in to what was previously the No. 3 warehouse, for instead of rows of maturing casks he would find the town's public baths warmed by the waste heat from the distilling process. The reason for this inspired piece of local philanthropy was partly due to the rising cost of fuel and the need to do something about it. By 1980 the distillery's fuel bill had reached £100,000 a year. Earlier the company had won praise from the green lobby for its work at the Glen Garioch distillery where heat had been recovered and used to grow a commercial crop of tomatoes in greenhouses next-door.

The swimming pool is not the only unique feature at Bowmore however. As well as being the oldest distillery on the island, it has been a focus for the community from the day the town was built. It may employ nothing like the number it once did, but without its distillery and all the visitors drawn here as a result, the town of Bowmore would suffer badly.

As you approach the town the first striking landmark is the round church built in 1769 to deny the devil any corners to hide and possibly lure the congregation into sin. The church was one of the earliest buildings to appear in what was to be the new economic and social centre of the island, replacing Killarow, now Bridgend, a few miles north at the foot

Bruichladdich Beside Loch Indaal
Somehow the scent of iodine and seaweed seeps into the spirit of Bruichladdich to give it the unmistakable stamp of Islay despite the relatively low levels of peating.

of Loch Indaal. The decision to create this new town was Daniel Campbell's, the laird of Islay, whose grandfather had bought the island in 1725. Among the first to arrive was a farmer and part-time distiller from Killarow called David Simson who was granted rights to open a quarry and build houses here as well as cut turf from the moss. He was also the local postmaster and ran a steam packet from Port Askaig to Tarbert on the mainland, but somehow found time to establish a distillery at the bottom of Hill Street down by the water-front. At one point he was even doing a bit of distilling on Jura, but soon found himself over-stretched.

Bowmore remained a very small-scale operation, until William and James Mutter, merchants from Glasgow, bought the distillery in 1837. According to one report there was only space to mash 100 bushels a week – enough to make 800 gallons of spirit. But things soon changed, for James Mutter, as well as being Glasgow's Ottoman, Portuguese and Brazilian Vice-Consul, was determined to drag Bowmore into the industrial age. The still house was expanded and new kilns and warehouses were added. Meanwhile the number of stills had grown to four by the 1880s. According to a contemporary etching these were all different and included a weird double-headed still that fed into two separate worms – a radical design that never caught on. Because of the expansion, the old lade from the river Laggan had to be diverted into a nine-mile aqueduct to carry sufficient water to feed the mash. By now production of this 'pure Islay malt' had risen to 200,000 gallons a year, making Bowmore second only to Ardbeg. The Mutters had their own 145-ton steamship to carry the casks to the mainland where it was aged and bottled beneath the arches of Glasgow's Central Station.

The whisky was being sold as far afield as Canada, but something went wrong and by 1890 the family firm had gone out of business. Over the next 70 odd years various new owners came and went until another Glasgow-based whisky firm, Stanley P. Morrison Ltd, bought Bowmore for £117,000 in 1963 and seriously cranked up production. Within five years the distillery was pumping out 880,000 gallons per annum – fourteen times what it had produced the year before the sale. What was now Morrison Bowmore finally became part of the Japanese spirits group, Suntory, in 1994.

In keeping with the idea that Bowmore is different, the barley is malted on site in the distillery's three malting floors to produce a moderately peated, and therefore atypical Islay malt whisky. The grain is smoked with a precise quantity of Islay peat and then dried by blowing air from radiators filled with waste water from the distilling process. Meanwhile low temperature steam is taken from the condensers to heat the stills and the coppers, thus doing away with the need for heavy fuel oil. The system cost the best part of £300,000 to install, but given the energy savings that resulted it took less than three years to recoup the money spent. It doesn't seem to have done the whisky any harm either – the standard 12 year-old is a beguiling, aromatic malt, sweet and floral, quite dry and smoky on the finish.

BRUICHLADDICH

Pronunciation: broo-ee**khlad**eekh

Founded: 1881

Founder: William, Robert and John Harvey

Region: Islands

Production capacity: 1,500,000 litres

Address: Bruichladdich, Islay, Argyll PA49 7UN

Tel: 01496 850221

website: www.bruichladdich.com

Parent Company: Bruichladdich Distillery Company

Visitor Centre: Contact distillery for details

When Bruichladdich was built in 1881 it was the ultimate, state-of-the-art distillery and boasted cavity walls and even concrete made from pebbles from the sea shore which was pretty radical in those days. By a curious twist of fate it has now become one of the most old-fashioned distilleries in Scotland, and proudly so. For a start its current owners are delighted that not one computer is used to produce Bruichladdich's single malt whisky. They bought the distillery in December 2000 and clearly see themselves as the true anti-heroes of the whisky industry. 'Bruichladdich – the independent Scottish company owned by real people NOT anonymous corporate conglomerates' declares the company website. Some years before, the company had fallen foul of one of these corporations and ended up in court for bringing out an independent bottling of Laphroaig and having the cheek to call it 'Leapfrog', but that's another story.

Bruichladdich is the most westerly distillery in Scotland, sitting on the jug-handle peninsula of Kilchoman facing east across Loch Indaal towards Bowmore. It was founded by Robert, William and John Harvey, a family whose experience of distilling went back for at least a century. The Harveys already owned two Glasgow distilleries, Yoker and Dundashill, the latter being Scotland's largest malt distillery at that time.

Their venture on Islay, built a couple of years before Bunnahabhain, came relatively late. By the 1880s blended Scotch was rapidly replacing malt whisky, and the blending houses were tending to

Stillroom at Bruichladdich

From being a true state-of-the-art distillery when it was built in 1881, Bruichladdich is now gloriously old-fashioned – its new owners proud that not one computer is used to make the single malt.

Polishing the Glass
From the Spirit Safe
at Bruichladdich

move away from the assertive, more dominant malts associated with Islay. For this reason, both Bruichladdich and Bunnahabhain have always had a reputation for being lighter and therefore different from the heavily peated malts of the Kildalton distilleries like Laphroaig and Lagavulin.

The fact that it was designed from scratch and had not evolved out of the farmyard which was so often the case, allowed the contractor, John MacDonald of Glasgow's Tollcross, to build an efficient, thoroughly modern distillery. MacDonald was said to be 'an excellent and expeditious builder... [and was] sole holder of a patent for concrete'. Assuming he had a good patent lawyer for this revolutionary new building material, he should have done quite nicely. The distillery buildings were

grouped around a spacious, square courtyard with the old floor maltings in front facing the water – a layout that has barely changed since.

Soon Bruichladdich's two stills were pumping out 94,000 gallons of malt whisky a year. This was sent over to the mainland for blending and bottling in a trade that grew to a speculative climax and then burst at the start of the twentieth century. In 1901, the Harvey brothers were approached by the Distillers Co. who had embarked on their great distillery buying spree to try and impose harmony on an industry where the bond between supply and demand had become so unhinged. The Harveys declined, but lost all their interests on the mainland a couple of years later and were left with just Bruichladdich which they shut down in 1929 and then finally sold to Joseph Hobbs eight years later for £23,000.

Hobbs was a recently returned Scottish born entrepreneur who made and lost money in North America. He was convinced that boom times were just around the corner for Scotch whisky once the US Government bowed to the inevitable and repealed prohibition. Backed by the American spirits firm of Train & Macintyre he had already bought Glenury in Stonehaven, and went on to buy Glenesk, Ben Nevis and Lochside.

After the war Bruichladdich was sold off to the Glasgow whisky brokers, Ross & Coulter, for a hefty £205,000, though this was mainly due to large stocks. With its old steam engine and the barley hoisted up to the barley loft by horse until the late

1950s, the distillery had rather lost its cutting-edge design. Then two more sell-offs left it in the hands of Invergordon Distillers in 1975, who were later purchased by the Americans and then merged with Whyte & Mackay. The new owners began a much-needed programme of investment – the mash-house and tun room were expanded, and a new pair of stills was added to boost potential output to 800,000 gallons, if there was the demand. Sadly things were looking fairly bleak on that front when the distillery celebrated its centenary in 1981. Spirit dribbled out in fits and starts until the boiler was shut down and the stills went cold in 1995, the same year as Ardbeg. Technically Bruichladdich was now in 'mothballs', waiting for the cyclical up-turn in whisky's fortunes which was due any day, but with each passing year resuscitation becomes that much harder and more expensive.

But with Ardbeg now back in business with Glenmorangie and Islay malts very much the flavour of the month there was a glimmer of hope. A week before Christmas 2000 the 'real people' we met at the start, just managed to raise the last few thousand pounds needed to clinch the deal. After spending the winter months preparing all the machinery and buildings the first spirit began to flow at the end of May 2001. At the party to celebrate the event, one very old Ileach, or native of Islay, was heard to say: 'This is better than the Coronation'.

Two whiskies are now made at the distillery. There is the traditional Bruichladdich, which comes as a 10, 15 and 20 year-old which uses a lightly peated malt less than a tenth as strong as Laphroaig. This, together with the tall, slender stills, gives a crisp, elegant spirit that lacks the lush, oily character often found in a more typical Islay malt. The other whisky is Port Charlotte, made from the stills but with fairly heavily peated malt.

Content to make malt whisky on its own without supplying others for blends, the distillery can engage in 'trickle distillation', then age all the casks on site before shipping them over to the bottling line on the mainland. Even then water is shipped over from Islay to dilute the whisky to its bottle strength of 46 per cent abv. Whether you can really detect this last point I'm not sure, especially when you have diluted the whisky with water from the tap, but it is a fine dram nonetheless.

CAMPBELTOWN

*Campbeltown Loch I wish you were whisky
Campbeltown Loch, Och Aye!
Campbeltown Loch I wish you were Whisky
I would drink you dry!* Andy Stewart

Of all the great whisky regions, the story of Campbeltown – its slow rise to glory and dramatic fall from grace – is one of the most intriguing. Not that Campbeltown whisky has disappeared for good, indeed the mighty Springbank is hailed as one of the finest malts in Scotland. But

**Campbeltown –
at the Head of the Loch**

At its peak there were over twenty distilleries in Campbeltown, or 'whiskyopolis' as it was dubbed. Thanks to the profits from Scotch, it was said that Campbeltown once enjoyed the highest income per capita of any town in Britain.

where once the town's distilleries outnumbered all but Speyside's, there are now just two that remain.

The Kintyre peninsular, the great arm of Argyll that slips southwards into the Irish sea between the isles of Arran and Islay, was known to be producing whisky by the end of the sixteenth century. Just under a hundred years after Friar John Cor made history with the first ever mention of distilling in Scotland, a quantity of 'aquavytie' was delivered to the village of Tayinloan, 15 miles from Campbeltown. If this is the first written record, many believe distilling had been practised in the region for some time before then. If you hold with the belief that this is a Celtic drink which came originally from Ireland. That the coast of Antrim is just twelve miles across the water, and that St Columba stayed here for three years before sailing to Iona in the sixth century. Then perhaps Campbeltown was the true cradle of Scotch whisky – yet, the truth is we will never know.

The first licence to produce whisky in the town was awarded shortly afterwards to John Boyl in 1609. It was a good time to start, for that same year the 'Statutes of Icolmkill' had decreed that the Western Highlands should stick to home-made drink and desist from imported wines and spirits. As for what drew the early distillers to Campbeltown, it was the abundant supply of barley, and the fact there was a well-established malting industry here with as many as 40 malt barns in the town by the mid eighteenth century. The Mitchells, whose descendents still run the Springbank distillery, were a family of farmers and maltsters when they moved from the Lowlands to settle in Campbeltown in the seventeenth century. Already by 1713 distilling had become a sufficiently important industry for the Town Council to appoint three inspectors to ensure no-one was producing watered-down whisky or 'insufficient stuff' as it was called. By the end of the century the *Statistical Account*

for the Parish of Campbeltown mentions 22 licensed distilleries. These were clearly modest operations with a combined output of just 19,800 gallons.

There was also plenty of whisky being made at home until the law first reduced the permitted size of the stills from ten gallons to two and then banned private distillation altogether in 1781. And there would doubtless have been a fair bit made on the side – taking advantage of Campbeltown's remote location right on the southern tip of Kintyre and thus well away from the main concentration of gaugers or excisemen. It was still taking six hours by coach from Tarbert, a century later. In any event the draconian laws of 1797 which raised the licence to £9 per gallon of still capacity made it almost impossible to produce whisky legally on a commercial scale, and remain in business. Over the next three years the authorities seized as many as 292 illicit stills in this one town. There was a slow realisation by the Government that their hostile tax regime had backfired, at least it was not bringing in the revenue it once was. There were several half-hearted measures to try and bring the licensed whisky trade back into being, but it was not until 1817 that anyone in this part of the world could be lured back into the fold to take out a licence. Six years later, the Excise Act finally made legal whisky a worthwhile enterprise and within little over a decade the number of distilleries in the parish leapt from three to thirty. They were well placed to corner the market in Glasgow, having long supplied the city with contraband whisky across the Firth of Clyde. Glasgow's population had already overtaken Edinburgh and was now the fastest-growing city in Britain. Its principal industry was textiles, and working in the heat and dust of these dark satanic mills brought on a terrible thirst.

Some of the new distilleries lasted only a matter of years, a few more were added in the 1870s until numbers settled at around twenty. It was still a vast number, nonetheless, of distilleries concentrated in such a small space. Only Speyside boasted more whisky production and that was spread out across the whole of Strathspey. By the end of the nineteenth century Campbeltown had become something special. This was no ordinary market town, this was the great 'Whisky Metropolis' of the west coast. The local distillers even set up their own draff refinery to process all the by-products disgorged by their distilleries. Wet grains and draff were sold locally at 4d a bushel, while dried grains were reportedly shipped to Rotterdam to feed the horses of the German army.

There had been sufficient local barley when this was still a cottage industry run on a part-time basis, but by now huge quantities of grain were being shipped in from other parts of Scotland and from as far afield as Denmark and Russia. When one of the great Baltic grain ships was in dock, it was reported that every horse and cart in the town had to be requisitioned in the town. Watching the barley come and the whisky go, the editor of the local paper declared:

'There is no saying where the Campbeltown whisky ends, or what it sets in motion as it flows along, but the volume set agoing from Campbeltown … [is] enough to make a navy as well as men's heads to swim'.

In his book *In the Hebrides*, written in 1886, C.F. Gordon Cumming put Campbeltown's annual production at 2,657,000 proof gallons. With duty charged at 10 shillings a gallon this meant this one town was contributing over £1 million to the Treasury each year.

The original house-style of the region had been for a strongly peated malt approaching Islay in its intensity. In fact the smell wafting down Campbeltown Loch from the chimneys of the town's many distilleries must have been quite something for anyone approaching by ship. During the second half of the nineteenth century Campbeltown enjoyed enormous demand from the big blending houses. As the fashion moved to a gentler, more Speyside-style of malt to use in the blends, the town's distilleries began to switch to coal to malt their barley instead of peat. Luckily there were plentiful deposits of cheap coal nearby.

By now some serious money was pouring into the bank accounts of the town's great whisky families. The Colvilles, Mitchells, McTaggarts and Fergusons all built large mansions to reflect their newfound wealth and status. It was claimed in 1891 that Campbeltown, with its population of just under two thousand, had the highest income per capita of anywhere in Britain. And if Gordon Cumming's figures were correct, it meant every citizen was contributing the equivalent of almost £30,000 a year in duty in today's money.

With production approaching 2 million gallons a year, it was almost too good to be true — surely it couldn't last? The answer was not long coming, though no-one could have foreseen how swift and devastating the collapse would be. Hedley Wright, the current owner of Springbank, believes that Campbeltown's phenomenal success contained the seeds of its own destruction. Such strong demand had inevitably fostered a sense of complacency among some distillers, a feeling that demand for their whiskies would always be around and that there was no need to plough the profits back into the business. There were also outside forces to contend with. Speculators bought large quantities of whisky which in turn boosted production to unsustainable levels.

When the bubble burst, as inevitably happened, it brought the speculators and the distilleries involved crashing through the floor.

The hangover from overproduction hit the whole industry in the years before 1914, as did the pernicious tax hikes of the Liberal Chancellor, Lloyd George. Once war-time restrictions eased, Campbeltown's home market of Glasgow was soon facing a crippling recession and mass unemployment. To add to their woes, the local coal field was pretty much exhausted. Desperate to hang on to their business, a number of distilleries were content to cut corners and do anything to shave a few pence off the price.

It was about this time that the highly pejorative term, 'stinking fish', began to appear as a way of describing the Campbeltown reek. Whether anyone really did use old herring barrels discarded by the town's fishing fleet is hard to say, the result would have been quite undrinkable. But inferior spirit was

No Malt Today

The malt store at Glen Scotia firmly locked.

Glen Scotia

Campbeltown's other distillery, still going if not as famous as Springbank

Empty Casks at Springbank
Having been emptied prior to bottling, casks such as these can be re-used up to 4 or 5 times.

Repairing the Roof at Springbank
Hector's plans for a quiet birthday were not to be.

compares to 16s for Craigellachie and 18s 3d for Ardbeg on Islay.

There had been some export trade across the Atlantic already established before US prohibition kicked in. A number of distilleries continued to ship their whisky across to Nassau from where it was bootlegged into the States. But it was not enough, and by 1925 the number of distilleries had fallen to 12 and by 1930 to just three. Soon there was just Springbank, until Glen Scotia came back from its slumbers to produce again.

GLEN SCOTIA

> **Pronunciation:** glen**skoash**a
> **Founded:** 1832
> **Founder:** Stewart, Galbraith & Co.
> **Region:** Islands
> **Production capacity:** 750,000 litres
> **Address:** High Street, Campbeltown PA28 6DS
> **Tel:** 01586 552 288
> **Parent Company:** Loch Lomond Distillery
> **Visitor Centre:** Contact distillery for details

being filled into poor-quality casks and this did nothing for the region's reputation.

Distilleries from Speyside and elsewhere were keen to move in on Campbeltown's patch and sell their whisky in Glasgow particularly to the big blending houses there. In 1924 the market price for spirit produced at Hazelburn, then part of Peter Mackie's White Horse empire and the largest distillery in Campbeltown, was just 8s a gallon. This

The demise of Campbeltown was brutally swift. Isolated down the far end of the Kintyre peninsula, the town found itself unable to compete with Speyside which was giving the blenders just what they wanted – reliable, well-balanced malts to pop in their blends. In desperation, Campbeltown looked west to America. But with the advent of prohibition and no brand names to push, the distilleries were soon pitching their anonymous Scotch against bathtub gin. They may have just won on quality, but they could not come close on price. The odds were so heavily weighted against survival, that all but two had disappeared for good by the mid 1930s.

Glen Scotia was established in 1832 on Campbeltown High Street by Stewart Galbraith & Co., who held the licence right up until the end of the First World War. After such a promising start, things started to go downhill rapidly. In 1930, the then owner, Duncan MacCallum threw himself into Campbeltown Loch after a dodgy business deal went wrong. They say his ghost still haunts the stillroom.

After a brief spell with the Bloch brothers, who cannot have found Campbeltown too convenient, given their other distillery was on Orkney, Glen Scotia eventually ended up with its present owners, Glen Katrine. Until recently its two stills have spent more time resting than making whisky, but is currently in production. Having spent much of the last century in crisis, perhaps Campbeltown's day will come again.

SPRINGBANK

Pronunciation: springbank
Founded: 1828
Founder: John and William Mitchell
Region: Islands
Production capacity: 2,000,000 litres
Address: 85 Longrow, Campbeltown, Argyll PA28 6ET
Tel: 01586 552 009
website: www.springbankdistillers.com
Parent Company: J & A Mitchell
Visitor Centre: Contact distillery for details

The story of Springbank is of one of gritty determination to survive against the odds. First there is the way the distillery itself managed to weather the terrible backlash of the 1920s and 30s which left the rest of the town's tight-knit whisky community in tatters. Then there is the story of the Mitchells themselves, the family of distillers who founded Springbank and still own and run it to this day. That is no mean feat in a world which has

Old 'Hoggies' of Springbank

become so dominated by corporate ownership, such that today just half a dozen companies control over four fifths of the Scotch whisky industry. Other than J&G Grant and Glenfarclas, it is hard to think of any other distillery that still belongs to the original family.

The Mitchells moved across from the lowlands and settled around Campbeltown on the southern tip of the Kintyre peninsular in the latter part of the seventeenth century. As a family of farmers and maltsters, they were almost certainly doing some distilling as well, if only in the form of home brew for their own consumption.

Springbank was established in 1828, and was officially the town's fourteenth distillery. It was on

A Barrowfull of Peat

Those distilleries with their own floor maltings like Springbank, fire their kilns with coke to produce the heat to dry the malt and then add peat for its fragrant smoke.

John Walker in Kilmarnock before the first year of trading was over. It may have been many years before the world-famous 'Johnnie Walker' blend was even thought of, but it was a nice, early endorsement all the same. The price paid per gallon including tax was just 8s 8d, which is roughly £35 in today's money, a sum that would not even cover the duty nowadays.

Unfortunately the two brothers fell out over their other interest – sheep farming, and William left to join Rieclachan, before eventually setting up on his own with the Glengyle distillery in 1872. By then, through partnerships, the extended Mitchell family had interests in four distilleries in the town, though Springbank, now registered under the name J & A Mitchell and Co, was easily the largest.

It would seem that Campbeltown's nineteenth-century whisky boom began relatively early. With one or two exceptions like Glengyle, the town's battery of distilleries were all in place within a decade of the 1823 Excise Act which turned legal malt whisky distilling into a viable reality. All the raw ingredients were close to hand including local peat and coal from the mine at Machrihanish. At first there was a healthy thirst among whisky drinkers in Glasgow to satisfy and this gradually gave way to a strong demand from the city's blending houses. Apart from a certain amount of spirit from Islay, and the ever-famous Glenlivet whiskies of Speyside, there was little in the way of competition. With a fast sea route up the Firth of Clyde, casks of Campbeltown malt could be shipped straight to the blenders' warehouses in the Broomielaw.

At its peak, this one industry town with its twenty lums (chimneys) all reeking away, must have felt safety in numbers. Whisky was by far the biggest employer in the region and demand was seemingly insatiable. Dufftown on Speyside could mimic Rome and boast of being built on seven stills instead of hills, but seven stills was nothing compared to Campbeltown, 'the Whisky Capital of the World'. Being all in the same place may have led to some useful economies of scale when it came to shipping in the grain and shipping out the whisky, but it had a serious downside as soon became clear.

Lumped so close together, the town's distilleries shared a collective reputation. When a few of them got a bad name for poor spirit and earned the epithet 'stinking fish' it poisoned the image of Campbeltown whisky as a whole. From this distance it is hard to know which came first. Maybe the blenders turned towards Speyside out of fashion, or perhaps they were provoked because the quality of Campbeltown had become simply too unreliable. If people really had grown so complacent that they were ageing their whisky in herring barrels as if no one would notice, you can hardly blame the blending houses for

Longrow in the centre of Campbeltown on the site of some old malt barns erected by Archibald Mitchell. Judging by the private ledger of a local coppersmith, Archibald had clearly diversified into producing whisky, or rather moonshine, since he never bothered to take out a licence. His son was a founding partner in Rieclachan which kept going right up until 1934, making it the third-last distillery in town to survive.

It was actually the Reid family, in-laws of the Mitchells, who built Springbank, but they soon found themselves in trouble financially and the distillery was bought by Archibald's two youngest sons, John and William, in 1837. The reputation of the Mitchell's malt whisky spread quickly and reached

switching their allegiance. Then again, that could have been just a vicious rumour put about by the east-coast distillers. It was certainly true, however, that Speyside malts tended to be much milder and this made them easier to absorb into a young blend. Either way the results for Campbeltown were disastrous and by the mid 1930s all but Glen Scotia and Springbank had collapsed.

Frank McHardy, the present distillery manager, claims they survived because of luck and because Springbank was always different from the heavy Campbeltown style. There was also the fact that the quality was never compromised. This was not going to be enough to protect the distillery from the 1980s whisky loch which left the few big players in the industry with more than enough stock of their own. The only solution was to become self-sufficient. In 1992 it was decided to restore the floor maltings and malt all the barley required using peat from Tomintoul. At the same time the distillery stopped selling fillings to blenders to concentrate on its three single malts. By having three stills, itself highly unusual, and carefully controlling the amount of peat in the kiln, McHardy can produce the triple-distilled, unpeated Hazelburn and the heavily peated, double-distilled Longrow. Between these two extremes, Springbank is moderately peated and distilled two and a half times. Add in the vagaries of different vintages and the effects of different casks that previously held anything from rum to Oloroso sherry [but not herring!] and this maverick distillery produces a wonderfully eclectic range of whiskies. For its part Springbank malt is characterised by its thick malty flavour, a discernible waft of peat smoke and a lively salty tang.

Malting one's own barley is a labour-intensive business, unless regularly turned the little rootlets of the sprouting barley are liable to matt together.

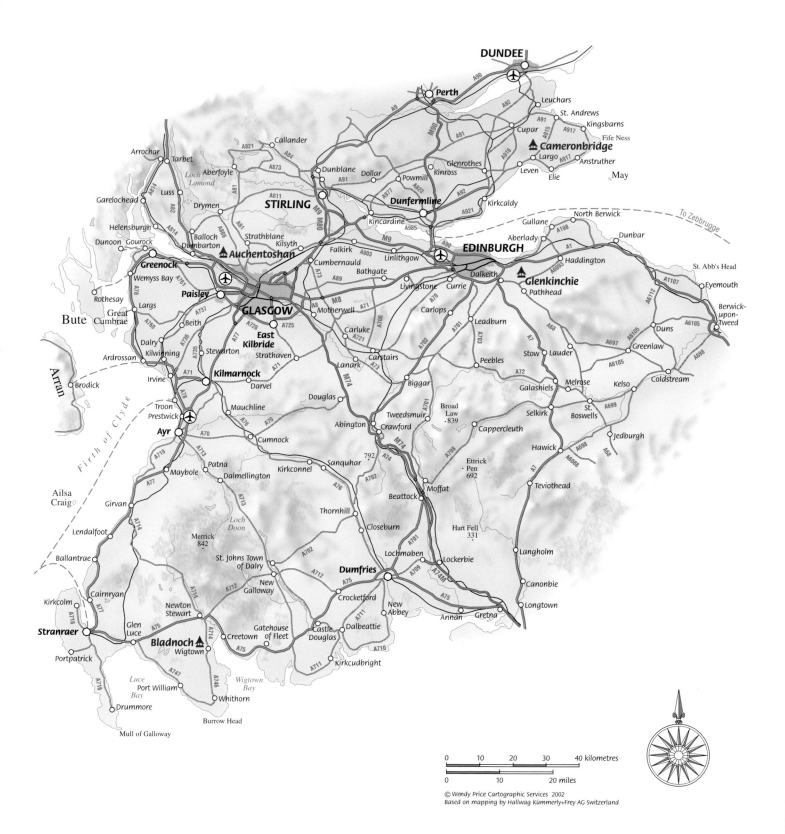

DUNDEE

Perth

Leuchars
St. Andrews
Kingsbarns
Cupar
Fife Ness
Callander
Glenrothes
Cameronbridge
Arrochar
Dunblane
Dollar
Largo
Anstruther
Tarbet
Powmill
Kinross
Leven
Elie
May
Loch
Aberfoyle
Lomond
Kilsyth
Kincardine
Kirkcaldy
Garelochead
Luss
Dunfermline
Drymen
STIRLING
North Berwick
Helensburgh
Strathblane
Falkirk
Linlithgow
Gullane
Dunbar
Balloch
Cumbernauld
Aberlady
Dunoon
Gourock
Dumbarton
Auchentoshan
Bathgate
EDINBURGH
Haddington
To Zeebrugge
Greenock
Livingstone
Dalkeith
Glenkinchie
St. Abb's Head
Wemyss Bay
Currie
Pathhead
Eyemouth
Paisley
Carlops
Rothesay
GLASGOW
Motherwell
Leadburn
Berwick-upon-Tweed
Largs
Bute
Great
Cumbrae
East
Kilbride
Carluke
Carstairs
Peebles
Stow
Lauder
Duns
Greenlaw
Dalry
Beith
Lanark
Galashiels
Melrose
Kelso
Ardrossan
Kilwinning
Stewarton
Strathaven
Biggar
St.
Boswells
Coldstream
Arran
Kilmarnock
Darvel
Irvine
Mauchline
Douglas
Tweedsmuir
Broad
Law
·839
Cappercleuth
Selkirk
Hawick
Jedburgh
Brodick
Troon
Prestwick
Abington
Crawford
Ettrick
Pen
692
Ayr
Cumnock
792
Teviothead
Ailsa
Craig
Maybole
Patna
Kirkconnel
Sanquhar
Hart Fell
331
Langholm
Girvan
Dalmellington
Thornhill
Beattock
Moffat
Loch
Doon
Closeburn
Lochmaben
Lockerbie
Lendalfoot
Merrick
842
St. Johns Town
of Dalry
Canonbie
Ballantrae
New
Galloway
Dumfries
Longtown
Kirkcolm
Cairnryan
Newton
Stewart
Crocketford
New
Abbey
Annan
Gretna
STRANRAER
Glen
Luce
Creetown
Gatehouse
of Fleet
Castle
Douglas
Dalbeattie
Bladnoch
Wigtown
Portpatrick
Luce
Port William
Bay
Whithorn
Wigtown
Bay
Kirkcudbright
Drummore
Burrow Head
Mull of Galloway

Firth of Clyde

0   10   20   30   40 kilometres
0   10   20 miles

© Wendy Price Cartographic Services 2002
Based on mapping by Hallwag Kümmerly+Frey AG Switzerland

LOWLAND
DISTILLERIES

———◆——◆——◆———

Before Sir Walter Scott, the so-called 'Wizard of the North', effectively re-branded Scotland in time for the State Visit of George IV in 1822, the Highlands were truly another country. It was a dim twilight zone full of menace and savagery, way beyond the dazzling enlightenment radiating from Edinburgh. Then as if by magic, the barbarous Highland warrior was transformed into the great 'Noble Savage', and suddenly all things tartan and Celtic became hugely trendy. If the whole romanticism of the Highlands was set in motion by Walter Scott, the Victorians hammered it home with a vengeance.

At the start of the nineteenth century, however, the Highland–Lowland divide had rarely felt so distinct. For one thing the revolution in farming and industry just beginning to sweep through the south, left the north virtually untouched. Thanks to better crop rotation, improved ploughing methods, the advent of new fertilisers and proper drainage, yields from Lowland arable farms improved dramatically. Meanwhile the big commercial whisky operations like James Stein's Kilbagie Distillery in Clackmannanshire with its staff of over 300, were swallowing up ever more barley, oats and wheat. At one point Lowland farmers were competing head on with the corn barons of East Anglia over who could supply the grain to produce the cheapest grain spirit. This would be rectified into gin, for which London had an insatiable craving.

As Lowland farming grew in scale, so too did whisky making. The farmers and the distillers developed a remarkable symbiotic relationship - a cycle of growing grain to feed the stills whose residue would be compressed into a nutritious source of protein for the animals.

The laws of the eighteenth century designed to raise revenue from whisky and curb smuggling, reinforced the north-south divide and pushed the few big licensed distillers to pursue quantity rather than quality. Nevertheless there were over 200

licensed distilleries set up in the Lowlands, the vast majority producing malt spirit in pot stills. But for Auchentoshan, founded in 1800, and Glenkinchie 37 years later, none of the malt distilleries have survived, although there is the resurgence of Bladnoch, way down in the south-west in Wigtown. Reopened as a museum, Bladnoch whose production is limited to 100,000 litres a year — is now the ultimate boutique distillery. Its closure by United Distillers back in 1993 was no great surprise. Though the malt whisky produced here was considered just as fine as Glenkinchie, it was simply too far away. Bladnoch was never really cut out to survive the modern cost-cutting approach of having one distillery manager to oversee a clutch of nearby distilleries.

Meanwhile near Glasgow, the last malt whisky trickled from the stills of Inverleven in 1991. This was built in the 1930s inside the giant Dumbarton distillery, which continues to pump out an awesome quantity of grain whisky, which disappears into such big blends as 'Teacher's Highland Cream' and 'Ballantine's Finest'.

The idea of making malt and grain whisky inside the same plant goes back to the nineteenth century, when the big Lowland distilleries converted to continual distillation with the new Coffey stills. To make grain spirit from wheat or maize you need a little malted barley to add to the mash tun to help the grist convert its starch into soluble sugar. If this meant you were malting your own barley, you might as well have an old pot still to make a little malt whisky on the side. These early distillers would produce anything. The Caledonian distillery was happy to sell that 'variety known as Irish,' even though its 5-acre site in Edinburgh was a long way from the Emerald Isle. You would not catch a modern Lowland grain distillery doing that now. They are far too busy pumping out Smirnoff Ice and Malibu to have time for that; besides, it is probably illegal.

Before Inverleven closed, most Lowland grain

GLENKINCHIE

Pronunciation: glen**kinsh**ee
Founded: 1837
Founder: John & George Rate
Region: Lowlands
Production capacity: 1,700,000 litres
Address: Pencaitland, East Lothian EH34 5ET
Tel: 01875 342004
website: www.malts.com
Parent Company: Diageo
Visitor Centre: April–May, Mon–Fri, 10am–4pm. June–September, Mon–Sat, 9.30am–5pm. Sun, 12–5pm. October, Mon–Fri, 10am–5pm. Sat and Sun, 12–5pm. November–March, Mon–Fri, 11am–4pm.

T he Lowlands' most productive distillery lies about 15 miles southeast of Edinburgh, beyond the coastal resorts of the Firth of Forth and on the edge of the Lammermuir hills. With its rich alluvial soil, this is prime east-coast barley country.

In 1745, just to the north of here at Prestonpans, Bonnie Prince Charlie's Highland army won possibly the fastest victory in history when they defeated the dragoons of General Sir John Cope in just ten minutes. Earlier it had been the favoured route for English armies coming up from the south to lay siege to the Scottish capital and trash the surrounding countryside in the process. The whole area has a gentle, west-country feel to it, so perhaps the English soldiers felt at home as they reduced the nearby town of Haddington to rubble yet again.

Once the fighting fizzled out, the Lothians became the cradle of the agricultural revolution in Scotland. Just across the fields from the distillery, in the village of Ormiston, John Cockburn founded the Society of Improvers of Knowledge of Agriculture in the early eighteenth century. Among other claims to fame the Society is credited with introducing the turnip and the potato.

A century later, John and George Rate, whose farm bordered that of Cockburn, established the Milton distillery in 1825. It was a small-scale farm distillery which grew its own barley, mashed it with the waters of the Kinchie burn and distilled it into a mellow Lowland malt. The name 'kinchie' comes from the de Quincey family who held the land round here in the fourteenth century. By 1837 the distillery was called Glenkinchie

So with a good crop of barley on the doorstep and a plentiful supply of water to steep the grain and cool the worms, this little glen just beyond the village

Glenkinchie – A Lowland Survivor

When United Distillers launched their 'Classic Malts' in the early 1980s, they wanted to present a broad regional spread of single malts. While Cragganmore faced plenty of competition on Speyside, Glenkinchie was the uncontested candidate for the Lowlands.

distilleries were producing malt whisky for blending. Some would appear bottled as Single Malt under names like Kinclaith, Glen Flagler and Ladyburn. Of course none of these supposed 'malt distilleries' had visitor centres, which was probably just as well. The charm of a malt called 'Ladyburn' might wear off if you found it being made in William Grant's industrial grain distillery at Girvan.

Malt whisky feeds off the romance of Scotland, and that is something inextricably bound up with the Highlands. The Glenkinchie distillery a short drive south of Edinburgh, may well produce a pleasant dram; but without that backdrop of heather-clad peaks and the sound of water chuckling in the burn, something is missing somehow. Perhaps the Old Wizard has more to answer for than just the resurgence of tartan whimsy and all those Celtic dreams.

Bringing in the Barley – East Lothian
Another crop safely gathered in. Depending on the harvest Scotland can account for over three quarters of the barley used to make malt whisky.

of Pentcaitland would seem a pretty ideal spot for making whisky. There was a large, prosperous market in Edinburgh to supply, and there was soon a railway which ran within a few hundred yards of the distillery. But by 1853 the stills at Glenkinchie went cold and the Rates sold up. For the next 30 years the place was turned into a sawmill and the beery fumes of the wash and the sweet, ethery aromas of new-make spirit gave way to freshly cut timber.

By the 1880s, the whisky industry had been transformed by the boom in blended Scotch. The port of Leith was at the forefront of this revolution, supplying bottled whisky throughout Scotland and helping to open up new markets in England and beyond. Demand from the big blending houses for casks of good-quality malt had never been so great. The Glen Kinchie Distillery Co. was born and the stills were quickly fired up once more. The partners behind the company were a Mr Hannah of the Boroughloch Brewery in Edinburgh and a couple of wine merchants from Leith. They were later joined by two more wine merchants, including Robertson Sanderson & Co., whose main brand of whisky was the 'Celebrated Mountain Dew'. The blend most closely connected with Glenkinchie however, was that of Haig – sold as Gold Label and Dimple Scotch. The distillery was licensed to John Haig & Co. of Markinch in Fife, the oldest whisky dynasty

of them all.

The new owners completely rebuilt the distillery, and transformed Glenkinchie into what it is today – a relatively substantial, four-storey affair. With its red brick it has a functional, somewhat municipal feel about it, but it was clearly efficient. In no time its pair of old pot stills were pumping out almost 80,000 gallons of malt whisky a year, while the local railway line was connected via a siding which ran right to the malting house. Inside there were overhead railways to carry the barley to the malting floor and a mechanical elevator to take the grain from the grist hopper to the mash tun which was stirred by mechanically powered rakes. Compared to some of the malt distilleries in the Highlands which had only recently evolved out of the farmyard, this operation was plainly at the cutting edge of industrial design.

Glenkinchie became one of the early foundation stones of the giant Distillers' Company in 1914 when it was grouped together with four other Lowland distilleries to become Scottish Malt Distillers Ltd. It was shut down for a couple of years during the First World War, but managed to escape the next time. Most distilleries were forced to close during World War II because the Government clamped down on the use of barley for making whisky, but a small, uninterrupted flow trickled from Glenkinchie's stills throughout.

AUCHENTOSHAN

The distillery stopped malting its own barley in the spring of 1968. Watching this age-old process come to an end, was a moving experience for the then manager – Alistair Munro. 'That brought it home to me how much and how fast our industry was changing; and I felt that something of that disappearing past should be preserved and recorded for the future.' The result is the Museum of Malt Whisky Production whose most striking exhibit is a fully-working scale model of a Highland distillery, built for the Empire Exhibition at Wembley in London in 1925. There is also a quirky collection of devices for smuggling spirit out of the distillery. You could secrete it in something like a curved, metal hot-water bottle worn round the belly, or slip it down the trouser-leg in a pair of 'dogs'. These were small cylinders made of copper to be dipped into a cask when the manger's eyes were turned.

Alistair Munro's predecessor as distillery manager used to farm the adjoining 85 acres as well as oversee the stills. His Aberdeen Angus cattle obviously flourished on all the nutritious by-products from the whisky making process. And as if to reaffirm that symbiotic relationship that distilling and farming have always shared – the Glenkinchie beef herd were unbeaten champions at the Smithfield Show three years in a row. Luckily not all the goodness in the grain ends up as cattle-cake, for as a 10 year-old single malt this is a sweet, beguiling whisky – pale and clean with the scent of freshly cut grass.

Pronunciation:	okhen**tosh**an
Founded:	1823
Founder:	John Thorne
Region:	Lowlands
Production capacity:	1,750,000 litres
Address:	Dalmuir, Dunbartonshire
Tel:	01389 878 561
website:	www.morrisonbowmore.co.uk
Parent Company:	Suntory
Visitor Centre:	Contact distillery for details

From the mouth of the River Tay, the great Highland Line heads southwest in a gentle slant across Scotland. En route it skirts south of Perth, slips between Stirling and Dunblane, passes just north of Dumbarton and heads off down the Firth of Clyde. This last stretch coincides with an ancient Roman wall built by Antoninus Pius as the final northwestern limit of the Roman Empire, beyond which lay the Barbarian hordes. Being built of peat and turf it has not survived like Hadrian's wall to the south.

Here beside the Clyde, on what is now the A82 by the Erskine bridge, stands Scotland's other Lowland distillery. If the region's Roman roots have been

Triple Distillation at Auchentoshan

completely buried, so too has any sense of rural life – all thanks to the explosion of activity during the last 200 years when Glasgow became the fastest-growing city in Britain.

In 1800, the date when the Auchentoshan distillery was said to have been founded, all this was yet to happen. It was built at the foot of the Kilpatrick hills, in Old Kilpatrick which was then a free-standing village surrounded by open country. In fact the name Auchentoshan means 'corner of the field'. The fields have long since been swallowed up by the Clydebank suburb of Dunochter.

The first mention of Auchentoshan by name dates back to 1649, which shows the present site was once a monastery. The monasteries in Scotland were dissolved in 1560, which led to a steady stream of monks leaving their sheltered cloisters to join the community. Those that had moved on from the old monastic tradition of brewing beer to making spirits, were thus able to pass on their knowledge of distilling to the population at large. If this was the case here, then the roots of whisky-making at Auchentoshan may be very old indeed.

The tobacco trade of the eighteenth century had put Glasgow on the map. No other port in the country could compete on price or speed with reaching the eastern seaboard of North America and the plantations of Virginia and Maryland. By 1776 and the American War of Independence, Glasgow was importing two fifths of Britain's tobacco. If the great weed was in demand at home, some profitable use for the cargo space had to be found for the out-bound voyage. The answer was to take advantage of the local hand-weaving industry and start shipping linen – a business which had grown to nearly two million yards by the outbreak of the war.

This particular trade came to an abrupt end, but the city's tobacco barons had been careful to reinvest their wealth in new ventures which were beginning to

take off with the industrial revolution. From textiles and then chemicals Glasgow progressed to iron and steel and the manufacture of tramcars, trains and of course ships.

All this was witnessed from little Auchentoshan on the banks of the Clyde. Just as Glasgow was preparing to overtake Edinburgh as the biggest city in Scotland, Auchentoshan quietly took out a licence and went legal in 1823. The distillery's first recorded owner was a man called Thorne. Other early owners included the Filshie family from whom it passed to a firm from Greenock called C.H. Curtis & Co. in 1878. They were still in charge when Alfred Barnard made a brief visit a decade later. Barnard describes it as a 'little distillery ... situated in a romantic glen with a stream of water running past it.' He then adds, 'at the time of our visit the haymakers were busy in the fields connected with Distillery and consequently the Works were almost abandoned.' The operation included a barley barn and floor malting connected to a malt kiln. There were four washbacks and a 'good sized Mash Tun' and two 'old pot stills'. There were only nine people employed and the production was a modest 50,000 gallons a year. With no mention of any warehouses, this was presumably taken straight off to Greenock.

At some point Auchentoshan acquired another still to begin its famous triple distillation. This was a traditional Lowland method, similar to the one used for making Irish whiskey. By using an intermediate still to separate the higher alcohols and strong feints from the low wines prior to the final distillation, you

can achieve a more refined spirit in the end. Compared to the standard double distillation, the yield is lower but the strength is higher – around 80 per cent alcohol by volume. The first distillation lasts an hour, the second five and the third nine hours.

While there was certainly a taste for robust Highland-style whiskies in Glasgow to judge by the popularity of Islay and Campbeltown, there was also a strong immigrant community to satisfy. The prospect of jobs and the need to escape the potato blight back home, had sent wave after wave of Irish up the Clyde. Many brought with them a thirst for that triple-distilled taste of home.

Auchentoshan spent much of the twentieth century in the hands of various brewers starting with Maclachlans and then Tennents who were absorbed into Bass in the 1960s. During the Second World War, the distillery suffered during the blitz which killed a thousand people on Clydebank. As with the Yoker distillery in Glasgow its warehouses were hit; on one occasion, on the night of 13th March 1940, it lost 53 butts of whisky.

It 1969 it was bought by Eadie Cairns who completely modernised the distillery before selling it on to its current owners, Morrison Bowmore, for £325,000 in 1984. Since then the distillery has been overhauled again, and now produces a range of delicate single malts, with the scent of hay and lemon peel and a fresh, grassy, slightly oily flavour. They are classically Lowland, but curiously the water, from the Cochna Loch in the Kilpatrick hills, comes from the Highlands.

CAMERONBRIDGE

> **Pronunciation: kam**eron**bridge**
>
> **Founded:** 1824
>
> **Founder:** John Haig
>
> **Region:** Lowlands
>
> **Production capacity:** 65,000,000 litres of alcohol, two-thirds to make grain whisky
>
> **Address:** Windygates, Fife
>
> **Tel:** 01333 350 377
>
> **website:** www.diageo.com
>
> **Parent Company:** Diageo
>
> **Visitor Centre:** Contact distillery for details

Fife's claim to fame in the history of Scotch whisky came early. Having scooped the prize for the first, recorded mention of 'aqua vitae' in 1494, the county's contribution to the story begins to fade. In fact in most books on whisky, any mention of Fife begins and ends on the same day. So to redress the balance and pulverise any notion that whisky is still some couthy cottage industry, let us turn our attention to Cameronbridge.

The mighty Cameronbridge, there is no other way to describe it, is the engine room of Diageo, the biggest producers of Scotch whisky by a mile. Here is made the grain whisky for everything from Bells to J&B to Johnnie Walker Red and Black, the latter being the best-selling brand of whisky in the world. But that is not all. About a third of the current annual production of 65 million litres disappears into the company's brands of gin and vodka. Since Gordon's and Smirnoff moved their production to Cameronbridge over the last 20 years, four fifths of the UK's white spirits are now produced in Scotland, which is some small consolation, when Smirnoff Ice has become the country's national drink, at least in Glasgow. To this must be added all the Malibu, Pimms, sloe gin and Archer's Peach Schnapps also made here. In fact, Cameronbridge must single-handedly be stocking tens of thousands of bars and drinks cabinets around Britain and beyond.

The numbers are compelling. Each week 40-50 million litres of water, 3500 tonnes of wheat and 15 tonnes of yeast are boiled up, vaporised and turned into alcohol and animal feeds. Much of the wheat comes from local farms — a welcome side-effect of Britain joining the European Union. Before then the grain was mostly maize shipped into the Port of Leith from South Africa and the United States.

Yet like all distilleries one constant remains — the need for a plentiful and reliable source of water. This must have been uppermost in the mind of John Haig when he first came here in 1822 to survey the

**Cameronbridge –
The Gin Palace**

Since Gordon's and
Smirnoff moved their UK
production to
Cameronbridge over
the last twenty years, four
fifths of Britain's white
spirits are now
produced in Scotland.

site. One can imagine him, fresh out of university, the fifth in an unbroken line of whisky distillers, looking up the river Leven from the old Cameron Brig - and deciding this was where his future lay.

Pride of place was given to the first-ever continuous still, which his cousin, Robert Stein, had patented a few years later. The Stein still turned the wash into a fine mist and sprayed it through a series of hair-cloth diaphragms. It worked, but not half as well as the Coffey still invented by Dublin's former Inspector of Excise, Aeneas Coffey, in 1830. The improvement was due to replacing the diaphragms with copper plates. Haig soon decided to set family loyalty to one side and switch stills. An intriguing footnote to this, was that Coffey had initially tried to tempt Irish distillers with his new invention, but they simply were not interested. Had they seized the chance they would have been perfectly placed to dominate the great revolution about to sweep the industry – that of blended whisky, in which case 'Irish' would have been far bigger than 'Scotch'. Of course that might have kept Scotch 'pure' in some people's eyes, though it is hard to believe there would be 80 malt whisky distilleries, or anything like that number, still in production if it were not for blends.

Not that Cameronbridge whisky was solely grain – there were pot stills in operation as late as the 1920s. As Alfred Barnard wrote in his book *The Whisky Distilleries of the United Kingdom*, [published in 1887] 'There are several kinds manufactured [at Cameronbridge] first patent 'Grain Whisky' second 'Pot Still Irish' third 'Silent Malt' and fourth

'Flavoured Malt.' 'Pot Still Irish' may have been stretching things a little, but then Fife had become a home from home for thousands of Irish navvies, there to build the two great rail bridges over the Tay and the Forth.

This was the age of steam when the desire to drive a railway straight up the east coast, linking Edinburgh, Dundee and Aberdeen in a straight line, had become an obsession. Until the wide, tidal estuaries that split Fife from the rest of Scotland could be spanned, passengers and freight would continue to have to make a wide loop inland.

As the workers were assembled into camps to start work on the Tay bridge in 1872, they naturally brought with them a taste for Irish whiskey which Cameronbridge was more than happy to supply. By the time Barnard paid his visit in the 1880s, construction of the Forth Rail bridge was in full swing. Every detail was recorded, from the 8 million rivets used, right down to the 8000 workmen's caps blown into the water and later recovered. Strong drink and high winds proved a lethal cocktail, as one of the designers of the bridge, Benjamin Baker, duly noted. 'The Hawes Inn flourishes too well for being in the middle of our works, its attractions prove irresistible for a large proportion of our 3000 workmen. The accident ward adjoins the pretty garden with hawthorns, and many dead and injured men have been carried there, who would have escaped had it not been for the whisky of the Hawes Inn.'

And that whisky, with its triple-distilled taste of Jameson's, undoubtedly came from Cameronbridge. Who can say how many of the 57 men who were killed building the bridge went to their graves with a bellyful of 'Pot Still Irish'? This later evolved into a single grain whisky called Cameron Brig which is also available as a 12 year-old and still has a strong following in the bars and hotels of Fife and Dundee.

In his book Barnard devoted four pages to this 'famed distillery' on the banks of the River Leven, compared to just one paragraph on Macallan. At the time Cameronbridge, the former power-base of the Haigs, had become part of the foundations of the recently created Distillers Company, or DCL. In the following century DCL quickly became the dominant force in the trade, and in their current guise, as Diageo, they remain so. In the intervening years, Cameronbridge had grown five times. As the grain spirit divides to become whisky, or goes for further distillation and rectification into white spirits, one can picture the accountant shaking his head in dismay. On the one hand Smirnoff on the shelf in a week, on the other Bells, in cask for eight years – it doesn't make a lot of sense. It does if you like whisky.

BLADNOCH

Pronunciation: blad**nokh**

Founded: 1817

Founder: McClelland family

Region: Lowlands

Production capacity: 100,000 litres

Address: Bladnoch Bridge, Wigtownshire DG8 9AB

Tel: 01988 402 605

website: www.bladnoch.co.uk

Parent Company: Co-ordinated Development Services

Visitor Centre: Mon–Fri, 9am–5pm. Tours, 10am–4.15pm. Open bank holiday weekends.

While Benromach aims to produce just 150,000 litres of alcohol a year, the ambitions of the Bladnoch distillery are even more modest. In fact under the contract he signed with its previous owners in 1994, Raymond Armstrong of County Down in Northern Ireland, is only allowed to make two thirds that amount. In fact current production is a mere 51,000 litres which is what a self-respecting Speyside distillery might make in a week.

The distillery is way down in Wigtown in the south-west corner of Scotland, miles from the nearest distillery, which is one good reason why Bladnoch has always suffered more than most from the ups and downs of the whisky business. When times are tough, when cost-cutting is at the top of the agenda, isolated 'production units' are bound to be the first to go. Having been idle for ten years, United Distillers reckoned it was going to cost at least £300,000 to bring it back to life, and were therefore keen to let it go. In the end Armstrong managed to spend around half that amount to resuscitate Scotland's most southerly distillery and he now runs it as a working museum.

It was said to have been founded in 1817 by the McClelland family who clung on to it until 1930 before selling to a firm from Belfast who sold it on six years later for £3,500, at which point Bladnoch shut down. Between this first Northern Irish connection and the present, it has changed hands no less than five times.

WHISKY GALLERY

an A to Z of Enjoying Whisky

HOW TO ENJOY WHISKY

To get the most out of a good drop of whisky, you need to be blessed with a magnificent nose and a perfect palate. You need the right glass, the right water, complete concentration and if possible total silence. At least that's the conclusion you could draw from some books on the subject, which take themselves not a little seriously. It is almost as if the makers of whisky stood around in subdued reverence as the spirit flowed from the still (which they don't), and therefore we should do the same as it pours into our glass. It hardly sounds a bundle of laughs.

Fortunately 99% of Scotch is not drunk that way. As I wrote in the introduction what matters most is where, when and with whom the whisky is being drunk - whether it is swigged from a flask on a mountain top, drunk at home among friends or sipped on a hot summer's night from a tall glass packed with ice. Whisky is above all a drink for sharing, a social lubricant for loosening tongues and letting the conversation flow where it will. It is only by association that it becomes something wonderful. On its own, without props, it is never quite complete.

TASTING

Having said that, if we want to learn more about the different combinations of taste and smell that make each whisky unique, and here we are really talking malt whisky, we have to try and focus on what lies inside the glass.

Imagine lining up four single malts, and wanting to decide which one you like best. Most people would pick up each in turn and take a sip, naturally assuming their taste buds would be able to pick up any differences there might be. The problem with this approach is that your taste buds are only able to

Pot Still, Glasgow

212

distinguish five basic flavours - those that are sweet, sour, salty, savoury and bitter. You only need to have a stinking cold to realise what a blunt instrument your tongue is.

So before taking a slug, pick up the glass and hold it to the light. Though most whiskies come in various shades of gold, the full spectrum ranges from pale straw to almost chocolate brown. The transformation from the clear spirit produced in a distillery to the amber nectar in your hand occurs in the barrel. Yet the intensity of colour says more about the barrel itself than the age of the whisky. A dram the colour of golden syrup might suggest a relatively young sherry cask, while one that resembles white wine might have spent twice as long in an old Bourbon cask that has been used so often it has nothing left to give. Either way the colour can provide a first clue of what to expect as you bend down to take a sniff.

Though under-used and far less sensitive than that of many animals the human nose is a pretty sophisticated organ. It picks up aromas as they waft from the glass and when the whisky's on your tongue because your nose is connected by a passage to the back of your mouth. This explains the nose trick and why it is hard to taste anything much when you are feeling completely blocked up.

The aroma of whisky will change as you add water – it opens up in the glass as the hot, tickling sensation in your nose caused by the strong, alcoholic vapours disappear. And as you take your first sniff, what initial thoughts come to mind? What do the aromas suggest? Is there a trace of Christmas pudding there? ... or pear drops ... or kippers? It could be anything – the fact that such random ingredients were never used (as far

as one knows) - is unimportant. What counts are first impressions however bizarre they might be.

Alternatively it might just smell of whisky. For most of us it is not that our nose is not up to the job, but that our brain has a real problem making the comparisons needed to put it into words. That can only come from experience and having a good memory, and even then it's an inexact science to say the least.

Though let's not forget, the aim of all this is simply to work out one's own preference based on what is in the glass, not the label on the bottle, nor whether some 'expert' has awarded it a high score. Some drink writers are obsessed with marking everything out of 100. This is something I have never understood – the idea that something as personal as taste can be totted up like items on a shopping bill?

Now it's time to take a sip, but before swallowing,

Whisky Tasting, The Malt Whisky Society, Leith

roll the whisky round your tongue and sense how it feels – is it smooth and luscious or is it sharp and fiery? And savour it for a moment, giving the nose one last chance, before it trickles down the throat. Then enjoy that delicious sensation of spreading warmth as it travels out to your finger-tips and toes.

MIXERS

Scotch has always been an extremely versatile drink. Before the art of distillation and the benefits of ageing were properly understood, it was mixed with all manner of herbs and spices, and sometimes drunk as a hot punch. The added ingredients were there to dampen the impact of drinking something as rough and raw as eighteenth-century whisky fresh from the still. With the arrival of smooth, consistent blends, the herbs gave way to fizzy water, and Scotch & Soda joined forces with gin & tonic to lubricate the British Empire. Later whisky played its part in the cocktail revolution of the twenties and for years Scotch and Orangina was a popular, if not hugely sophisticated choice at the Crazy Horse in Paris. While over in Glasgow there were often bottles of lemonade on the bar for drinkers to mix with their dram.

Somewhere along the line came a counterblast to this frivolity - a belief that real men drank whisky neat or with water from the tap. The 'first dram' was a male rights of passage in which the nervous young recruit was 'inducted' into the ritual by his elders. And if he survived he might one day develop a taste for the harsh, fiery spirit. Unfortunately the new generation of drinkers who have more choice than ever before, appear reluctant to sign up unless the pain barrier can be softened. Our tastes tend to progress from sweet to dry as we get older, so today's alcopop drinkers might eventually, if left to their own devices, move on to Scotch, and perhaps malt whisky. How they get there should be entirely up to them.

Famous Whisky Cocktails

BLUE BLAZER

Ingredients: 2 1/2 ozs Scotch Whisky, 2 ozs boiling water, 1 tsp honey, lemon twist. Warm the whisky and pour into a flame-proof mug. Pour boiling water and honey into another flame roof mug. Set the whisky alight and carefully pour it and the water from one mug to another until the flame goes out. Add lemon and cool before drinking.

CLANSMAN'S COFFEE

Ingredients: 1oz Scotch whisky, 3/4 oz Sambucca, black coffee, whipped cream, sugar to taste. Dip the rim of a goblet in brown sugar and add whisky and coffee. Top with whipped cream.

FLYING SCOTSMAN

Ingredients: 1 oz Scotch whisky, 1oz sweet vermouth, 1 dash bitters, 1/4 tsp sugar. Shake all ingredients with ice, strain and serve.

HIGHLAND SLING

Ingredients: 1tsp sugar, 2 tsp water, 1 oz lemon juice, 2oz Scotch Whisky, lemon twist. Combine ingredients with ice and shake well. Strain into tall glass.

HOT TODDY

Ingredients: 2 parts Scotch whisky, 1 tsp honey, boiling water, dash of lemon juice. Dissolve honey and lemon juice in a small amount of water. Top up glass with whisky and more water, and stir.

RUSTY NAIL

Ingredients: 1 1/2 oz of Scotch whisky, 1/2 oz Drambuie. Combine and serve with ice.

SCOTCH HORSE'S NECK

Ingredients: 2 measures of Scotch whisky, 2 measures of French vermouth, 2 measures of Italian vermouth, double dash of Angostura, ginger ale, lemon peel spiral. Stretch lemon peel from rim to the bottom of the glass and add ice. Add and mix in ingredients and top up with ginger ale.

WHISKY MAC

Ingredients: 1 1/2 oz Scotch, 1oz green ginger wine or other measures to taste. Combine and serve.

WHISKY SOUR

Ingredients: 1 1/2 oz Scotch whisky, juice of half a lemon, 1/2tsp sugar. Shake together and serve with ice and a top up of soda water.

VIEWING THE GALLERY

Below is a gallery of brands of blended Scotch and single malts on sale in the UK, together with a few famous names only available abroad. During the last twenty years, ownership of the whisky industry has contracted from over a dozen to just 4 or 5 publicly quoted companies, led by Diageo (previously Guinness UDV) and followed by Allied Domecq and Pernod Ricard – the French drinks group who bought the whisky interests of Seagram in 2000. These three multi-nationals account for just over 50% of all the Scotch whisky produced. The two leading independents are the Edrington Group who control Highland Distillers with their Famous Grouse and Macallan, and William Grant & Sons, owners of Glenfiddich.

Availability is rated from 'rare' or one star for a whisky occasionaly available in specialist whisky shops, to a maximum of five stars for a whisky like Bells or Glenmorangie that is on sale in all the major supermarkets.

ABERFELDY

ABERLOUR

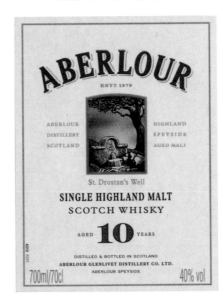

Description: This big, modern distillery has the capacity to pump out 4 million gallons of spirit a year – all but a drop goes into blends.

AN CNOC

Name:	Aberlour
Type:	Single Malt (Speyside)
Produced by:	Pernod Ricard
Availability:	★ ★ ★ ★ ★
Description:	This top selling malt comes in various ages, including the award-winning 10 year old – luscious, mildly spicy and typically Speyside.

Name:	Aberfeldy
Type:	Single Malt (Speyside)
Produced by:	Bacardi
Availability:	★
Description:	Most of this minty, vanilla-scented malt disappears into blends - notably Dewar's White Label.

ALLT-A-BHAINNE

Name:	Allt' A Bhainne
Type:	Single Malt (Speyside)
Produced by:	Pernod Ricard
Availability:	rare

Name:	Knockdhu – An Cnoc
Type:	Single Malt (Speyside)
Produced by:	Inver House
Availability:	★
Description:	The 12 year-old has a malt-loaf sweetness with a lingering, smoky finish.

ARDBEG

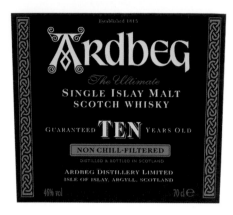

Name: Ardbeg
Type: Single Malt (Islay)
Produced by: Glenmorangie
Availability: ★ ★ ★ ★
Description: Despite the pungent aromas of peat smoke and tar, this hefty Islay malt is a gentle giant in the mouth.

ARDMORE

Name: Ardmore
Type: Single Malt (Highland)
Produced by: Allied Domecq
Availability: rare
Description: But for the odd independent bottling, Ardmore's principal role is to supply the heart and soul to Teacher's Highland Cream.

AUCHENTOSHAN

Name: Auchentoshan
Type: Single Malt (Lowland)
Produced by: Suntory
Availability: ★ ★
Description: As a 10 year old, this lowlander has a light, malty flavour with the aroma of cut grass and hay.

AUCHROISK

Name: Auchroisk ('Singleton of Auchroisk')
Type: Single Malt (Speyside)
Produced by: Diageo
Availability: ★ ★
Description: Sold as the 'Singleton of Auchroisk' this smooth toffee-flavoured malt only appears once the blenders at 'J&B' have taken their fill.

AULTMORE

Name: Aultmore
Type: Single Malt (Speyside)
Produced by: Bacardi
Availability: ★
Description: Despite the sweet scent of apple peel, this relatively rare malt tastes drier than you would expect.

BAILIE NICOL JARVIE

Name: Bailie Nicol Jarvie
Type: Blend
Produced by: Glenmorangie
Availability: ★ ★ ★
Description: At the time of its 'rediscovery' by Glenmorangie in 1994, this venerable, Victorian blend had long disappeared as had anyone who could remember what it tasted like. This gave the company's blender a free hand to create a really cracking whisky.

BALVENIE

Gordon and Macphail Whisky Shop, Elgin

Name: Balvenie
Type: Single Malt
Produced by: William Grant & Sons
Availability: ★ ★ ★ ★
Description: Made under the shadow of Glenfiddich, its sister distillery, Balvenie comes as a rich, opulent 10 year-old, and a smooth, sherry-scented 12 year-old.

BALBLAIR

Name: Balblair
Type: Single Malt (Highland)
Produced by: Inver House
Availability: ★ ★
Description: Quite spicy and dry in style, this long-time component of Ballantine's Finest is now being bottled by Inver House who bought the distillery in 1996.

BALLANTINE'S FINEST

Name: Ballantine's Finest
Type: Blend
Produced by: Allied Domecq
Availability: ★
Description: Cross over the Channel, especially to Spain and it's hard

to avoid Allied's best selling Scotch. As indulgent parents, the company has just pledged £80 million to promote their pride and joy to make it even more popular. This well balanced blend of 57 malts deserves its success.

BALMENACH

Name: Balmenach
Type: Single Malt (Speyside)
Produced by: Inver House
Availability: rare
Description: Now back in production under new owners who bought the distillery in 1997, it will be some while before they have the opportunity to bottle Balmenach as a single malt.

BELLS

Name: Bells
Type: Blend
Produced by: Diageo
Availability: ★ ★ ★ ★ ★
Description: In the race to become Britain's biggest-selling whisky, Bells went through a dismal phase in the seventies and early eighties. It returned to form as a clean, well-balanced blend in 1994 when its new owners relaunched it as an 8 year-old.

BEN NEVIS

Name: Ben Nevis

Type: Single Malt (Highland)

Produced by: Nikka

Availability:: rare

Description: The odd bottle of aged, cask strength Ben Nevis, occasionally appears in specialist whisky shops. The only alternative is to buy your own cask direct from the distillery.

BENRAICH

Name: Benriach

Type: Single Malt (Speyside)

Produced by: Pernod Ricard

Availability: ★ ★

Description: This sweet smelling, distinctly floral whisky, is a classic Speyside malt.

BENRINNES

Name: Benrinnes

Type: Single Malt (Speyside)

Produced by: Diageo

Availability:

But for the odd bottle, this relatively full-bodied, sweetish malt is swallowed up by Diageo's vast stable of blends.

BENROMACH

Name: Benromach

Type: Single Malt

Produced by: Gordon and Macphail

Availability: very rare

Description: After fifteen years lying in mothballs, Benromach finally began producing again in 1998, which means the first bottle of fully matured malt is some way off.

BLACK BOTTLE

Name: Black Bottle

Type: Blend

Produced by: Edrington Group

Availability: ★ ★ ★ ★

Description: While many whiskies disguise their roots, Black Bottle is an unashamedly Islay-based blend of all the island's malts under the banner of Bunnahabhain. For a real mouthful of peat and black treacle, try its big, 10 year-old brother.

BLADNOCH

Name: Bladnoch

Type: Single Malt (Lowland)

Produced by: Raymond Armstrong

Availability: rare

Description: Run as a working museum, Scotland's most southerly distillery produces around 50,000 litres a year which makes this malt rare indeed.

BLAIR ATHOL

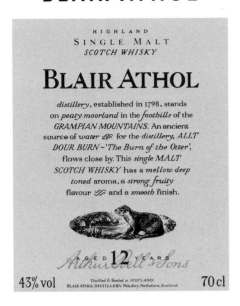

Name: Blair Athol
Type:: Single Malt
(Central Highlands)
Produced by: Diageo
Availability: ★
Description: An age-old component of Bells, some Blair Athol does seep out as a rich, nutty single malt, though mostly through the distillery shop.

BOWMORE

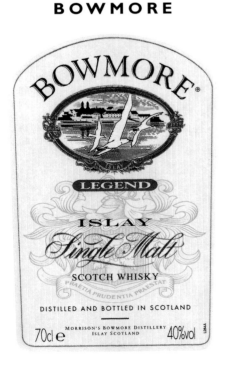

Name: Bowmore
Type: Single Malt
(Islay)
Produced by: Suntory
Availability: ★ ★ ★ ★
Description: With less of the peat-reek you find with Laphroaig, Lagavulin and Ardbeg, this Islay whisky is a complex, smoky and sweetly aromatic malt.

BRAEVAL

Name: Braeval
Type: Single Malt
(Speyside)
Produced by: Pernod Ricard
Availability: rare
Description: Built in the early seventies by Seagram, Braeval now has five stills and the capacity to pump out of 4 million litres of spirit a year to feed the big Chivas Brothers blends now owned by Pernod Ricard.

BRUICHLADDICH

Name: Bruichladdich
Type: Single Malt
(Islay)

Produced by: Bruichladdich Distillery Co. Ltd
Availability: ★ ★ ★
Description: A combination of tall-necked stills and lightly peated malt make Bruichladdich an elegant, less oily whisky than most Islay malts.

CAOL ILA

Name: Caol Ila
Type: Single Malt
(Islay)
Produced by: Diageo
Availability: ★ ★
Description: This full-bodied pungent, delightfully smoky whisky has been such a favourite among blenders, that little was allowed to dribble out as a single malt. Now one of Diageo's 'Hidden Malts', more will become available.

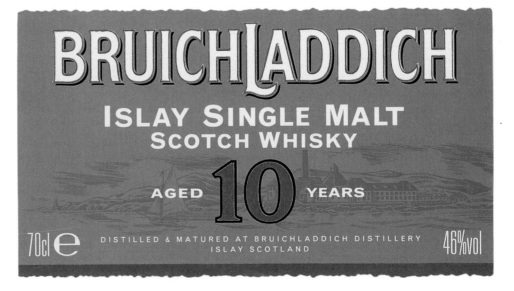

CAPERDONICH

Name: Caperdonich

Type: Single Malt (Speyside)

Produced by: Pernod Ricard

Availability: rare

Description: Forever under the shadow of its sister distillery - Glen Grant, Caperdonich has never developed any real character of its own.

CHIVAS REGAL

Name: Chivas Regal

Type: 12 year-old deluxe blend

Produced by: Pernod Ricard

Availability: ★ ★ ★ ★

Description: Since its creation by the Chivas brothers in Aberdeen in the 19th century, this sumptuous, creamy, Speyside-dominated blend has gone on to conquer the world with sales of around three million cases.

CLAN CAMPBELL

Name: Clan Campbell

Type: Blend

Produced by: Pernod Ricard

Availability: Not in UK

Description: Hugely popular in France, this relatively light blend of mainly Speyside malts with a dry, grassy flavour claims to be one of the fastest growing brands of Scotch whisky around.

CLAYMORE

Name: Claymore

Type: Blend

Produced by: Kyndal

Availability: ★ ★ ★

Description: As its name suggests, this was another Victorian creation using Highland mythology - in this case the chieftain's sword

– to reinforce its Scottish credentials. Having disappeared from view it re-surfaced as a price-fighting blend in the seventies.

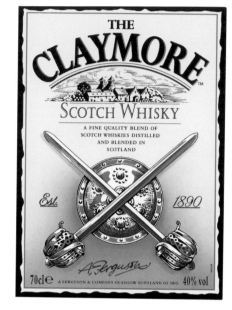

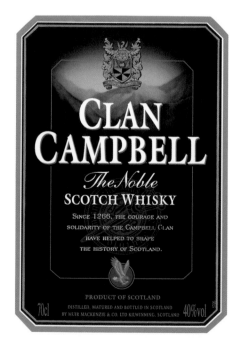

CLYNELISH

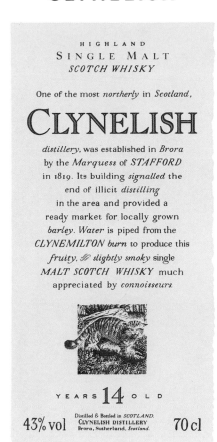

Name: Clynelish

Type: Single Malt
(Highland)

Produced by: Diageo

Availability: ★ ★

Description: Though made beside the North Sea, Clynelish has a definite west coast flavour with notes of seaweed and smoke, drying to a peppery finish.

CRAGGANMORE

Name: Cragganmore

Type:: Single Malt
(Speyside)

Produced by: Diageo

Availability: ★ ★ ★

Description: This subtle, smoky Speyside whisky with an attractive herbal flavour stands beside the mighty Talisker and Lagavulin as one of Diageo's 'Classic Malts'.

CRAIGELLACHIE

Name: Craigellachie

Type: Single Malt
(Speyside)

Produced by: Bacardi

Availability: ★

Description: With its lush, malty sweetness this typical Speyside is well worth tracking down.

CUTTY SARK

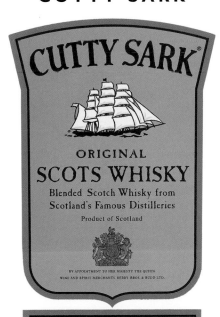

Name: Cutty Sark

Type: Blend

Produced by: Cutty Sark International

Availability: ★

Description: Invented in the 1920's to satisfy American thirst for 'gen-U-ine Scotch whisky' during prohibition, this pale, crisp, faintly herbal blend got off to a flying start. Still popular in the States, its biggest market is now Spain.

DAILUAINE

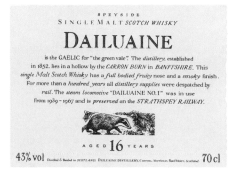

Name: Dailuaine

Type: Single Malt
(Speyside)

Produced by: Diageo

Availability: rare

Description: Popularity with blenders, has meant only occasional bottlings of Dailuaine as a single malt. It has a spicy, almost peppery aroma with a flavour that starts off sweet and nutty.

DALLAS DHU

Name: Dallas Dhu

Type: Single Malt

Produced by: Historic Scotland

Availability: no longer available

Description: The stills went cold in 1983 and Dallas Dhu is now a museum where you can sample the last remaining drops of Dallas Dhu via the blend – Roderick Dhu.

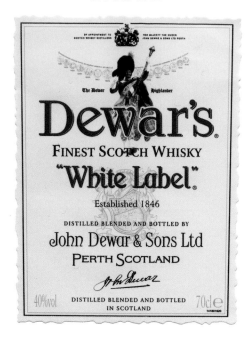

DEWAR'S WHITE LABEL

DALMORE

Name: Dalmore

Type: Single Malt
(Highland)

Produced by: Kyndal

Availability: ★ ★

Description: This smooth, sumptuous
Highland malt deserves to be
far better known, and now
under new management with
Kyndal, perhaps it will be.

Description: Perfumed and smoky on the
nose, with a honeyed richness
in the mouth, Dalwhinnie is
another of Diageo's
'Classic Malts'.

DEANSTON

Name: Deanston

Type: Single Malt
(Central Highlands)

Produced by: Burn Stewart

Availability: ★

Description: If you like your malt whisky as
smooth as honey, with no
pungent whiff of peat smoke,
Deanston 12 year-old could
be the one.

Name: Dewar's White Label

Type: Blend

Produced by: Bacardi

Availability: Only at Aberfeldy distillery
in the UK

Description: Thanks to that
irrepressible salesman,
Tommy Dewar, White
Label was once up
there with Johnnie Walker
as the world's favourite
Scotch. Today 'Doo-ers',
is fighting hard to re-establish
itself in the States with
advertising support from
a bare-chested Highlander
clutching a surfboard.

DUFFTOWN

Name: Dufftown

Type: Single Malt
(Speyside)

Produced by: Diageo

Availability: ★

Description: As one of the ingredients
in the 25 million bottles
of Bells sold around the
world, little of this lean,
sweet-natured malt is
bottled as such.

DALWHINNIE

Name: Dalwhinnie

Type: Single Malt
(Highland)

Produced by: Diageo

Availability: ★ ★ ★

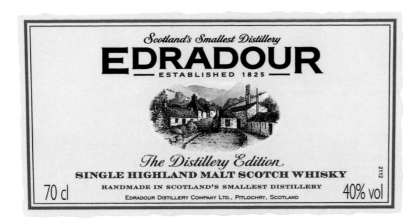

into Perthshire for the start of the grouse shooting season, local blender William Gloag recognised an opportunity when he saw one. Today this balanced, deliciously malty blend is now Scotland's favourite, and number two in the UK.

EDRADOUR

Name: Edradour

Type: Single Malt

Produced by: Signatory Vintage Scotch Whisky Ltd

Availability: ★

Description: Not much of this lush, minty malt makes it beyond the distillery shop, for the simple reason that so little is produced.

FAMOUS GROUSE

Name: Famous Grouse

Type: Blend

Produced by: Edrington Gloag

Availability: ★ ★ ★ ★ ★

Description: As Victorian sportsmen poured

GLEN ELGIN

Name: Glen Elgin

Type: Single Malt (Speyside)

Produced by: Diageo

Availability: ★ ★

Description: While Glendullan helps feed the Old Parr blend, Glen Elgin is employed to give White Horse, a sweet dollop of classic Speyside malt. Now one of Diageo's 'Hidden Malts' more will become available.

GLEN GARIOCH

Name: Glen Garioch

Type: Single Malt

Produced by: Suntory

Availability: ★ ★

Description: Less peaty than before, Glen Garioch's delicate flavours of spice and heather-honey are now more apparent.

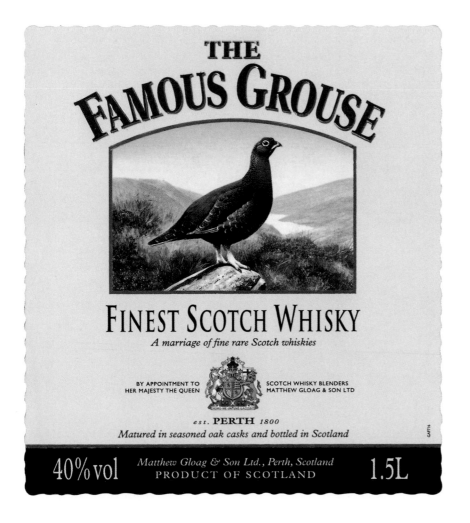

GLEN GRANT

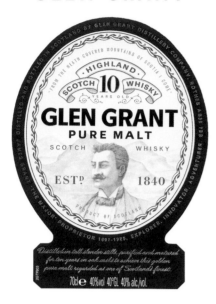

Name: Glen Grant
Type: Single Malt
(Speyside)
Produced by: Pernod Ricard
Availability: ★ ★
Description: On the dry side of Speyside, and somewhat thin as a 5 year-old, but nicely mellow with a slight nutty taste as a 10 year-old.

GLEN KEITH

Name: Glen Keith
Type: Single Malt
Produced by: Pernod Ricard
Availability: rare

Description: This spicy little number from Speyside tends to disappear into big-selling blends like Passport and Chivas Regal.

GLEN MORAY

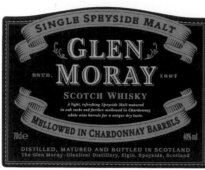

Name: Glen Moray
Type: Single Malt
(Speyside)
Produced by: Genmorangie
Availability: ★ ★ ★ ★ ★
Description: Another of the drier styles of Speyside malt, Glen Moray's real purpose in life is to provide ballast to an heroic blend - Bailie Nicol Jarvie.

GLEN ORD

Name: Glen Ord
Type: Single Malt
(Highland)
Produced by: Diageo
Availability: ★ ★
Description: This fine, well-balanced whisky with a sweetish middle and a

dry, slightly spicy finish is now one of Diageo's 'Hidden Malts'.

GLEN ROTHES

Name: Glen Rothes
Type: Single Malt (Highland)
Produced by: Edrington Group
Availability: ★
Description: A key component of Famous Grouse and Cutty Sark, Glen Rothes has a rich, sherry-scented aroma and a smooth, slightly drier taste.

GLEN SCOTIA

Name: Glen Scotia
Type: Single Malt
(Campbeltown)
Produced by: Glen Katrine
Availability: ★
Description: As one of only two Campbeltown distilleries still going, Glen Scotia may soon be launching a 5 year old malt. The 14 year-old has that tangy salt-laden taste of the sea.

GLENALLACHIE

Name: Glenallachie
Type: Single Malt (Speyside)
Produced by: Pernod Ricard
Availability: rare
Description: Built to supply blending fluid in the late sixties, the distillery's role remains unchanged, though the principal blend is now Clan Campbell.

GLENBURGIE

Name: Glenburgie
Type: Single Malt
Produced by: Allied Domecq
Availability: rare
Description: But for the odd cask that slips into the hands of an independent bottler, Glenburgie's role is to supply malt for the likes of Ballantine's.

GLENDRONACH

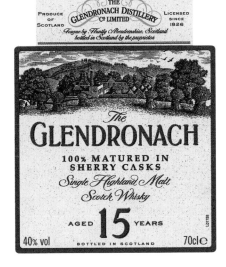

Name: Glendronach
Type: Single Malt (Eastern Highlands)
Produced by: Allied Domecq
Availability: ★
Description: A deep hued, sherry-scented malt, much used in Teacher's.

GLENDULLAN

Name: Glendullan
Type: Single Malt (Speyside)
Produced by: Diageo
Availability: ★
Description: Limited amounts of this straw-coloured, medium bodied, oak-flavoured malt are bottled by Diageo from time to time.

GLENFARCLAS

Name: Glenfarclas
Type: Single Malt (Speyside)
Produced by: J & G Grant
Availability: ★ ★
Description: For John Dewar it contained 'the hum of the bee & the breath of May .. (and) the distant purple of heather in the mountain mist' - sink a bottle of the dark, sherried, buttery 15 year old and see what you think.

GLENFIDDICH

Name: Glenfiddich
Type: Single Malt (Speyside)
Produced by: William Grant & Sons
Availability: ★ ★ ★ ★ ★
Description: This pale, light-bodied, yet refreshing whisky may not be the last word in complexity, but it remains the world's most popular single malt, despite 40 odd years at the top.

GLENGLASSAUGH

Name: Glenglassaugh
Type: Single Malt
Produced by: Edrington Group
Availability: rare
Description: Battered by the worst of North Sea weather on the Aberdeenshire coast near Banff, Glanglassaugh has just managed to cling on, though for how much longer one can only guess.

GLENGOYNE

Name: Glengoyne

Type: Single Malt (Highland)

Produced by: Edrington Group

Availability: ★ ★

Description: Within half an hour of Glasgow, yet just north of the Highland Line, Glengoyne produces a soft, creamy ten year-old malt that deserves to be better known.

GLENKINCHIE

Name: Glenkinchie

Type: Single Malt (Lowland)

Produced by: Diageo

Availability: ★ ★ ★

Description: The survival of this gentle, straw-coloured malt was assured the day Diageo invited it to become a 'Classic Malt', though on a plinth beside heavyweights like Talisker and Cragganmore it appears out of its depth.

GLENLIVET

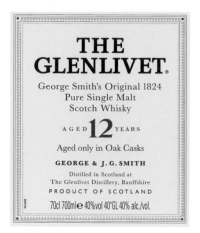

Name: Glenlivet

Type: Single Malt

Produced by: Pernod Ricard

Availability: ★ ★ ★ ★ ★

Description: The glory days of Glenlivet may be long gone, yet as a12 year-old this flowery Speyside with traces of sherry and vanilla still has plenty of charm.

GLENLOSSIE

Name: Glenlossie

Type: Single Malt (Speyside)

Produced by: Diageo

Availability: ★

Description: A gentle, cleansing malt, with a scent of apple peel, that makes an occasional appearance in specialist whisky shops.

GLENMORANGIE

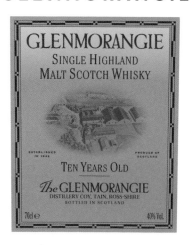

Name: Glenmorangie

Type: Single Malt (Highland)

Produced by: Glenmorangie

Availability: ★ ★ ★ ★ ★

Description: Despite the welter of different expressions, the standard 10 year-old with its subtle taste of candied fruit and orange peel remains Scotland's favourite malt whisky and one can see why.

GLENTAUCHERS

Name: Glentauchers

Type: Single Malt (Speyside)

Produced by: Allied Domecq

Availability: rare

Description: Another big production unit, pumping out over 3 million litres of malt to supply Allied's portfolio of blends. The occasional independent bottling does exist.

GLENTURRET

Name: Glenturret

Type: Single Malt (Central Highlands)

Produced by: Edrington Group

Availability: ★ ★

Description: Visitors to Glenturret now get the full Famous Grouse Experience, but should look out for the single malt - a rich, appetising, toffee-scented dram.

GRANT'S

Name: William Grant's
Type: Blend
Produced by: William Grant & Sons
Availability: ★ ★ ★ ★
Description: The man who built Glenfiddich and founded a whisky dynasty that's still proudly independent, was a monument to the Victorian can-do spirit. His name lives on, in this big-selling, Speyside-dominated blend.

HANKEY BANNISTER

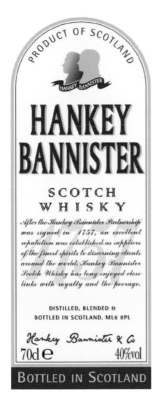

Name: Hankey Bannister
Type: Blend
Produced by: Inver House
Availability: ★
Description: Named after a London wine merchant who took up blending whisky in the 1890's, the odd bottle of this light, unpeated blend still surfaces from time to time.

HIGH COMMISSIONER

Name: High Commissioner
Type: Blend
Produced by: Glen Katrine
Availability: ★ ★ ★ ★ ★
Description: This no-frills blend from the Loch Lomond distillery, has been quietly climbing the charts. Its low price may be the main attraction, but it is now firmly in the top ten brands in the UK.

HIGHLAND PARK

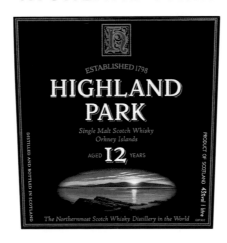

Name: Highland Park
Type: Single Malt (Highland)
Produced by: Edrington Group
Availability: ★ ★ ★ ★ ★
Description: They no longer lay sprigs of heather on the smouldering peat used to malt the barley,

but Highland Park has retained its delicious heather-honey richness.

IMPERIAL

Name: Imperial
Type: Single Malt (Speyside)
Produced by: Allied Domecq
Availability: Rare
Description: Some malt whiskies were made to stand on their own two feet, and some should be hidden away in blends. This is one of the latter.

INCHGOWER

Name: Inchgower
Type: Single Malt (Speyside)
Produced by: Diageo
Availability: ★
Description: Though principally used in blends, limited bottlings of this floral, slightly sweet and sour malt are sometimes made available.

THE INVERARITY BLEND

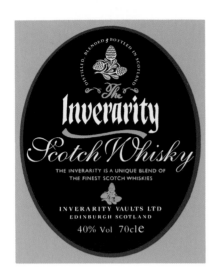

Name: The Inverarity Blend
Type: Blend
Produced by: Inverarity Vaults
Availability: ★ ★
Description: For anyone tired of blended Scotch that is shallow and unfulfilling, this mouth-filling, silky smooth blend is a winner.

ISLE OF ARRAN

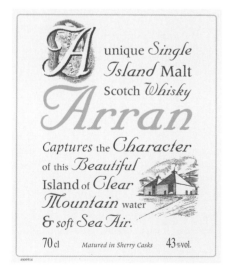

Name: Isle of Arran
Type: Single Malt (Island)
Produced by: Isle of Arran Distilling Co.
Availability: ★

Description: As a 5 year-old, this fast maturing malt has a pleasantly refreshing flavour with a slight prickly, peppermint note.

ISLE OF JURA

Name: Isle of Jura
Type: Single Malt (Island)
Produced by: Kyndal
Availability: ★ ★ ★
Description: Jura's big stills produce an oily, relatively light malt that fades from sweet to dry in the mouth.

ISLE OF SKYE

Name: Isle of Skye
Type: Blend
Produced by: Peter J Russell
Availability: ★ ★ ★
Description: Deservedly popular in Scotland, Isle of Skye shares the same, mellow West Coast charm of Black Bottle.

J & B

Name: J&B
Type: Blend
Produced by: Diageo
Availability: ★ ★
Description: This light, grassy, whistle-clean blend has built up a huge fan-club in mainland Europe, especially Spain where it is drunk, long, on ice and often with Coke. In the UK it is being pushed in the right bars and clubs as an 'irreverent spirit that just happens to be whisky'.

JOHNNIE WALKER BLACK LABEL

Name: Johnnie Walker Black Label
Type: 12 year-old deluxe blend
Produced by: Diageo
Availability: ★ ★
Description: Given the care lavished on this thoroughbred, plus the massive promotional support, Black Label has become the last word in premium Scotch whisky for much of the world. If only all blends tasted half as good.

JOHNNIE WALKER RED LABEL

Name:	Johnnie Walker Red Label
Type:	Blend
Produced by:	Diageo
Availability:	not available in the UK
Description:	With sales of 7-8 million cases a year the world's favourite Scotch is certainly 'still going strong' even if 'born 1820' is a slight exaggeration for a brand patented in 1908. In contrast to its J&B stable-mate, it is richer and more oily, thanks to added weight from Talikser and Caol Ila.

KNOCKANDO

Name:	Knockando
Type:	Single Malt (Speyside)
Produced by:	Diageo
Availability:	★ ★
Description:	Released in vintage years as a ripe, succulent malt with a creamy taste and a dry-ish finish.

LAGAVULIN

Name:	Lagavulin
Type:	Single Malt (Islay)
Produced by:	Diageo
Availability:	★ ★ ★ ★
Description:	This big, beefy slow-maturing whisky fills the mouth with rich

malty flavours before the bitter taste of peat smoke kicks in.

LANG'S SUPREME

Name:	Lang's Supreme
Type:	Blend
Produced by:	Edrington Group
Availability:	★ ★
Description:	Though the old firm of Langs has long gone, their namesake blend survives with the pure, honeyed malt of Glengoyne, still at its heart.

LAPHROAIG

Name:	Laphroaig
Type:	Single Malt (Islay)
Produced by:	Allied Domecq
Availability:	★ ★ ★ ★
Description:	If like Prince Charles you want something pungent to put in your glass, nothing quite beats this heavily peated malt with its stench of tarred rope and TCP.

LINKWOOD

Name:	Linkwood
Type:	Single Malt (Speyside)
Produced by:	Diageo
Availability:	★
Description:	A fine, complex malt with a curious aroma of Irn-Bru, and a luscious, mouth-filling taste that finishes dry.

LONGMORN

Name:	Longmorn
Type:	Single Malt
	(Speyside)
Produced by:	Pernod Ricard
Availability:	★ ★
Description:	An award-winning whisky, with a faint trace of sherry and a pleasant malty sweetness.

MACALLAN

Name:	Macallan
Type:	Single Malt
	(Speyside)
Produced by:	Edrington Group
Availability:	★ ★ ★ ★ ★
Description:	If you spent ten years in an old sherry barrel this is what you would smell like. But beneath the rich aroma lies a beautifully balanced whisky with notes of candied fruit and butterscotch.

MACDUFF/GLEN DEVERON

Name:	Macduff / Glen Deveron
Type:	Single Malt
Produced by:	Bacardi

GLEN DEVERON
PURE HIGHLAND
SINGLE MALT

Availability:	★
Description:	Just to confuse things, the Macduff distillery sells its single malt as 'Glen Deveron' - a light, faintly sweet n' sour Speyside.

MANNOCHMORE

Name:	Mannochmore
Type:	Single Malt
	(Speyside)
Produced by:	Diageo
Availability:	★
Description:	This seventies neighbour to the Victorian Glenlossie, shocked a few people with its famous black whisky - Loch Dhu in 1996. Since when little has been heard of Mannochmore.

MILTONDUFF

Name:	Miltonduff
Type:	Single Malt
	(Speyside)
Produced by:	Allied Domecq
Availability:	rare
Description:	Apart from specialist whisky shops, the best place to find this malt is in one of the 55 million bottles of Ballantine's Finest sold each year.

230

MORTLACH

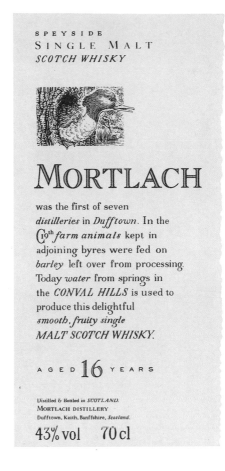

SPEYSIDE
SINGLE MALT
SCOTCH WHISKY

MORTLACH

was the first of seven *distilleries* in *Dufftown*. In the C19th *farm animals* kept in adjoining byres were fed on *barley* left over from processing. Today *water* from springs in the *CONVAL HILLS* is used to produce this delightful *smooth, fruity single MALT SCOTCH WHISKY.*

AGED 16 YEARS

Distilled & Bottled in *SCOTLAND.*
MORTLACH DISTILLERY
Dufftown, Keith, Banffshire, *Scotland.*
43% vol   70cl

Name:	Mortlach
Type:	Single Malt (Speyside)
Produced by:	Diageo
Availability:	★
Description:	A firm favourite with blenders looking for a classic rich, fruity Speyside malt to enhance their blends.

OBAN

OBAN
'Little Bay of Caves'
SINGLE MALT
WEST Highland MALT
SCOTCH WHISKY
43% vol   70cl

Name:	Oban
Type:	Single Malt (West Highland)
Produced by:	Diageo
Availability:	★ ★ ★ ★
Description:	With guaranteed demand as one of Diageo's 'Classic Malts', and no room to increase supply, this smooth, lightly peated malt is sitting pretty.

OLD FETTERCAIRN

ESTABLISHED 1824
Aged 10 Years
OLD FETTERCAIRN
Single Highland Malt
SCOTCH WHISKY
THIS RARE OLD SINGLE MALT SCOTCH WHISKY
HAS BEEN MATURED IN OAKWOOD CASKS FOR TEN LONG YEARS
CREATING A SUBTLE PEATY FLAVOUR
PRODUCT OF SCOTLAND
70cl e   40% vol
Distilled & Bottled in Scotland
Fettercairn Distillers Company, Kincardineshire, Scotland

Name:	Fettercairn
Type:	Single Malt (East Highlands)
Produced by:	Kyndal
Availability:	★ ★
Description:	Many miles from the nearest distillery on the southern edge of the Cairngorms, Fettercairn produces a smooth, toffee-scented malt mainly for the Whyte & Mackay blend.

OLD PULTENEY

Name:	Old Pulteney
Type:	Single Malt
Produced by:	Inver House
Availability:	★ ★ ★
Description:	The northernmost distillery on the mainland, produces a clean aromatic malt with a refreshing sea-side tang.

POIT DHUBH

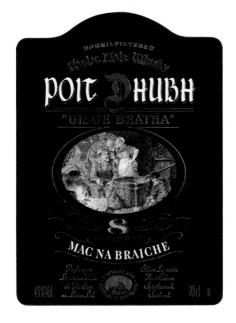

UNCHILLFILTERED
Gaelic Malt Whisky
POIT DHUBH
"UISGE BEATHA"
8 YEARS
MAC NA BRAICHE
43% vol   70cl

Name:	Poit Dhubh (pronounced: 'Potch ghoo')
Type:	Vatted Malt
Produced by:	Pràban na Linne
Availability:	★ ★
Description:	Depending on who you talk to, this is either a vatting of various Hebridean malts, or something smuggled off the Isle of Skye. Either way 'Poit Dhubh' - Gaelic for 'black pot' or 'illicit still' is robust and full of character.

231

Description: Having long supplied own-label whiskies to the supermarkets, Burn Stewart bravely decided to take on Famous Grouse and Bells, with a brand of its own in the UK. It has far more character than you would expect for the price and deserves to do well.

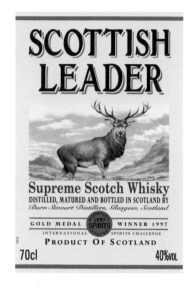

ROYAL BRACKLA

Name: Royal Brackla
Type: Single Malt (Highland/Speyside)
Produced by: Diageo
Availability: rare
Description: Occasional bottlings of this medium-bodied malt with a savoury edge do appear, though most is used in blends.

SCAPA

Name: Scapa
Type: Single Malt (Highland)
Produced by: Allied Domecq
Availability: rare
Description: One of only two distilleries on Orkney still in production - the other being the more famous Highland Park. Scapa's malt has a seaside aroma, quite oily and rich at first, fading to dry.

ROYAL LOCHNAGAR

Name: Royal Lochnagar
Type: Single Malt (Highland)
Produced by: Diageo
Availability: ★ ★
Description: With capacity to produce just 400,000 litres of spirit a year, this delightfully rich, Christmas pudding of a malt will never be in the mainstream.

SCOTTISH LEADER

Name: Scottish Leader
Type: Blend
Produced by: Burn Stewart
Availability: ★ ★ ★ ★

SPEYBURN

Name: Speyburn
Type: Single Malt (Speyside)
Produced by: Inver House
Availability: ★ ★
Description: A typical Speyside, with a delicately floral scent and honeyed flavour.

SPEYSIDE

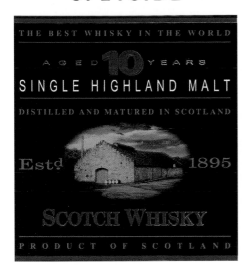

THE BEST WHISKY IN THE WORLD
AGED 10 YEARS
SINGLE HIGHLAND MALT
DISTILLED AND MATURED IN SCOTLAND
Estd 1895
SCOTCH WHISKY
PRODUCT OF SCOTLAND

Name: Speyside
Type: Single Malt (Speyside)
Produced by: Speyside Distillery Co.
Availability: ★
Description: As the first drop of spirit only began flowing in 1991, the malt from this boutique distillery is only now being bottled as a 10 year-old.

SPRINGBANK

ESTABLISHED 1828
SPRINGBANK
Scotch S Whisky
Campbeltown
SINGLE MALT
Aged 10 Years
Distilled by J. & A. MITCHELL & CO. LTD.
· Campbeltown · Scotland
PRODUCT OF SCOTLAND
70cl 46%vol

Name: Springbank
Type: Single Malt (Campbeltown)
Produced by: J & A Mitchell

Availability: ★
Description: Made with great care, this mellow, moderately peated whisky has achieved cult status among malt whisky aficionados.

EST 1786
STRATHISLA
CHIVAS BROTHERS
STRATHISLA
PURE HIGHLAND MALT
SCOTCH WHISKY
AGED 12 YEARS
700ml/70cl   DISTILLED AND BOTTLED BY CHIVAS BROTHERS LTD., STRATHISLA DISTILLERY. KEITH. AB55 5BS. SCOTLAND   43°GL/43%vol.

STEWART'S CREAM OF THE BARLEY

Name: Stewart's Cream of the Barley

Type: Blend
Produced by: Allied Domecq
Availability: ★ ★
Description: The last big blend to be made in Dundee was bought by what became Allied Distillers in the sixties. It is a light, undemanding whisky often lurking in the bargain basement at the supermarket.

EST 1831

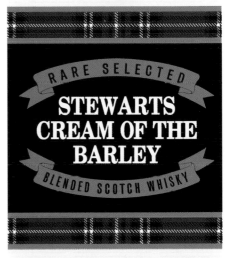

RARE SELECTED
STEWARTS
CREAM OF THE
BARLEY
BLENDED SCOTCH WHISKY
DISTILLED BLENDED & BOTTLED IN SCOTLAND
STEWART & SON OF DUNDEE LIMITED
DUNDEE SCOTLAND
100% SCOTCH WHISKIES
40% vol   70 cl

STRATHISLA

Name: Strathisla
Type: Single Malt (Speyside)
Produced by: Pernod Ricard
Availability: ★ ★
Description: As the spiritual home of Chivas Regal, Strathisla's main role is clear, but it also appears as a sherry-scented malt with a fruitcake flavour finishing dry.

233

STRATHMILL

Name: Strathmill
Type: Single Malt (Speyside)
Produced by: Diageo
Availability: rare
Description: Yet another raw ingredient for Diageo's blenders to play around with. In this case much of it slips into J&B.

TAMDHU

Name: Tamdhu
Type: Single Malt
Produced by: Edrington Group
Availability: ★
Description: A fragrant, relatively sumptuous single malt which trails off in a wisp of smoke.

Availability: ★ ★
Description: Gaelic for the 'little feminine one' or 'wee dram', whose gentle dryness gives way to something sweeter and more heathery.

TALISKER

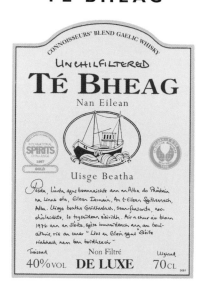

Name: Talisker
Type: Single Malt (Island)
Produced by: Diageo
Availability: ★ ★ ★ ★
Description: A 'Classic Malt' beloved by fans of intense, pungent, peppery West Coast whiskies.

TÉ BHEAG

Name: Té Bheag (pronounced: 'chey vek')
Type: Blend
Produced by: Pràban na Linne

TEACHERS

Name: Teachers
Type: Blend
Produced by: Allied Domecq
Availability: ★ ★ ★ ★ ★
Description: This famous brand, known as 'Teacher's Highland Cream' since 1884, has come a long way from its Glasgow roots. As ever the malt of Ardmore lies at the heart of this dark, fruity, defiantly robust blend.

TEANINICH

Name: Teaninich
Type: Single Malt
Produced by: Diageo
Availability: ★
Description: A lively, gently peat-smoked, citrus flavoured single malt.

Royal Mile Whisky Shop, Edinburgh

FOUNDED 1798
TOBERMORY DISTILLERS LTD
THE ISLE OF MULL
70cl   PRODUCT OF SCOTLAND   40%vol

famous for its double marriage where over thirty malts are vatted together, before being mixed with six grain whiskies for four months to produce a plump, spicy, fruit-cake style of Scotch.

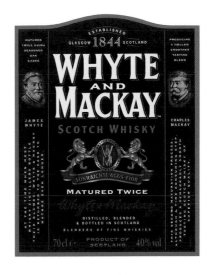

TOBERMORY

Name:	Tobermory
Type:	Single Malt (Island)
Produced by:	Burn Stewart
Availability:	★ ★
Description:	In contrast to the heavier, more oily styles of whisky associated with Islay, the malt from Mull has a fresh, slightly minty flavour.

WHITE HORSE

Name:	White Horse
Type:	Blend
Produced by:	Diageo
Availability:	★
Description:	For years, the world-wide success of White Horse ensured the survival of the distillery that makes its core ingredient. Then came the great malt whisky boom, and today the blender of White Horse must almost have to beg Lagavulin for each barrel of precious malt.

WILLIAM LAWSON

Name:	William Lawson
Type:	Blend
Produced by:	Bacardi
Availability:	★
Description:	When Bacardi bought Dewars, its existing brand of Scotch must have felt like a 2nd Division footballer having David Beckham join the squad. For all that, William Lawson has plenty of fine Speyside malt in the mix.

TOMATIN

Name:	Tomatin
Type:	Single Malt
Produced by:	Tomatin Distillery Co.
Availability:	★ ★
Description:	A nicely caramelised, quite peppery single malt available in various ages from 10 years and up.

TORMORE

Name:	Tormore
Type:	Single Malt
Produced by:	Allied Domecq
Availability:	★
Description:	Definitely on the dry side of Speyside this malt is probably best left to the blenders.

WHYTE & MACKAY

Name:	Whyte & Mackay
Type:	Blend
Produced by:	Kyndal
Availability:	★ ★ ★ ★
Description:	This late-Victorian blend is

235

GLOSSARY

AGE: as stated on the label refers to the youngest whisky in the bottle. All Scotch whisky must be at least three years old by law.

ANGEL'S SHARE: the proportion of spirit, usually around 2% a year, lost through evaporation during the ageing process.

BARLEY: The raw ingredient for making MALT

BLEND: A mixture of GRAIN WHISKY and MALT WHISKY. The proportions vary, but well-known blends like Bells and Famous Grouse contain around a third malt, two thirds grain. A higher malt content does not necessarily mean a better whisky, what matters is balance.

BLENDING: the art of marrying malt and grain whisky.

BONDED WAREHOUSE: A place where whisky can be aged and stored before DUTY becomes payable.

CARAMEL: A neutral colouring agent, used to ensure a consistent colour, usually in blends.

CASK: the standard vessel made of oak staves and metal hoops used to age and store whisky, usually comes as a 'Hogshead' containing 250 litres (55 gallons) or a 'Butt' - 491 litres (108 gallons)

CASK STRENGTH: Casks are originally filled with spirit at 63.5 per cent alcohol by volume (abv), and slowly lose strength during maturation. The term 'cask strength whisky' means whisky bottled straight from the cask and not diluted to the standard 40% abv.

CHILL-FILTERING: A method of filtering the whisky at a low temperature before bottling to stop it turning cloudy.

COFFEY STILL: see PATENT STILL

CONDENSER: the device for condensing alcoholic vapours into liquid form asthey rise off the still. It consists of copper tubes and an outer shell through which cold water is run, and is found in all distilleries except those still using a WORM.

COOPERAGE: A place where casks are made or reassembled from staves of ex-Bourbon barrels imported from the USA. Some larger Scotch whisky distilleries have their own cooperage.

DARK GRAINS: Cattle cake produced by distilleries from draff (malt husks left behind in the MASH TUN) and pot ale (residue in the WASH STILL).

DISTILLATION: Separation of alcohol from a mixture of alcohol and water using evaporation and condensation.

DRAM: Originally an 18th-century measure of around a third of a pint of whisky at about 60%abv – now considerably less.

DUNNAGE: An old-fashioned method of stacking maturing casks on top of each other in a warehouse, often with an earthen floor.

DUTY: The tax on whisky levied by HM Customs & Excise, currently around £5.70 per 70cl bottle in the UK, (not including VAT)

FEINTS: The heavier of the undesirable alcohols in the SPIRIT STILL and therefore the last to be driven off during the second distillation.

FEINTS RECEIVER: A Tank where the FORESHOTS and FEINTS are kept before being pumped into the WASH STILL for redistillation with the LOW WINES.

FERMENTATION: The chemical process whereby yeast enzymes break down the sugars present in organic substances like malted barley and convert them into CO_2 and alcohol.

FIRST FILL CASKS: those casks which have never held Scotch whisky before.

FLOOR MALTINGS: The traditional method of turning barley into MALT by spreading it over a stone floor to germinate, after first STEEPING it in water.

FORESHOTS: The lightest of the undesirable alcohols in the SPIRIT STILL and therefore the first to be driven off during the second distillation.

GERMINATION: the moment a seed grain starts sprouting at the start of its growth cycle.

GRAIN WHISKY: Whisky made in a PATENT STILL from cereals other than malted barley such as maize (corn) and wheat. However a little malted barley is used at the start to provide the necessary enzyme, known as diastase, to allow the conversion of starch into sugar.

GRIST: grain that has been pulverised in a mill with a consistency somewhere between porridge and flour.

HIGHLAND LINE: A line drawn up by Act of Parliament in 1784 to split Scotland in two from Greenock in the west to Dundee in the east. Distilleries north of the line are classified 'Highland' and in the 17th–18th centuries were taxed differently from their 'Lowland' cousins.

KILN: a large oven for drying the malted barley and thus stopping further growth which would eat up the supply of soluble starch in the grain.

LOW WINES: The technical term for the product of the first distillation which comes off the WASH STILL at about 25% abv and is stored in the Low Wines Charger until the SPIRIT STILL is ready.

LPA: Litres of pure alcohol

LYNE ARM: The copper pipe connecting the neck of the still with the CONDENSER or WORM, also referred to as a Swan neck.

MALT: Barley which has germinated and then dried to prevent further growth.

MALTINGS: A building for producing malted barley under controlled conditions.

MALT WHISKY: Whisky made entirely from malted barley which has been fermented using hot water and yeast, and then distilled.

MASHING: the method of dissolving all the fermentable sugars by soaking the GRIST in hot water in a MASH TUN.

MASH TUN: large circular tank, traditionally made of wood, now increasingly stainless steel, in which the MASHING takes place.

MATURATION: the ageing process where the spirit becomes whisky after three years and continues to mellow in cask until it is thought ready for bottling.

MIDDLE CUT: The part of the spirit flowing off the SPIRIT STILL that is worth keeping, after the FORESHOTS and before the FEINTS.

MOTHBALLED: The term used for a distillery that has been shut down and kept in readiness for better times. In practice some 'mothballed' distilleries have had their stills ripped out and are highly unlikely to produce again.

NEUTRAL SPIRIT: Grain spirit over 94.7% abv used to make other spirits like gin and vodka. By law GRAIN WHISKY has to be produced below this strength.

NEW-MAKE SPIRIT: The clear spirit that flows from the SPIRIT STILL.

NOSING: A way of sampling whisky by sense of smell alone.

PAGODA: The Chinese-style roof above a distillery kiln, first designed by the architect Charles Doig on Speyside in the 19th century and much copied since.

PATENT STILL: A still made of two columns - an analyser and a rectifier - which can be run continuously for distilling GRAIN WHISKY and spirits like gin and vodka.

PEAT: fuel made from decomposed organic matter half-way to becoming coal, used for drying the malt in the KILN.

PEAT REEK: the pungent aroma of peat smoke in the finished whisky.

POT STILL: a large, bulbous copper pot for distilling MALT WHISKY, one batch at a time.

PROOF: The traditional measurement of alcoholic strength, now calculated as alcohol by volume, with most Scotch whisky sold at its minimum legal strength of 40% abv.

REFILL CASKS: Casks which have already been used to hold Scotch whisky.

REFLUX: The vapour that boils off only to condense on the neck and run back into the still.

RUMMAGER: A rotating arm inside the still which scours the bottom with strips of chain mail made of copper rings. In the days when stills were direct fired, before internal steam coils took over, they were all fitted with rummagers to prevent the build-up of burnt deposits on the bottom of the still.

SCOTCH WHISKY: the water of life or if you want to be technical: 'A spirit obtained by distillation from a mash of cereal grains saccharified by the diastase of malt' Either way, it has to have been distilled in Scotland, must be at least three years old and a minimum of 40% abv.

SILENT SEASON: A time when water levels dropped in mid-summer and the distillery would shut down for a month or two to allow annual maintenance.

SINGLE MALT: A malt whisky from a single distillery - i.e. not blended or VATTED.

SPARGING: pumping hot water into the MASH TUN to mix with the GRIST.

SPENT LEES: Residue left in the SPIRIT SAFE, mostly de-oxygenated water.

SPIRIT RECEIVER: The tank for holding the MIDDLE CUT when it first comes off the SPIRIT STILL.

SPIRIT SAFE: A brass box with a glass front, through which the spirit flows. Though locked, the stillman can re-direct the flow to capture the MIDDLE CUT.

SPIRIT STILL: The second still in the process, used for refining the first distillation, or LOW WINES, and increasing its strength from around 25%abv to around 68% abv.

STARCH: Carbohydrate food material stored in plants.

STEAM COIL: A coiled pipe inside a still for heating the liquid which works on the same principal as the element in an electric kettle.

STEEPING: The process of soaking the grains of barley in cold water to wake them up prior to germination.

STILLHOUSE: the part of the distillery containing the stills.

STILLMAN: the distillery worker in charge of operating the stills and deciding when to make the MIDDLE CUT.

SWITCHER: The rotating blade beneath the lid of the WASHBACK which keeps the foaming liquor from overflowing

TRIPLE DISTILLATION: The method of distilling whisky using an intermediate still between the WASH STILL and the SPIRIT STILL. Once traditional in the Lowlands, now more commonly associated with Irish Whiskey.

TUN ROOM: The room containing the washbacks.

UNDERBACK: The vessel attached to the MASH TUN to receive the WORT as it drains off.

VATTED MALT: A mixture of two or more MALT WHISKIES.

VATTING: the process of mixing or marrying various MALT WHISKIES.

WASH: The beer-like substance produced in the WASHBACK with a strength of around 7-8% abv.

WASHBACK: Deep, cylindrical tub, traditionally made of larch or pine now often stainless steel, where the WORT is fermented into WASH.

WASH STILL: The first of the (usually) two stills used to produce MALT WHISKY.

WORM: The coiled copper pipe for condensing the alcoholic vapour coming off the still into a liquid. The traditional method and still the best, some would say, because it ensures a slow, gentle distillation.

WORM TUB: A large tank containing the WORM into which cold water is continually pumped to condense the spirit inside.

WORT: The liquid full of fermentable sugars drawn off the MASH TUN.

YEAST: a mould of living cells that in the right conditions feeds on any fermentable sugars present, converting them into alcohol and CO2, until the alcoholic strength eventually kills off the yeast.

BIBLIOGRAPHY

Andrews, Allen - *The Whisky Barons* (Jupiter, 1977)

Barnard, Alfred - *The Whisky Distilleries of the United Kingdom* (Harpers, 1887)

Barr, Andrew - *Drink - A Social History* (Pimlico, 1998)

Bergius, Adam - *Make Your Own Scotch Whisky* (1972)

Boswell, James - *The Journal of a Tour of the Hebrides, with Samuel Johnson* (Charles Dilly, 1786)

Brander, Michael - *The Original Scotch* (Hutchinson 1974), *The Essential Guide to Scotch Whisky* (Johnston & Bacon, 1975)

Brown, Gordon, *Whisky Trails* (Prion, 2000)

Chisnall, Edward - *The Spirit of Glasgow: The Story of Teachers Whisky* (1991)

Cooper, Derek - *Guide to the Whiskies of Scotland* (Pitman 1978), *A Taste of Scotch* (Andre Deutsch, 1989), *The Balvenie* (Private, 1993)

Collinson, Francis - *The Life & Times of William Grant* (Private, 1979)

Craig, Charles - *The Scotch Whisky Industry Record* (Index Publishing, 1994)

Cribb, Stephen & Julie - *Whisky on the Rocks* (NERC, 1998)

Daiches, David - *Scotch Whisky: Its Past and Present* (André Deutsch, 1978)

Dewar, Thomas - *A Ramble Round the Globe* (Chatto & Windus 1894)

Graham, Duncan & Wendy - *Visiting Distilleries* (NWP, 2001)

Gray, Alan - *The Scotch Whisky Industry Review* (MIM 2001)

Gunn, Neil - *Whisky and Scotland* (Routledge 1935)

Hamilton, Henry - *An Economic History of Scotland in the Eighteenth Century* (OUP 1963)

Hills, Philip et al - *Scots on Scotch* (Mainstream, 1991)

House, Jack - *Pride of Perth* (Hutchinson 1983)

Jackson, Michael - *The World Guide to Whisky* (Dorling Kindersley 1987), *Scotland and its Whiskies* (Duncan Baird Publishing, 2001)

Johnson, Samuel - *A Journey to the Western Isles of Scotland* (1775)

Johnson, Tom - *Berry Bros. & Rudd* (Private, 1985)

Lamond, John - *The Malt Whisky File* (Canongate 1995)

McDowall, RJS - *The Whiskies of Scotland* (John Murray, 1967)

MacLean, Charles - *The Pocket Whisky Book* (Mitchell Beazley, 1998), *Malt Whisky* (Mitchell Beazley, 1997)

Martin, Martin - *A Description of the Western Islands of Scotland* (1716)

Martine, Roddy - *Scotland: The Land and the Whisky* (John Murray, 1994)

Millroy, Wallace - *Malt Whisky Almanac* (Lochar, 1991)

Morewood, Samuel - *Inebriating Liquors* (Dublin, 1838)

Morrice, Philip - *The Schweppes Guide to Scotch* (London, 1983)

Moss, Michael and Hume, John - *The Making of Scotch Whisky* (Canongate, 1981)

Murray, Jim - *Classic Blended Scotch* (Prion, 1996)

Pennant, Thomas - *A Tour of Scotland* (1774)

Ross, James - *Whisky* (Routledge & Keegan Paul, 1970)

Skipworth, Mark - *The Scotch Whisky Book* (Hamlyn, 1987)

Smith Gavin & John McDougall - *Wort, Worms & Washbacks* (NWP, 1999)

Spiller, Brian - *Cardhu, the World of Malt Whisky* (John Walker & Sons, 1985)

Townsend, Brian - *Scotch Missed - the Lost Distilleries of Scotland* (NWP, 1995)

Wilson, Neil - *Scotch and Water* (Lochar, 1985)

ACKNOWLEDGEMENTS

Apart from the obvious debt I owe my family, and Charlie MacLean for proposing the book in the first place, I would also like to thank the following in no particular order for all their help.

Bill Bergius, Mark Hunt, Dr Nicholas Morgan, David Robertson, Stuart Thomson, Ronnie Mennie, Jacqui Macdonald, Neil Boyd, Ian Millar, Colin Ross, Raymond Armstrong, David Hardy, Jim McEwan, Isabel Coughlin, Peter Warren, Stuart Robertson, Piers O'Hegarty, Liz Miller, Graham Eunson, John Peterson, Russel Anderson, Iain Henderson, Kay Fleming, Rob Starling, Alan Greig, Alistair Roberston, Peter Smith, Jonathan Driver, Billy Mitchell, Iain MacMillan, Alan Gray, Cameron Evans, Mark Reynier, Gordon Wright, Lucy Pritchard, Dr Jim Beveridge, Tara Serrafini, Babara Nimmo, Jacqui Stacey and Vanessa Wright.

Tom Bruce-Gardyne

Colin Baxter Photography would like to add their thanks to the following people for their kind assistance with the production of this book:

Isabel Coughlin, **Bruichladdich**; Alison Winship and Sharon Tait, **Burn Stewart Distillers Plc**; Jim Long and Vanessa Wright, **Chivas Brothers**; Jo Burrell, **Cutty Sark International**; Jacqui Seargeant and Jacqui Macdonald, **John Dewar & Sons Ltd**; Eileen Kelly, **The Drambuie Liqueur Company Ltd**; Simon Cullingford, **Glen Catrine**; Christine Fraser and Barbara Nimmo, **Glenmorangie Plc**; Janette Moore, **Gordon & MacPhail**; Christine Jones, Sharon Maxwell and Lucy M. Pritchard, **Diageo**; Tara Serafini, **Highland Distillers Ltd**; Jacqui Stacey, **Inver House**; Katie Cryden, **Isle of Arran Distillers Ltd**; Rebecca Richardson, **J & G Grant**; Denise Marshall and Lisa Wilson, **Kyndal Spirits Ltd**; Euan Mitchell, **J & A Mitchell**; Nicola Mackinlay and Matthew Mitchell, **Morrison Bowmore Distillers Ltd**; Skip Clary, **Pràban na Linne**; Jacqui Cooper, **Peter J Russell**; Sive Megson and Emma Smith, **The Scotch Malt Whisky Society**; Jim J. Gordon, **Speyside Distillers Company Ltd**; Heather Brunton, Scottish Life Archive, **National Museums of Scotland**; Dennis Klindrup, **www.whiskyportal.com**; Andreas Jacobs, Germany; **The Scotch Whisky Association**; Charles MacLean.

PUBLICATIONS & USEFUL CONTACTS

Harpers
Harper Trade Journals Ltd
47 Brunswick Place
London N1 6EB, UK
Tel: +44 (0)20 7575 5600
Fax: +44 (0)20 7608 6520 (Main)
http://www.harpers-wine.com/
Weekly trade magazine

The Malt Advocate
3416 Oak Hill Rd.
Emmaus,
Pa 18049
Voice: (610)-967-1083
Fax: (610)-965-2995.
http://www.maltadvocate.com/
http://www.whiskeypages.com/
American glossy magazine

Whisky Magazine
Paragraph Publishing
St Faiths House.
Mountergate
Norwich,
Norfolk NR1 1PY
Tel: 01603 633 808
Fax: 01603 632 808
http://www.whiskymag.com
http://www.whisky-world.com/
UK monthly magazine

TRADE ORGANISATIONS

The Scotch Whisky Association
20 Atholl Crescent
Edinburgh
Tel: 0131 222 9200
Fax: 0131222 9237
contact@swa.org.uk
http://www.scotch-whisky.org.uk

The Wine and Spirit Association
Five Kings House
1 Queen Street
London EC4R 1XX
Telephone: + 44 (0)207 248 5377
Fax: + 44 (0)207 489 0322
Email: info@wsa.org.uk
http://www.wsa.org.uk/

GENERAL INFORMATION

Scotch Whisky Heritage Centre
354 Castlehill
Royal Mile,
Edinburgh
Tel: 0131 220 0441
http://www.whisky-heritage.co.uk/
Heritage Centre Tour brings 300
years of Scotch Whisky history to life.

The Whiskyportal.com
http://www.whiskyportal.com/
The Whisky Portal is a private and
independent site that offers basic
information (and links to more information) about all whisky distilleries,
bottlers and blenders in the world.

www.whisky-world.com/
Popular, up to date website

www.scotchwhisky.net
In-depth website

WhiskyWeb
18 Albany Street
Edinburgh EH1 3QB
Tel: +44 0131 557 5663
Fax: +44 0131 556 7397
http://www.whiskyweb.com/
News, facts and figures and
a discussion forum

www.distillers.com:
Publish http://www.scotchwhisky.com/
and http://islaywhiskysociety.com.
They also run The Whisky School.
21-23 Hill Street,
Edinburgh, EH2 3JP,
United Kingdom
E mail@distillers.com.
Tel +44 (0) 131 624 9150
Fax +44 (0) 870 161 2606

Alternative Whisky Academy
Large collection of information and
links http://www.awa.dk/

CLUBS AND SOCIETIES

**The Scottish Malt Whisky
Society**
The SMWS Ltd,
The Vaults
87 Giles Street,
Edinburgh EH6 6BZ
Tel: +44 (0) 131 554 3451
Fax: +44 (0) 131 553 1003
enquiries@smws.com
http://www.smws.com/

Overseas Contacts
SMWS Benelux and Germany
Vijfhuizenberg 103,
PB 1812,
4700 BV Roosendaal,
The Netherlands.
Tel: +31 (0)165 529905
Fax: +31 (0)165 540067
puntnl@planet.nl
http://www.smws.com/other/index-
d.html

SMWS France
5, Square du Trocadéro,
75016 Paris,
France.
Tel: +33 1 5626 6000
Fax: +33 1 5626 6111
contact@smwsfrance.com
http://www.smwsfrance.com/

SMWS Italy
c/o Ferrigato Srl,
Via Veneto 2/c,
36015 Schio (VI), Italy
Tel: +39-0445-579344
Fax: +39-0445-579343
info@smws.it
http://www.smws.it/

SMWS Switzerland + Austria
Entfelderstrasse 7,
5012 Schönenwerd, Switzerland
Tel: +41 62 858 7030
Fax: +41 62 858 7031
smws@smws.ch
http://www.smws.ch/
http://www.smws.at/

SMWS Japan
Garden Terrace Jingumae 101,
Jingumac 3-33-17 Shibuya-ku,
Tokyo 150-0001, Japan
Tel: +816 3405 7779
Fax: +816 5772 2675
smws@whisk-e.co.jp

SMWS North America
4604 North Hiatus Road,
Sunrise, FL. 33351
Tel: 1-954-749-2440
Fax: 1-954-749-2257
smws4604@aol.com

**The Spirit of Speyside
Whisky Festival**
http://www.spiritofspeyside.com/
This celebration in Malt Whisky
Country has become an established
fixture on Scotlands tourism calendar.

The Gillies Club, Australia
46 Debra St, Rowville 3178
Victoria, Australia
torresan@bigpond.net.au
Possibly one of the oldest malt whisky
associations outside Scotland

Sociedade Braileira Do whisky
Av. Rui Barbosa
830 AP 102,
Rio de Janeiro
22250-020, Brazil
Tel : (021) 551 2297
Email: whisky.sbw@radnet.com.br

An Quaich
The Scotch Malt Whisky Society of
Canada
198 Promenade Des Bois
Russell, Ontario,
K4R 1C4, Canada
Fax : +1 613 445 2628
http://www.anquaich.ca/

Companions of the Quaich
Canadian Malt Whisky Appreciation
Society
http://www.thequaich.com/

Dansk Maltwhisky Akademi
The Scotch Malt Whisky Society in
Denmark
Gl. Hovedvej 3
8410 Rønde,
Denmark
Tel : + 45 8615 2072
Fax : + 45 8637 1945
scottishcountrycottages@post.tele.dk

La Maison Du Whisky
20 Rue D'Anjou
Paris 75008,
France
Tel : 01 42 65 03 16
info@maisonduwhisky.fr
http://www.whisky.fr
The club of the famous shops

Le Clan des Grand Malts
44 Avenue des Terroirs de France
Paris 75012,
France
Tel : +33 (0)1 43 43 38 90
Fax : +33 (0)1 43 07 08 66
http://www.grandsmalts.com
A French malt whisky club

**The International Malt Whisky
Society**
Netherlands
http://www.whiskysociety.nl

Beathas Vänner
http://www.beatha.nu/
One of the oldest Swedish whisky
societies

**Single Malt Academy
of Dalecarlia**
Sweden
http://www.smad.nu
http://w1.241.telia.com/~u24103214/
One of the biggest whisky societies
in Sweden.

Scotland Online
http://www.scotlandonline.com/her-
itage/heritage_whisky.cfm
Detailed information about scotch

Celtic Malts
http://www.celticmalts.com/
Many articles about whisky, and
whisky-related matters.

INDEX

Entries in **bold** indicate main entry